GROWTH AND
PROFITABILITY

Optimizing the Finance Function
for Small and Emerging Businesses

To a loving family
(Mom, Dad, Pam, Lorraine, and Christine)
and a God that *is* love

GROWTH AND
PROFITABILITY

Optimizing the Finance Function
for Small and Emerging Businesses

Michael C. Donegan

John Wiley & Sons, Inc.

Library of Congress Cataloging-in-Publication Data
Donegan, Michael C.
   Growth and profitability : optimizing the finance function for small and emerging businesses / Michael C. Donegan.
      p. cm.
   ISBN 0-471-21216-4 (CLOTH : alk. paper)
   1. Small business—Finance. 2. Financial statements. I. Title.

HG4027.7 .D66 2002
658.1—dc21   2002001893

Printed in the United States of America.

10 9 8 7 6 5 4 3 2 1

FOREWORD

Liquidity. No company can successfully operate without it. Access to cash, when it's needed, becomes so important that all other considerations are secondary. The recent bankruptcies of industry giants Enron and Kmart and the severe liquidity struggles at Lucent Technologies are sobering reminders of the need to maintain healthy cash flow at all times. One might ask: *if the "sophisticated" giants can fall on their collective faces, then what hope does the small or emerging business owner have?*

The answer lies in having a solid plan. Actually, the *plan* is less important than the act of *continuously planning.* The road to business success is full of unexpected twists and turns, and ongoing planning allows for the necessary adjustments that make the journey worthwhile. Additionally, planning by its very nature commits the owner/executive to the visualization and preparation needed for the future—a necessity when put in a financial context.

But how should companies do it? This book lays the foundation for a solid start. As Michael Donegan deftly points out, no entrepreneur *starts* with a finance function, or a plan for strategically building that function. Yet, every transaction in which the entrepreneur engages is ultimately measured by dollars and cents with the medium of measure born from the finance function—data. Ignoring or minimizing this function is certain to lead to trouble.

Although most owner/executives have an exclusive sales and operations focus, sooner or later an appreciation for the strategic necessity of the finance function is recognized as a key ingredient to success. Missing revenue or profitability targets can happen multiple times but companies will only run out of cash once. Don't let it happen to your business.

Thomas F. Donahue
Corporate Finance Consultant
Former Corporate Treasurer—Sensormatic Electronics
Corporation and Citibank Universal Card Services Corp.
July, 2002

ACKNOWLEDGMENTS

Because writing a book is no easy task, I am truly indebted to Heidi Oneacre for her diligence and persistence in editing this work. Her ability to deliver criticism balanced with careful measures of sensitivity and encouragement was invaluable and greatly appreciated. Additionally, I would like to thank Tim Oneacre for his hospitality and keen insight into the English language.

Special thanks go to Chris Muccio, with whom much of the material for this book was developed. I would also like to thank Mike Fredericks for being a worthy partner in the trenches and a continuing source of technical knowledge rivaled by none. A thank-you goes out to Jean Nelson for giving me the opportunity to excel. Finally, I'd like to thank Michael Sincere for providing direction when it was most needed.

PREFACE

Information is the life-blood of decision making. While companies are willing to dedicate resources to advertising, marketing, and sales initiatives, they are oftentimes reluctant to devote the same to garnering accurate and timely financial information to make business decisions. Very few executives and business owners will deny the value of building and maintaining reliable mechanisms for handling the financial data needs of the organization. However, actions often fall short of this intention. It is not unusual to see the proliferation of annotated information systems and inadequate processes throughout the business community. Whether it is the potentially ambiguous value proposition or the sheer complexity involved with creating a reliable finance function, many organizations unintentionally discount the need for a strong one or, worse, relegate it to the status of a necessary evil. Understanding why this happens is second only to recognizing the telltale signs that it is happening in the first place. Can the organization translate its business to financial statements quickly and accurately? Can the reporting process rapidly reflect changes in the business organization? A more overt hint may come in the unwillingness to dedicate budget dollars to the finance area on an ongoing basis. While marketing, sales, or other key operations people can dictate major policies and resource commitments, can the finance area do the same? Companies, especially in their early years, will live and die with the success of marketing and sales efforts. However, their capacity to translate financial data from the business environment into knowledge will either bolster marketing and sales efforts or negate them altogether. Ensuring the long-term stability of information flow and the decision support system requires alignment of priorities in thought and action.

I have witnessed many times this juxtaposition in thought and actions. The minimization of the accounting and finance aspect of the business is rarely intentional, but rather a function of ignorance, misinformation, or misguided business culture. Many executives and business owners are simply not equipped with an adequate perspective of the finance function or the value it provides. Additionally, they may not be committed to cultivating this aspect of their business. Executives reared on the operations side often are led to believe that this area is *overhead* and must be strictly controlled from a fiscal standpoint. The extreme return on investment (ROI) business culture that prevails has fueled this misconception. Having spoken on the topic of strategizing the finance function to large and small groups, I receive all sorts of feedback, most of which deals with the fact that there simply

is not a definitive base of knowledge that addresses the finance function in its entirety. Many finance and nonfinance people want to address this aspect of their
business but find very little accessible guidance. Because easy-to-understand lit-
erature is lacking, many companies resort to engaging high-priced consultants
and/or hiring expensive finance executives to develop comprehensive finance
strategies. Much of the dialog I have with finance professionals comes about as a
result of a marked breakdown in the finance area that is manifesting itself in some
harmful way. Comments are often preceded by "Had I known . . ." or "If someone
had only told me." Throughout my career, I have designed, implemented, and
maintained finance applications on a global scale and discovered firsthand the
staggering lack of accessible knowledge on the overall topic of defining the finance function. The frustration I experienced in following through with my objectives in this realm was the chief motivator for this book.

This book was almost titled *Guerrilla Accounting,* the premise being that it
does not take considerable depth and breadth of knowledge to lay the groundwork
for a sophisticated finance function. The objective of this text is to address the general lack of knowledge and misinformation related to the finance area while creating the mind-set to establish a finance-friendly culture. Although no reader will
come away with all the answers to all the issues related to the finance function, it
is my hope that many will achieve that first breakthrough—realizing the need for
a finance function. The small and emerging business owner must recognize the
need for developing a culture in business that values a solid finance/accounting
function. A culture of awareness will breed the development of good fundamentals
related to a strong data flow dynamic. The danger is waiting until the need for one
is great. Much like runners who reach for the water bottle when thirst is already
upon them, waiting until a critical juncture in the business's life cycle to begin developing a solid finance/accounting organization may be too late. Laying the
groundwork early and developing sound fundamentals and awareness is much like
hydrating oneself before a race. The challenge is overcoming the subtle and sometimes long-term ROIs. Although ROIs are critical, establishing a mind-set of
growth and progressivity in the finance area will preempt the awkward recurring
rationalization of expenditures for seemingly unproven and expensive finance
projects.

My intention in pulling these thoughts together is to provide readers a definitive starting point in dealing with this often confusing and complex area of their
business. The central focus of the book is the methodology for gathering all the
considerations that factor into developing the finance/accounting area of a business. Because certain considerations are more fundamental to overall finance function development than others, these areas of focus are arranged in a pyramidlike
structure with the more fundamental business considerations appearing at the bottom of the pyramid and the more finance specific considerations arranged at the

top. The small and emerging business owner, who may be short on time, money, and know-how, can benefit greatly from referencing this model. It will provide a knowledge base from which a relevant finance function can be developed and maintained. The model itself is universal and applies to all businesses, large and small, and can be utilized by business executives/owners regardless of their knowledge level in the finance/accounting area. The essence of this multilevel approach to strategizing the finance function is to provide insight on what needs to be done and when. The model itself provides guidance in the initial setup and design of a finance function as well as its evolution and adaptation as the business grows. The considerations arranged in this pyramid form will allow the owner/executive to make well-informed, relevant decisions related to employing systems technology, designing processes, hiring professionals, and developing financial analysis tools. The small and emerging business owner will face many challenges in the early years of the business. This focus on the living, breathing data-flow dynamic will preclude unnecessary attention on accounting issues related to properly employing generally accepted accounting principles (GAAP). This book concentrates on developing concepts, imparting knowledge, and developing actionable strategies. The object is to convey and develop a perspective and approach to addressing overall developmental finance and accounting matters and spur action as it relates to developing a suitable finance function. Developing a methodology for approaching this area as opposed to defining particular solutions will serve the small and emerging business owner well as the business evolves and data needs change.

The best way to use this book is to identify and make note of similarities between your business circumstances and those highlighted in the examples discussed. Recognizing circumstances that prevail with your business peers and/or competition is also recommended. Understanding what is being done wrong is as important as recognizing what is being done right. Then use this as a reference in troubleshooting or anticipating issues that may put your organization at a disadvantage. Particular areas of reference will be the chapters dealing with the multilevel approach (Chapter 4), processes (Chapter 6), information systems (Chapter 7), and writing the strategy document (Chapter 9). There are no right answers or premier solutions for the informational needs of a business; however, developing the discipline to corral the issues and questions that must be addressed is imperative. Developing and maintaining a sound finance function is an iterative process and will take time and patience. While trial and error may be a necessary component of development, this book will help clarify what needs to be done and when. Be patient and open-minded as your finance function evolves. Change is unavoidable; in fact, it will be critical in the finance area if the finance function is to remain relevant and value-added for the organization.

The key to success in this area is an open mind and a willingness to embrace new and innovative ideas in systems and process design. We are living in exciting times where technology is developing at what seems to be warp speed. Achieving success will mean matching up well-defined needs with carefully crafted solutions. More important, success in this area will be manifested by a thriving business. Evolving data needs will mean the business is growing. It is critical that an awareness of the finance function be maintained as the business matures. I wish you well in developing your new business or growing your existing one.

CONTENTS

1

DOING BUSINESS IN TODAY'S ENVIRONMENT

KEY TAKEAWAYS

- Understanding the objectives of this book.
- Understanding common misconceptions regarding the finance function.
- Defining small and emerging businesses.
- Understanding the role data management plays in the enterprise.
- Understanding the core motivation for staying in business as well as the business owner's roles/responsibilities as leader of the organization.
- Understanding the need for data analysis.
- Understanding how the dynamic of converting data to knowledge impacts the capacity to be long-term vision oriented.
- Understanding that the changing business environment will impact operations as well as business strategies.
- Becoming familiar with eight high-risk business circumstances.

OBJECTIVE

The objective of this book is to cut to the core purpose of the finance function and create a context for laying the groundwork for a sound finance organization. Unlike traditional accounting and finance guides, this book does not address the esoteric (and complex) pronouncements issued by the accounting industry for interpreting transactions and events. Instead, it provides the conceptual framework for the small business owner to lay a sound foundation of finance infrastructure now that can be built on successfully in the future. In so doing, this book also addresses the necessary relationship between finance objectives and operational goals/initiatives of the enterprise. Additionally, the data flow dynamic is addressed as well as how it impacts the objectives of the business as a whole. Putting finance and accounting in the context of the "entire" business helps the small and emerging business owner create not only a sound finance function but also a culture of decision making and analysis that will enable the organization to devote more energy to making long-term strategic and day-to-day decisions that add value to the overall business.

Why focus on small and emerging business owners/executives? Perhaps the reason lies in the corporate mortality rate. Of the 800,000 to 900,000 businesses formed each year in the United States,[1] over 80% will close their doors within five years of inception. It is interesting to note that nearly 50% of these failures are due to management's lack of managerial and fiscal savvy. An additional 16% of these failures are due to the improper balance of operational and financial initiatives. There are many reasons for business failures, although it is clear that many are due to the inability of owners and executives to balance administrative and back-office functions like finance with operations. By tying the finance function to operations, small and emerging businesses that are inherently at risk can (at best) buoy themselves into profitability or (at the least) extend their lives through challenging times.

WHAT IS THE PERCEPTION OF FINANCE AND ACCOUNTING?

Small business owners and executives are compelled to wear many hats in carrying out their duties as leaders of a business organization. Often the accounting/ finance hat is the one most avoided. The small and emerging company's survival depends largely on the health of the finance function. Knowing this, any trepidation about handling issues that affect the finance/accounting function must be overcome before a tendency to avoid finance issues becomes a culture of neglect. Reluctance to address the finance function properly often stems from misconceptions and half-truths—these are dangerous because, left unchecked, they eventually will lead to bad decisions. Common misconceptions toward the finance function borne by small and emerging business owners are often expressed in one (or more) of five ways:

1. *Accounting and reporting are administrative/back-office functions not considered the front lines, so who cares?* The reality is the accounting/ finance function underscores virtually all aspects of the front lines of any business enterprise, whether it dictates the language of sales contracts, defines customer payment terms, or helps determine sales quotas. Unlike most areas of a small and emerging business, finance decisions may not yield that rush of instant gratification or obvious benefit. In fact, the return on investment (ROI) on a finance plan or investment in infrastructure may

be long term and/or extraordinarily subtle. This notwithstanding, the finance function is no less important as a primary driver for the organization.

2. *Between consultants, applications, and hardware, the accounting function is a money pit.* This is often the case with poorly thought out infrastructures or myopic strategies—a symptom of many emerging companies in swiftly moving industries. Decision making as it relates to information systems and applications must have a mid- to long-term focus. The speed at which software and hardware becomes obsolete forces organizations to face the same purchase decisions over and over again. When it comes to accounting and finance software packages and the technological platforms that drive them, user needs must play an equal or greater role in the purchase decision process.

3. *Accounting and finance issues are simply too complex to deal with. Rather than dealing with them incorrectly, I'll just ignore them.* These issues almost never become barriers to the business when they are identified and dealt with early on. Understanding the business itself and having a solid idea of the strategic direction go a long way toward addressing accounting and finance issues, whether they are changes in accounting/disclosure rules, infrastructure issues, or data availability issues. Knowledge of the business, the industry in which it operates, and the status of industry peers give the business owner the opportunity to at least recognize when a questionable finance issue is encountered. Sometimes it is just as important to know when to ask a question as how to answer it.

4. *As long as I have customers and revenues, the accounting will take care of itself.* Customer generation and retention may be the direct result of how well the company costs and bills customer jobs—a major part of the accounting and finance area. In this and other ways, the finance function dictates how effectively the organization approaches prospective customers and handles existing ones. Skill at budgeting and forecasting will drive positive relationships with suppliers, and the ability to close the books company-wide will drive positive relationships with owners, shareholders, and analysts.

5. *I simply do not have time to deal with the accounting function. I have to get revenues now or I am finished anyway.* The fact is, everybody is busy. The business owner can deal with the accounting and finance function now or wait until a problem arises as a result of neglect and put the fire out then. Short-term thinking is a slippery slope where many executives lose footing, especially if the company is publicly traded and has quarterly earnings expectations. Many executives and business owners see shortsighted decisions as the better alternative to neglect. This may be so; however, engaging in short-term decision making may be ultimately as damaging to the organization.

DEFINING SMALL AND EMERGING BUSINESSES

How are small and emerging businesses defined? It is difficult to suggest parameters that categorize businesses as small, emerging, or growth companies. The purpose of this book is to educate the business owner in how to deal successfully with circumstances that will be encountered as the company matures. With this in mind, definitions for *small* and *emerging* businesses will be suggested, knowing that each and every business has its own set of circumstances and challenges, regardless of its size or stage of development. The intent is to create a context to examine finance and accounting-related issues from the point of view of a developmental stage business. The idea is to capture the circumstances of the business owner/entrepreneur who is not well versed in the intricacies of finance and accounting and to present solutions to existing issues while preventing future difficulties. The following sections define small and emerging businesses.

Small Businesses

Businesses are defined and categorized based on any of a series of classifications: revenues, assets, number of employees, office/lease space, and so on. This text loosely follows the definition of small business used by the Small Business Administration (SBA):

- *Revenue.* Companies with revenues less than $100 million
- *Number of employees.* Companies with 500 or less employees[2]
- *Value.* Companies with a net worth less than $18 million[3]

A few categories of small businesses may be worth mentioning:

- *Mom & Pops.* This term is uniquely descriptive of a piece of Americana which connotes a single-site operation that serves more as a lifestyle endeavor to owners than a revenue-generating cash machine. A Mom & Pop is typically a mature, stable organization with little or no momentum or inclination to change. It usually does not have a succession plan if the owners leave or become unable to run the business.
- *Family owned.* These business types serve mostly to enrich the lifestyle and culture base for owners and their immediate family. The implied succession of the business to future generations assures a reasonable amount of forward momentum of the enterprise. It may be a single-site operation or be operating in multiple geographic and functional areas.
- *Start-up.* Start-ups, which are described in more detail under "Emerging Businesses", may have small or large revenue streams. The term refers to businesses with less than $100 million in revenues, less than 500 employ-

ees, and/or less than $18 million in equity (net worth). They may be public, private, or family owned.

■ *Net ventures.* Though net ventures have lost some of their luster of late, this ubiquitous business form deserves attention. This term refers to companies whose business model is driven almost exclusively by the Internet. *Business-to-Business, Web solutions, Dotcom,* and *E-Commerce* are a few of the terms that personify net ventures. It is worth mentioning this business type since so many high-profile net ventures have spanned the entire business life cycle in recent years. This category has been deemed the new predominant cottage industry due, in part, to the lack of entry barriers in taking an idea to a business form.

Emerging Businesses

An early-stage or *emerging* business is also referred to as a *start-up.* For purposes of this book, companies less than five years old are considered emerging businesses. These businesses often balance new products and technology with burgeoning markets. Typical of emerging businesses is the need for infrastructure—buildings, technology, business processes, and the people to manage them. Perhaps the most significant characteristic of emerging businesses is their likelihood of being headed by "green" leaders who may be long on hope and enthusiasm but short on experience. Emerging businesses may be public or private, large or small.

WHY IS THE BUSINESS OWNER IN BUSINESS?

Starting a business can be an exciting and rewarding undertaking. It also can be scary and, at times, overwhelming. Regardless of how one gets started or why, owners of a small or emerging business will find that their new life's purpose will be presiding over matters of operations and administration. As they drive the company forward, the intention is to strengthen the company, in turn increasing their own wealth or the wealth of absentee owners.

From a textbook perspective, the purpose of the corporation is to maximize shareholder wealth. In recent years the business culture has translated this into creating value for shareholders or owners. Regardless of how the motives for going into business are defined, most entrepreneurs do so with the intention of making their lives better. This objective may be achieved through a perpetual, steady upward trend or (as is the case with more mature, public companies) through a synergistic event such as a merger, an acquisition, or a necessary divestiture.

Owners of small and emerging businesses have the daily responsibility of focusing on the most fundamental matters of business. The pressure of applying seed money wisely and effectively in a lightning-quick business environment is a big enough challenge without having to learn the finer points of being an administrator, delegator, and firefighter. As the company matures, stabilization and making order out of chaos will be followed by the need to create structure that will endure. The business owner or chief executive's role is to build a sound management team as well as conserve and safeguard available resources. These objectives will be followed by the need to build a sound business strategy and put it in motion.

DATA NEEDS

Being the chief visionary in a small/emerging business means dealing with the daily struggle by subordinates and customers for time and attention. In spite of these demands, one objective always must remain at the fore: turning a profit and turning it quickly. For many small and emerging business owners, the formative years of the business are heavily dependent on getting results *now*. Time to develop markets, products, and a recognizable brand is often in short supply. The pressure to not only make decisions but to make good decisions seems overwhelming at times. To avoid guessing and/or consulting the crystal ball for answers, the small/emerging business owner will need to make sense out of the environment in which the company operates. Successfully managing data is the key to making sound decisions. Later chapters discuss the foundation of providing for data needs including data collection, analysis, and translation to knowledge.

As the data flow dynamic is explored, it is important to focus on the ultimate objective of data management, which is generating knowledge. It is through knowledge that solid decisions are made and strategies are built. Knowledge depends on data analysis; data analysis depends on data processing; and data processing depends on data gathering. The need to engage in all of these activities in a timely manner underscores the whole effort.

The most important use of knowledge is to develop and employ performance measures also referred to as *metrics*. Developing performance measures, whether they are revenue targets, expense ratios, or return on investment (ROI), will depend on the business owner's reliance on knowledge of the business and the environment in which it operates. It is not surprising that almost 35% of U.S. businesses (large and small) fail to create real value because they apply incorrect performance measures.[4] The superior organization will have not only a sound data flow dynamic but also the know-how to interpret or analyze the knowledge derived from the data it generates. Establishing a culture of analysis in the infant years of the organization will pay dividends as the company grows.

GOING FROM DAY TO DAY TO LONG-TERM STRATEGY

Understanding that business owner/executives need data to analyze and need it quickly is not enough to satisfy their decision-making requirements. They must determine the what, when, and how relative to creating the infrastructure and culture that will yield this capability. It is important to recognize that creating a finance function that serves the organization's needs is not easy and does not happen overnight. The ROIs are often mid to long term and subtle in nature—characteristics that may impede investment in this area for many small organizations.

Leaders of organizations often are overburdened and preoccupied with "right-now" issues. Although yielding revenue and cash in the short term is a necessity for small and emerging enterprises, it is imperative that some attention be diverted toward matters of data quality, flow, and timing—issues requiring long-term focus. The temptation is to think short term. The challenge, however, is to see into a longer time horizon when it comes to developing the finance function. Unfortunately, the reality is that because many companies make decisions to get them through the short term, they inadvertently derail the likelihood for mid- to long-term prosperity. This is especially true when it comes to investing in infrastructure. Consider this example:

Ira is an executive of a company that manufactures electronic components. Like thousands of other executives, he is struggling to come to terms with a series of decisions he has made regarding his company's information systems. About 15 months ago Ira gave the nod to an investment in an accounting software application and an accompanying server upgrade. The need, as he understood it, centered on pressure to enhance the accounting consolidation function (the gathering and processing of company-wide financial data). The push was to get something in place within a three-month window—in time for the year-end close. The application in question came highly recommended by his Information Systems (IS) department and was reputed to work best on this particular server. Although it could operate on a larger one, Ira opted for what he thought was a prudent decision not to spend any more money than necessary to provide the platform to run the application. He ultimately OK'd over $100,000 for this project. He was assured that he was getting off cheap, given the array of other server options that would also work. He was convinced his decision was fiscally prudent and made sense for his finance department, though they did not actually drive the decision. The project yielded mediocre results for the year-end close—as they experienced the usual snafus related to meeting deadlines, training, and so on. The fallout, however, came six months later when the company went forward with the acquisitions it had been planning since the prior year. The application was not scalable (it was difficult to expand upon) and the server environment was woefully inadequate for the company's expanded data needs related to the acquisitions. The consensus in the organization was that Ira wasted $100,000. Ira made the following mistakes common to many businesses:

- His *IS* department drove the evaluation and selection of an application used by his *finance* department, without understanding finance's requirements.

- The company's needs beyond the year-end close were not considered, particularly the future needs of the finance department.
- The package did not interface well with any of the company's other data management applications.
- Ira sank *another* $100,000 into a system recommended by his IS organization subsequent to the deemed failure.

This is a good example of how pressure to solve issues now can yield solutions that are inadequate in the mid and long term. In this case, Ira's $200,000 will no doubt yield another investment equal to or in excess of the original investment. Like thousands of executives discover everyday, this project will prove to be the gift that keeps giving (or taking). Would a larger investment on the first go-round have accommodated the company's needs over a greater time horizon? Would Ira have been better served if his finance department had been included in the purchase process along with the IS department? Should the purchase decision been part of a larger plan to enhance the finance organization? After going through such an experience, executives are more often in need of salve for their pride than hard advice on how to not perpetuate the situation. Unfortunately, many executives in small, mid-size, and large organizations react to short-term circumstances and make decisions that create more long-term problems than they solve.

Public companies face the temptation to be shortsighted on matters of process and infrastructure more often than private companies. If the motivation to improve the closing process and systems fades as the auditors sign off on another quarter, *be warned*. The quarters will not get any easier to close, and the data quality will not get any better if left alone. If a period close or data request paralyzes an organization, the first step in improving is a commitment to long-term initiatives that will improve the finance function.

The implosion of the Internet industry (and resulting impact on the stock market) shows the pitfalls of rationalizing short-term thinking. In the late 1990s the prevailing strategy of seeking brand over revenue and cash flow provided a recipe for disaster. Short-term strategies related to branding were easier and more gratifying to pursue from quarter to quarter than were the more heady strategies related to sustained revenue growth and profitability. The end result in this case is documented all too well. Using the downfall of many Internet companies as a metaphor for a mind-set that must be kept in check can be a fulcrum to transform views from that of day-to-day survival to that of long-term strategic vision.

DEALING WITH THE BUSINESS ENVIRONMENT

Conceiving and building a sound finance strategy involves working with the known and dealing with the unknown. Creating logical strategic initiatives in a stable business environment is a challenge in and of itself. The small and emerging business owner, however, must be prepared to strategize in the midst of a changing world. The shifting business environment always presents situations that threaten the organization's objectives. It is the job of the business owner to ensure that the finance strategy is prepared to deal with inherent threats and turn them into opportunities.

Any seasoned executive or business owner will agree that avoiding problems is better than dealing with them as they arise. This is the essence of strategic planning. Although it is impossible to identify all circumstances that the growing enterprise may encounter, it is important to identify those situations that may present the greatest hazards. If they are identified, the business owner sets the stage to diffuse circumstances before they become a true threat. Costly threats to the organization may arise from:

- Going public
- Regulatory requirements
- Doing business in foreign countries
- Litigation
- Technology needs of vendors and customers
- Employee needs
- Strikes
- Natural disasters

GOING PUBLIC

Private Companies

Many small and emerging businesses are private, closely held companies; that is, they have a small group of owners who represent neither institutions nor other individuals as owners. The owners themselves often are involved directly in operations. The business must remain focused on generating knowledge for the exclusive use of business owners to make decisions. The finance function may or may not be efficient in small privately held companies when it comes to ensuring that enough cash is being generated to keep the business going. The private environment lacks the distractions of nonoperational information needs (earnings and performance expectations by absentee owners [shareholders]), giving privately held companies the luxury of developing finance infrastructure in a less-frenetic environment.

Public Companies

Many small and emerging companies have sought and found financing in the equity markets. By participating in the equity markets and going public, they have availed themselves to adequate levels of capital to fund the business. Participating in the capital markets, however, comes with a price. Because a public company handles other people's money, it is subject to the myriad of accounting, disclosure, and reporting rules dictated by the U.S. Securities and Exchange Commission (SEC). These rules require a heightened level of functionality and sophistication in the finance function. Without adequate preparation, a small or emerging business organization that goes public can fall prey to the swiftly moving dynamics of public disclosure. The fallout from a lack of vigilance in this area could manifest itself in the form of shrinking market capitalization (number of shares outstanding × stock price) or a waning company image (brand). Both of these maladies could result in delisting (getting permanently or temporarily barred) from the exchange, paralyzing lawsuits from shareholders, or sanctions for company executives. The primary areas of risk for the small and emerging business seeking to go public lie in the nature of complying with disclosure rules which include employing generally accepted accounting principles (GAAP) (see next section), dealing with the shareholder/analyst community, and managing performance expectations of the public.

Disclosure Rules and Applying Generally Accepted Accounting Principles Methodologies

Public companies are required to adhere to the general framework of accounting guidelines, which are issued by the accounting profession and referred to as GAAP. To keep GAAP guidelines relevant, the profession constantly updates them and evolves this conceptual framework to keep pace with the business community. The reporting requirements are intended to lend a level of consistency to all financial statements issued by companies that are traded on the public exchanges. Depending on the industry and type of transactions engaged in, GAAP may be extremely complex or relatively straightforward. Regardless, management bears the burden of ensuring that the company is reporting its financial data in an accurate, GAAP format. Although professionals from the public accounting industry audit the financial statements of publicly traded companies to opine on the fairness of GAAP compliance, it is ultimately the responsibility of management to take reasonable steps to ensure consistency and accuracy in reporting. While it is easy to enlist professionals to help the business report the data generated by the organization, the real challenge is managing the changes to GAAP, in particular assessing the impact of the changes on the organization's financial statements. This includes keeping tabs on rules issued by the profession as a part of GAAP and monitoring disclosure rules issued by the SEC.

Because legally mandated disclosure rules and financial statements are the bases by which absentee shareholders judge the health of the company, it is important for management to understand the impact of accounting and disclosure rules on the shareholder community. What are their expectations? How will changes in reporting the company's financial results impact the stock price? When combined with the need to gather data to make general operational decisions, the ability to meet all federally mandated reporting requirements in a timely manner represents a formidable challenge for the finance function in small and emerging businesses.

Before exposing itself to these rigid reporting requirements, a company considering going public should assess its ability to gather, process, and analyze financial data with the dual objectives of reporting as disclosure rules require and creating knowledge for decision making. Any small and emerging business that has not examined itself for these capabilities is courting disaster. For example, disclosing worldwide data on the Form 10K (an annual filing with the SEC) on a geographically segmented basis as required by the SEC may be beyond the capability of an organization's systems and processes. Not being equipped to gather and report the data this way is not an excuse to not disclose it. In this instance the company would be forced to estimate this activity breakout if it could not get it from its finance department. Incorporating estimates into the reporting process puts the company at risk of providing misleading financial information to the public, whether intentional or not. The result can be severe sanctions for executives including fines, removal from office, or even jail time. Having adequate systems and personnel to interpret standards and company data is crucial to existing in a public environment.

In certain circumstances, companies in the public arena go overboard in developing data systems that are focused on meeting external reporting requirements to the exclusion of overall data needs. Keeping these two imperative needs in balance is a formidable challenge. Surprisingly, the data processing and analysis function in many public companies is much like the Maginot Line in its rigidity and one-sidedness. Built more toward complying with the public disclosure rules and statutory reporting requirements, these systems are focused on putting data into financial statement form as opposed to generating forward-looking knowledge. In this way, the lack of strategic thinking by business owners and management leaves many companies, large and small, with a data flow process that falls short of meeting the organization's internal information challenges.

Shareholder/Analyst Community

The needs of the shareholder/analyst community are an aspect of the environment the organization will have to deal with if it has a presence in the equity markets. As stewards of the finance data, it is the responsibility of management to understand the needs of shareholders and serve them. The cornerstone of this responsibility is the delivery of accurate and timely financial statements to Wall Street, or the general public. The company will have to go beyond this, however, if it intends to maintain a healthy relationship with this community of data customers, especially if it exists in a high-profile industry. With management's responsibilities traditionally focused on building and maintaining the finance organization for its own decision-making purposes, liaising with the Street may be beyond the scope of its abilities. Creating and managing reasonable expectations as well as adhering to fair disclosure laws in meeting shareholder needs are areas of responsibility that management must work into their strategy models.

Managing Expectations

A key component in dealing with the shareholder/analyst community for public companies is managing expectations. Maintaining a high stock price (and market capitalization) is a high priority if the plan is to use company stock to facilitate mergers and acquisitions, pay employees, or seek financing. With this in mind, the finance strategy should seek to manage this aspect of the business environment.

In the public arena, the company is evaluated from quarter to quarter. Depending on the industry or business sector, certain expectations may be thrust on the organization, including earnings growth, revenue growth, expense management, and acquisitions. Not being aware of these expectations could put management or the small business owner in the hot seat and put the company's market capitalization at risk. Strong companies are skilled at setting expectations.

Setting expectations involves understanding the industry in which the business operates as well as what the business is capable of doing. From a finance perspective, it is worthwhile to know what contemporaries in the company's peer group are doing. What financial multiples and ratios must be maintained? How robust must systems and processes be? Do peers make earnings each quarter? How do the stocks collectively perform? Are they in a volatile sector?

REGULATORY REQUIREMENTS

Complying with government regulatory requirements may present crippling consequences for organizations that are not prepared. Certain industries, from banking and insurance to mining and industrial chemicals, have a full slate of requirements dictated by state or federal governments that address certain aspects of doing business. As a result, some companies may be subject to costly regulatory requirements stemming from changing business circumstances, shifting laws, or unforeseen preexisting business conditions. Contaminated soil/property and pending product liability litigation are examples of circumstances that a business owner may have been oblivious to at one time and subsequently forced to deal with in quick order. The required response may tap out already thin cash reserves, devalue assets, alienate customers, and (worst of all) distract owners from operations. To determine if a company is prepared to deal with unforeseen regulatory issues, strategists should ask:

- Do adequate cash reserves exist?
- Is all the necessary insurance in place?

■ Have all foreseeable risks been identified?
■ Are owners in touch with industry peers regarding changing rules and regulations?
■ Does the company have quick access to legal counsel that knows enough about the industry to guide the enterprise through changing federal and local regulations?

From a financial standpoint, strategies should be in place that take into account unexpected regulatory barriers. Setting up adequate reserves and having the capability to quickly add the impact of new regulatory guidelines into budgets and forecasts may be the extent of a sound preventive finance strategy. If the organization is publicly traded, however, a process may have to be in place to communicate changes like these to the analyst community and shareholders in general, to manage expectations and optimize stock price. In this case the finance strategy may involve retaining an investor relations professional or firm to spin unexpected news and requirements to the public.

DOING BUSINESS IN FOREIGN COUNTRIES

The *new economy* (as dictated by the Internet boom) has created markets where they previously did not exist while enhancing those that were once modest, at best. Companies in the United States are finding that penetrating markets in North America may not be enough to remain competitive with rival industry players. Burgeoning economies in Latin America, Asia/Pacific, and Europe are driving a changing world of market and cultural demographics. Before diving headlong into a foreign market, it is prudent to weigh the risks of participating in cross-border commerce with an upside potential.

The Internet
The chief driver of the new economy, undoubtedly, is the Internet. By providing cheap, (relatively) low-maintenance access to the global community, companies of all sizes and means can deliver products and services to once-inaccessible consumers. What is the cost of this unbridled access? Is the company exposed to local tax liabilities if it sells to customers in certain countries? What local disclosure rules are the company subject to? Is the enterprise violating trade treaties or laws by selling to the international community? Is the enterprise prepared to deal with local authorities in the case of trade or import levies? Could U.S. or foreign authorities force the enterprise to shut down its website or stop offering products and services? Any or a combination of these scenarios could have an impact on the financial health of the organization. What is the best way to strategize around such bumps in the road?

Brick-and-Mortar Operations

To better address the issues of doing business in foreign markets, it is best to examine the situation from a bricks-and-mortar perspective—that is, how would the enterprise function if it had a physical presence in a certain country? Having a physical presence in a country avails the company to advantages it would not have if it had no physical presence. Avoiding exorbitant tariffs and duties not to mention glacial import protocols are some of the major advantages of having a physical presence in a foreign country in which a company wishes to do business.

With these advantages, however, come the responsibilities to comply with local tax and reporting rules. Regardless of the company's status (as a subsidiary, distributor, or manufacturing concern) in the foreign locale, foreign countries (with few exceptions) consider the company's mere presence grounds to assess it as a legitimate tax-paying entity. This means allowing local authorities access to all books, records, and information systems for statutory review. It also means complying with all tax laws. Doing so could include definitions of revenue, expenses, assets and liabilities that differ from those of the United States. Lack of compliance with even the mildest of provisions could mean fines, penalties, or a cessation of business. Additionally, accounting treatments prescribed by foreign bodies, whether by the countries themselves, by administrative bodies like the International Accounting Standards Committee, or by a combination of both, must be understood and applied properly. In some cases, local GAAP rules and tax rules are one and the same; in other cases they may be different. Examples of country-specific reporting rules are:

- *Thin capitalization rules.* Many countries require that certain threshold ratios of debt to equity be maintained. For example, if Germany requires that all companies doing business within its borders have no more than a 1.5 to 1 debt-to-equity ratio, any slippage below this ratio could deem a company bankrupt and require it to be liquidated. Companies often must institute drastic measures in circumstances like this, such as injecting cash into the enterprise or converting debt to equity. The solution required to address such a problem may be counter to the company's overall strategy.
- *Hyperinflationary accounting rules.* Certain countries with unstable economies require the revaluation of balance sheet and/or profit and loss (P&L) balances on a periodic basis to mitigate the impact of a weak local currency. Economies that are hyperinflationary have specific rules for revaluing balances in an effort to keep year-to-year comparisons of data accurate. This may include creating and maintaining specifically defined accounts on the general ledger. In Mexico, for example, this is called the *B-10 calculation* and is mandated for all companies that are traded on the public exchange.

Aside from reporting and tax rules, a company must take into account cultural norms and the potential for political instability. Other countries may deal with issues related to social costs (equivalent to Social Security in the United States), vacation time, and employee hiring/firing very differently from what is done in the United States. Social costs may be significantly higher in foreign countries, something that must be factored into budgets and forecasts. The norm for vacation time in some countries may be a minimum of six weeks or more per employee. Rules related to constructive termination (where employees are deemed terminated due to a change in work environment) play a huge factor in some countries, especially if a restructuring effort is undertaken by the U.S. parent company. Generous statutory severance also plays a factor in restructuring efforts. These costs must be taken into account in budgets and financial models, whether they are one-time charges or recurring expenses, especially when the viability of operations is considered.

Infrastructure issues also play a role in doing business in foreign countries. The level of reliability of certain aspects of infrastructure vary wildly from country to country. The condition of roads, public structures, water supplies, phone lines, and electricity ranges from excellent to poor depending on the continent, country, or city. It is not uncommon in some countries for phone lines and power grids to go down for extended periods of time. If a period-end closing of the books relies on the submission of data from a country with poor or unreliable phone lines, the closing may be held up or put in jeopardy, a particular concern for public companies with scheduled press release dates and filing deadlines.

LITIGATION

Litigation can have a direct and/or indirect impact on the enterprise. The impact of litigation filters down to the bottom line in the form of fines, penalties, inability to sell a product, or mandated recalls. In a more subtle way, litigation impacts the way an entire industry approaches a market or an individual company's brand image. A perfect example of both the overt and the subtle impact of litigation on the enterprise is embodied in the Microsoft antitrust litigation, *United States of America v. Microsoft Corporation,*[5] which extended from May 1998 to April 2000 (original trial). The economic fallout from this action has already been borne by Microsoft shareholders. Microsoft's market capitalization declined precipitously as the initial verdict was read and penalties proposed. The real and most far-reaching impact, however, will be felt by smaller, existing software makers and consumers. By mandating a change to the way Microsoft produces and markets its operating systems, the U.S. Justice Department can significantly alter the landscape of the computer software industry. The wide-open, hypercompetitive software industry sought by plaintiffs in the case may come to pass, which could change the financial fortunes for many.

Litigation also can have a direct impact on companies that do not follow reporting and disclosure rules. A good example is the case of Caterpillar Inc., a global manufacturer of heavy equipment. The company was subject to class action suits related to financial statements it issued in 1990. The lawsuits alleged, among other things, violations of certain provisions of the federal securities laws. The complaints alleged that company executives fraudulently issued public statements and reports during the period from January 19, 1990, to June 26, 1990, which were misleading in that they failed to disclose material adverse information relating to the company's Brazilian operations, its factory modernization program, and its reorganization plan. In this case the lack of disclosure of potential foreign currency risk in its Brazilian operations led to shareholder lawsuits filed when the economy of Brazil hiccupped, adversely affecting the company's financial statements. The precipitous drop in the price of the stock led to the lawsuits, which forced the resignation of key executives in the organization and led to other debilitating sanctions. The circumstances surrounding this case moved the SEC to issue specific guidance on disclosures in certain public filings.[6] Acute punitive damages for executives are becoming more common as the SEC continues to get tough with those who manipulate accounting and disclosure guidelines for their own benefit. This means jail time. Phar-Mor, Bennet Funding Group, Lumivision, Bernard Food Industries, and California Micro Devices are examples of companies whose executives served time for accounting/disclosure indiscretions.[7]

The key point is recognizing the need to evaluate risk in the organization. For the small and emerging business owner, this may be a challenge. The need to recognize the presence of risk in doing business and quantify it is the challenge of the finance organization. At the very least, reserves and insurance to cover potential litigation should be in place. However, as a growing business enterprise becomes more diverse in its offerings and the business environment becomes more complex, the finance organization must be suited to identifying and quantifying the risk associated with the direct or indirect impact of litigation.

TECHNOLOGY NEEDS OF VENDORS AND CUSTOMERS

The business owner must be in tune with suppliers and customers from an infrastructure perspective as well. The Internet has enabled business-to-business ordering, which greatly enhances the speed and accuracy with which orders for merchandise and services are communicated. This paperless model for handling customers and vendors, however, may require attention to system and application interfaces. Collaboration of the two is becoming more and more necessary for businesses with common supply interests or those that participate in similar vertical markets. Having adequate platforms and interfaces is a must to enable these tremendous cost-saving models.

Participating in these paperless models often opens up a whole new world of stewardship when it comes to systems maintenance. The intricate interdependencies of different companies and their interfaces or applications requires an all-or-nothing participation commitment. If one component/participant goes down, how does this affect the rest of the consortium? How vulnerable to viruses or damage is the consortium? Can a single participant crash the whole system? Issues like these must be addressed up front before such an endeavor is sought as a cost-savings solution. Business owners must be willing to commit time and dollars to such solutions in an amount equal to that of other participants.

EMPLOYEE NEEDS

Some of the most challenging decisions made by small and emerging company owners relate to employee-related benefits. Health insurance, life insurance, and 401k plans may be a part of the business owner's plan to retain top talent and foster loyalty. These plans have a cost, however, and the business owner has a responsibility to ensure they are appropriately funded and suit employees. Do these plans require a one-time outlay of cash to set up? How heavy will the funding obligations be over time? Will the funding obligations change over time? Is the company properly reserved to fund a huge liability to the program if needed? Employee benefit plans should be a part of any small and emerging business, but the business owner must be aware of the financial obligations of the particular programs that have been or will be put in place. The headache of switching programs for financial reasons may create confusion and bad will rather than peace of mind among employees.

STRIKES

Depending on the industry, labor strikes may impact the company either directly or indirectly. A company whose operations rely on organized labor (or other companies with organized labor) may be vulnerable in the event of a work stoppage. Work stoppages due to labor strikes could result in unfilled orders, slow returns, and supply chain slowdowns. For many small and emerging businesses, the impact of strikes may be more indirect. Merchandisers that rely on the Internet to reach customers may depend exclusively on the post office, UPS, or FedEx to deliver merchandise to customers. What type of provisions have been made to guard against the impact of strikes at courier companies? If a strike cuts off delivery to customers, how long could the company hold out? What is the run rate on cash? The company should have as a part of its strategy a finance model that addresses such a scenario.

NATURAL DISASTERS

All companies are subject to risk of some sort, not the least of which are acts of nature. Whether it is hurricanes in the Southeast, floods in the Midwest, or earthquakes in the far West, the most extreme circumstances must be considered when it comes to planning a business strategy. Provisions should be made not only for the operational aspects of the business in the event of a natural disaster (manufacturing, distribution, service support) but for the repository of financial data and the data flow dynamic as well. SEC filings, state and federal tax returns, debt compliance, and the like must be attended to regardless of circumstances. Although authorities make provisions for companies affected by such events, rarely if ever do they forgive a reporting requirement. In this age of electronic data storage, there is no excuse for losing all financial data and the capability to gather it in the event of a natural disaster.

Many companies in high-risk areas have insurance to guard against business disruption and physical plant damage in the event of a natural disaster. However, the life-blood of the organization—the ability to convert data to knowledge—must be preserved in all circumstances. Does the organization back up key data (financial or otherwise) daily? Is the data stored in an alternate offsite location? If the organization operates in a high-risk area, is this storage site in an alternate, less risky geographic area? How about provisions for the finance function itself to continue in the midst of a devastated area? It may take something less than a disaster to impair a company's ability to function. For businesses in the southeastern United States, heavy rains and flood conditions are common during the late summer and early fall. If offices are flooded and computer systems are damaged, how will the company continue to bill and service customers? How will it close the books if such an event happens during year-end? Do key personnel have alternate communication and workstation capability? Has an alternate "hot site" or rendezvous point been designated in the event of disaster? Does a plan exist to mobilize key finance personnel to continue with crucial finance tasks?

TEN QUESTIONS

This book provides guidance and insight on finance infrastructure, policies, and the culture of analysis. What this book does not provide is the inclination to act. The following 10-question self-examination serves to drive home the need to strategize the finance function.

  1. *How much time spent on finance matters is quality time?*   Are the decision makers really making decisions or performing clerical finance tasks? In a survey of over 1,000 large and small companies, Hackett

Benchmarking Solutions, a consulting group in Hudson, Ohio, found that throughout the 1990s, finance managers were spending an increasing amount of time on clerical tasks such as billing, compliance, and booking journal entries and less time on decision support, planning, and managing the finance function. They found that from 1996 to 1999, the amount of time spent on transaction processing increased from 41% to 47%. In that same time period, the amount of time spent on strategic planning, business performance analysis, and cost analysis declined from 18% to 16%.[8] Because the business executive's time is at a premium in the critical formative years of the business, it is worth the effort to set the stage for a well-oiled finance function that minimizes non–value-added tasks. Are the prime movers of the business making decisions or crunching numbers?

2. *How often does the organization focus exclusively on financial/accounting tasks?* Closing the books at the end of the month should not paralyze the organization. The objective should be to make a period-end close a non-event. More time spent on pulling the numbers together means less time for analysis and interpretation of the numbers. This point applies to nonstandard information requests as well. The finance function should be able to respond to all standard and (reasonable) nonstandard information requests relatively quickly. How well does the organization's finance function do this?

3. *How reliant is the organization on financing?* Growing a business with other people's money is what is great about being in business. The down side—it *is* other people's money, and strings *are* attached. Depending on the type of financing in place or being sought, the organization may be subject to audits or reviews that are a matter of law. Can the finance function hold up to scrutiny? If the validity of numbers is in doubt, the finance function is not adequate and the organization is not ready to use other people's money to grow the business.

4. *Does the flow of cash into the business move in proportion with earnings?* Hardcore analysts look at these two major indicators of company performance—cash flow and earnings—and draw an overall conclusion on the health of the organization. If both indicators move in tandem over time, that is good news. If they diverge for any significant length of time, then red flags pop up all over the place. Without getting too technical, the business may have good reason for earnings and cash flow to diverge (investment in infrastructure may be one reason). The important question to ask is: How quickly does revenue translate to cash? Does the organization have to wait an inordinate amount of time to collect cash from customers? This is often a problem and businesses do not even know it. Good customers may not be good after all if they deprive the business of cash owed on the sale of products and services. In the spawning years of any business, optimizing cash flow is a must. Does the finance organization have the capability to track this crucial indicator?

5. *Does the business have a manufacturing/supply chain?* If the business is a manufacturer, how well is it using technology to streamline the management of data related to the supply chain? "Managing the supply chain" refers to maximizing margins on goods sold rather than managing inventory. If the organization has not considered initiatives such as purchasing supplies online or sharing product purchase forecast reports with vendors online, it may be letting dollars slip through its hands. Has the business owner evaluated and strategized the supply chain?

6. *Is the industry in which the business operates reliant on the Internet?* According to the Small Business Administration, small companies that rely on the Internet for doing business have higher revenues than those that do not. Internet-savvy small businesses average nearly 40% higher revenues than the average of all small business revenue.[9] For all small and emerging businesses that are Internet ventures, it is no secret that the business environment is changing on a daily basis. These business owners must ask themselves if they are prepared to change their business model on a day's notice. In addition, they must have a feel for how well their data gathering, processing, and analysis tools suit their changing information needs. Can the finance function change its focus at the drop of a hat? Being able to thrive in this environment will mean being able to gather the particular data needed, when it is needed most. How well can the finance function react to the organization's changing needs?

7. *Does the company rely on nonfinancial databases?* The organization may be juggling a myriad of databases that gather both financial and nonfinancial data. The organization's marketing department may be presiding over a substantial cache of data that grows daily. Is the finance function plugged into this? Are business owners enabling forecasting and budgeting by accessing this nonfinancial data? The ability for the finance organization to access *all* data gathered by the enterprise (financial or otherwise) creates valuable synergies for the finance organization and magnifies its impact on operations. How well has the organization harnessed this data?

8. *Is the organization a new player in a new industry?* Being the new kid on the block is one thing, but starting up a business in an industry that is relatively new is quite another challenge. With nothing or no one to measure itself against, the organization will have a difficult time establishing meaningful metrics and benchmarks for growth. The need to be *transparent* (translate easily to financial statements) is more important than ever if

the business is alone in a new industry or niche. The challenge of the small and emerging business owner will be to navigate a nonstandard season or fickle marketplace while balancing seed money and other financing alternatives. Getting a hand on the pulse of the organization and getting it quickly will require a robust forecast and budget function as well as an agile closing process. The small and emerging business owner must determine if the finance function is up to the task.

9. *How does the small and emerging business owner visualize growing the business?* Do the owners and executives subscribe to the model of growth through acquisition, or are they more comfortable with the organic (internally generated) growth model? If they subscribe to the former, are they prepared to adapt a target company's finance model to theirs? If the business is predicated on an organic growth model, what metrics (measures) and analysis models are being employed to reach growth goals? As a practical matter, most business growth strategies should employ a fair mix of organic and acquisitive growth initiatives. If financing will play any role in growth strategies, having a sound data flow dynamic will be imperative to maintain compliance with loan covenants and financial statement deadlines. Is the organization prepared for this?

10. *How savvy is the management team?* As a small or emerging company, chances are the management team has a broad skill set with no consistent degree of depth in multiple areas. Most likely, the management team is heavy on the operations side, which can result in acute issues on the finance side going unaddressed (traditionally these are viewed as an administrative or back-office function). Waiting to deal with finance and accounting issues until they become a crisis will cost the organization in both dollars and/or lost opportunities. It is possible, however, to take steps in the early years of the business to set the stage for sound finance function development. Ignoring this part of the business in its infancy may put the organization's decision-making, operational strategies, and customer relationships at risk. The organization's management team must ask itself: How much attention has been given to the finance function?

FINAL THOUGHTS

Evaluating the current state of the organization and the finance function that supports it can be a sobering exercise, especially when it relates to a business entrepreneurs/owners may have spent their lives building. If the 10 questions above have cast doubt or concern on the state of the finance function and its effectiveness, let this book serve as a primer for organizing thoughts and developing a sound strategy for finance function development. The first step in creating a sound finance strategy is recognizing the need to develop one in the first place. The next step is to understand what the finance function is and why the need to strategize is so important.

NOTES

1. Small Business Administration (SBA), Office of Advocacy, Washington, D.C., *www.sba.gov/advo.*
2. SBA, Office of Advocacy, Washington, D.C., *www.sba.gov/size/guide.*
3. *Ibid.*
4. Jake Wengroff, "SEC Scrutiny: They'll Be Watching," *CFO,* July 2001, p. 12.
5. *United States of America v. Microsoft Corporation,* U.S. District Court for the District of Columbia, 2000.
6. *In the Matter of Caterpillar Inc.,* Exchange Act Release No. 30532, March 31, 1992.
7. Tim Reason, "Jailhouse Shock," *CFO,* September 2000, p. 113.
8. Eric Krell, "Finance Managers on the Wrong Track," *Business Finance,* July 2000, p. 10.
9. SBA, *www.sba.gov/advo.*

2

FINANCE FUNCTION DEFINED

KEY TAKEAWAYS

- Understanding the basic tasks of the finance function.
- Understanding the definition and purpose of the finance function.
- Distinguishing between two major components of the finance function: concrete components and soft components.
- Recognizing traditional perceptions of the finance function and how to overcome them.
- Understanding how and why to synchronize the finance function with operations.
- Understanding how to preserve the dynamic nature of the finance function and why it is important.
- Understanding why the finance function must preserve the integrity of financial representations of the company.

FINANCE FUNCTION IN ACTION

Conceptualizing, implementing, and maintaining a finance strategy requires an understanding of the finance function itself. This function has many components, some more easily defined than others. The finance function serves as the foundation for virtually all aspects of the business—from gathering data and converting it to knowledge, to performing due diligence on expansions, to disseminating financial data to the general public.

So what *does* the finance function do? Many aspects of the business are prompted, driven, or dependent on the finance function. However, some of the following areas also are considered an explicit part:

- Budgets and forecasts
- Closing the books
- External reporting
- Paying bills
- Billing and collecting cash from customers

- Paying salaries
- Financing
- Collecting and paying taxes
- Human resources

Budgets and Forecasts

For publicly traded companies, budgeting and forecasting play an integral role in relating to the external community. Because earnings and growth estimates drive stock price, garnering accurate budget and forecast data in a timely manner is key to achieving an optimal stock price and market capitalization for the enterprise. This aspect of the finance function is no less important for small and emerging businesses that are not publicly traded. Understanding raw material needs, personnel needs, and expansion requirements will force the small and emerging business owner to thoughtfully estimate their needs in the business environment.

Closing the Books

Also referred to as *the close,* this aspect of the finance function is the process by which all subsidiary ledgers and journals of the organization are summed up for a given time period while assets and obligations (liabilities) are valued. The close may be relatively simple for small, single-site organizations or complex for large, multinational organizations. The close may cover activity over a period of a month, quarter, or year. The value of a quick close is the ability to assess the organization and provide a basis to make business-wide, strategic decisions. An organization that has difficulty with the timing of a close or with the accuracy of the data this process yields is at risk if the industry in which it operates moves quickly and changes often.

At the heart of the close is the data flow dynamic, which is the process by which the data is gathered at the front lines of the organization and translated into meaningful information for management. A sound data flow dynamic is agile—it works quickly and can react to the changing environment. A sound data flow dynamic will yield complete and accurate information to the management team.

The ideal closing process can be done over a period of hours, which means it can be executed on any given day. Global organizations or organizations with multiple geographical locations rely heavily on a quick close. Small to midsize organizations also should have the capability to close their books organization-wide within a few days. This enables the business to look at the entire organization's performance on a monthly basis without disrupting operations.

External Reporting

Organizations with outside financing, absentee shareholders, and certain regulatory requirements to follow have standard external reporting requirements. Typical of many companies, this shows how banks, shareholders, and the general public are all *stakeholders* in the organization. Unlike owners who participate in day-to-day management, these stakeholders do not have ready access to the performance re-sults of the company. In spite of this *absentee ownership,* shareholders and debt holders (those lending money to the company) still have an interest in the company's performance. They rely exclusively on the legally mandated reporting requirements of the organization to gain an understanding of company performance.

Publicly traded companies are subject to comprehensive reporting requirements. These reporting requirements typically have hard deadlines (quarterly) and content requirements. Public companies must adhere to the detailed requirements of generally accepted accounting principles in preparing the details of account balances as well as additional nonfinancial disclosures mandated by the Securities and Exchange Commission. The final product must be subjected to audit or review procedures by a qualified professional (a certified public accountant).

Because the majority of owners (stockholders) of public companies are absentee (i.e., do not participate in day-to-day management or operations), they rely on the accuracy and predictability of the data coming from the companies in which they invest. They hold the company to performance predictions or forecasts and typically punish those companies that do not meet their expectations by *dumping* (selling) the stock. This fact underscores the need for good data and shows how external reporting may have both an actual and a budget/forecast component. Companies must realize that before going public or taking on outside stakeholders, they must ensure their reporting process is sound from the data flow dynamic to the dissemination of data to stakeholders. Maintaining credibility with the external community is key to optimizing stock price or future consideration of stakeholders.

Paying Bills

Managing cash in and cash out is critical for the small and emerging business. It is important to ensure that vendors, creditors, and service providers are paid the proper amounts at the proper time. Optimizing cash flow means staying adequately liquid (having as much cash on hand as possible) at all times. The finance function must record and maintain payment policies that balance the organization's cash needs (optimize liquidity) while paying bills within a reasonable time period. Rather than paying bills as they are received, organizations should take advantage of payment terms. Paying a bill the day it is received as opposed to waiting through a vendor-approved term of 30 days or more may deny the organization cash it needs to run the business. A sound finance function schedules cash payments that optimize the organization's cash management objectives—which means keeping as much cash on hand as possible while satisfying vendors and their payment terms.

Billing and Collecting Cash from Customers

Most important, an organization's success or failure is based on how well it can bring in cash. Many companies can have substantial difficulties in billing and collecting from customers. Terms and conditions of delivery and/or satisfactory installation of promised products can represent a substantial gap between recognizing revenue (signing contracts, etc.), and billing and collecting cash from customers. These circumstances can turn a nice revenue or sales number into a highly discounted or delayed payment term. Companies may have the sales process down but fall short when it comes to follow-through. At this crucial juncture of the organization's operations, the finance function must be in sync with the company, especially with the way in which it does business and relates to customers.

The growing availability of Internet software packages suited for billing and collections creates alternatives for companies in the area of cash management. Investigating these alternatives is important for the small and emerging business owner whose resources (time and money) are in short supply. The advantage of using these packages is that they are usually quick and easy to deploy and relatively inexpensive. Being linked online to customers facilitates quick, paperless orders as well as swift, simple billing and payment processes.

The cautious business owner may prefer the traditional method of delivering bills through the mail. Regardless of the preference, the finance function must pursue a reliable billing and collection methodology that suits both customers and management. When conceptualizing this aspect of the finance function, the organization has three basic alternatives:

1. *In-house billing and collections.*   This involves employing personnel to prepare, mail, and monitor bills. It also means maintaining a team to follow up on and execute the collection effort. This is the costliest option, although traditionalists see it as the most reliable route in billing and collections.
2. *Partial outsourcing.*   Some businesses hire third parties to bill customers, while they focus their own efforts on collections. This is an option for small and emerging businesses that are not yet equipped to handle the documentation aspect of billing.
3. *Complete outsourcing.*   In this case a third party handles all aspects of billing and collections. For the company that is growing quickly and does not have the internal resources to handle this function, complete outsourcing is a viable option.

Beyond the technological aspect of billing and collecting, what other challenges must be considered? Culture, especially for multinational companies, is a big issue. Selling merchandise to customers in foreign countries where owning a credit card is not common makes online billing and collection difficult. For brick-and-mortar (as opposed to virtual) operations that are in foreign countries, what is the custom for collecting cash? In some South American countries, for example, the custom is to collect receivables in person.

Paying Salaries

One of the most important aspects of dispensing resources may lie in the way businesses pay employees. Keeping employees satisfied includes paying them in a reliable and timely manner. Perhaps the most overwhelming hurdle a young company faces is dealing with the laws that govern payroll taxes—Social Security, withholding, Medicare, and so on. The finance function must make the process of paying employees quick and painless for both the employee and the employer. Many companies choose to outsource this aspect of the finance function (i.e., pay a third party to manage this task). Considering the record-keeping requirements plus the need to observe state and local laws, outsourcing is a good alternative. For companies that choose to save the money, some other considerations for employing a payroll system include direct deposit, stock purchase, 401k and retirement plan deductions, and benefits withholding. For many business owners this is the first hurdle in developing the finance function.

Financing

Financing the company's operations may be the single most important aspect of the finance function for the small and emerging business owner. Adding fuel to the company's fiscal engines is a challenge that never ends—although at the early stages of the organization it is particularly critical. What does financing mean? In simple terms, it means keeping the company's coffers full of cash to run the business. As a practical matter, it means doing this while maintaining a balanced capital structure (debt versus equity). The finance function lies at the core of financing efforts both in assessing needs and in maintaining access to the capital markets.

The first challenge in financing the organization is setting up the pipeline of cash. The small and emerging business owner may choose a credit line from a bank, mortgage loan, or equipment leases. Approaching local banks that participate in small business loan programs is often a good solution. The finance function will provide data on the health of the company and/or forecast its performance. The burden is on the small business owner to garner the required financial data to paint the company's financial picture for loan officers and answer necessary questions.

The second challenge, though no less important, is the maintenance of loan covenants. Do certain financial ratios or levels of performance have to be maintained? How equipped is the finance function at monitoring the covenants in loan agreements? Assembling sketchy documentation to secure a loan then subsequently failing to meet the loan covenants or conditions of financing may create a bigger headache than having never received the financing in the first place. Monitoring the capital structure, specifically keeping track of debt versus equity financing and what best suits the organization in the near, mid-, and long term, is crucial when dealing with financing needs. These issues are an integral part of the finance function.

Collecting and Paying Taxes

Regardless of the size or form of the company, the obligation to comply with tax laws is omnipresent. Whether it is compliance with federal, state, or local laws, the finance function must be prepared to gather the necessary information and documentation to support remittances to taxing authorities. Federal tax laws may require the finance function to compute alternative depreciation methods on assets, track nondeductible expenses, or gather specific data on manufacturing costs. State and local tax laws may require detailed documentation that validates sales and use tax remittances. Documentation requirements vary from state to state. This puts a burden on the finance function to accumulate adequate documentation in companies that provide products and services in multiple state jurisdictions. The finance function also is burdened with the task of interpreting the varying state tax laws appropriately to keep the company in compliance with the various jurisdictions in which it does business.

Human Resources

The small and emerging business owner must address staffing needs in the finance area—both hiring new, qualified professionals and attending to the needs of current employees. This may not be an issue if the finance function is outsourced. If the responsibility is to monitor an outsourcing contract, however, the business owner/manager still must search for, hire, and retain qualified, knowledgeable professionals. Networking with peers and placement agencies is a part of the task of finding the right finance professionals. What is the going rate? What skills are needed? When it comes to providing the small and emerging business with the "human" aspect of the finance function, overstaffing can be just as damaging as understaffing.

FINANCE FUNCTION DEFINED

The finance function consists of the people, technology, processes, and policies that dictate tasks and decisions related to financial resources of a company. Depending on the organization and the industry in which it operates, this function may be simple or complex. Some finance functions are "overstaffed"—that is, they rely on individuals to perform both advanced and simple tasks—while others are highly automated—relying on people for decision making and policy setting exclusively.

Regardless of the ratio of people to technology, the goal of the finance function is to serve the organization's financial/accounting needs while laying a platform for the future. This means handling clerical tasks, providing information to the organization, and setting financial policies and strategies that will serve the company in the future. To succeed in these three broad areas, the small and emerging business must be prepared to develop a finance function that both suits its needs and can adapt to the growth and changes of the business. The first step is to *develop* an adequate finance function. To do this, it is important to understand the component parts.

COMPONENT PARTS

The finance function consists of two basic component types: (1) concrete components and (2) soft components. Concrete components include all aspects of infrastructure including technology, software applications, and processes, as well as the people who manage them. Soft components include the standards, strategies, models, and vision that drive the finance/accounting aspect of the business. Each component stands on its own to an extent; however, ultimately all components must be woven together in a way that serves the overall organization objectives. It is not enough that all component parts exist; rather they must exist in harmony with one another, yielding synergies that serve the company's needs today and provide for the future.

Concrete Components

The term *infrastructure,* in this context, refers to all relevant concrete components of the finance function. These components may already exist in the organization in some fashion, although they are not thought of as infrastructure. Regardless of how they were classified, these components were assessed for their usefulness and either purchased or developed. In order for certain tasks to be undertaken on a regular basis, tools and processes must be put in place to manage them. Items of infrastructure can be classified into three major categories: (1) finance organization, (2) information systems, and (3) processes.

FINANCE ORGANIZATION The term *finance organization* refers to the people responsible for conceptualizing, implementing, and following through with all finance and accounting related tasks and initiatives, as well as the technological tools they employ. The finance function works best when people with the right qualifications are matched with the right tasks. When the proper technological tools are put in the mix, the finance organization will excel and serve the needs of the organization. Chapter 4, "Multilevel Approach," addresses issues related to developing the finance organization in more detail. Here the focus is on issues related to the two major components: staffing and technology:

- *Staffing.* Enlisting the right people for the job is a challenge in any business. When certain aspects of the finance organization (namely infrastructure) are lacking, it is easy for employers to lose sight of essential employee skill needs. For example, the position of Director of Budget and Forecasting may require Information Systems (IS) skills because no IS organization exists.

Finding a Director of Budget and Forecasting may be difficult enough, but finding one with advanced IS skills may be impossible. Finance personnel typically rely on technological tools to do their jobs; however, they may not be so knowledgeable at maintaining the technology. If substandard tools are provided to professionals, they may have to fend for themselves when it comes to managing the secondary demands of the job (making their computer work or administering software) rather than focus on their primary objective (managing the budget and forecasting process).

This human element of the finance organization can be a powerful resource for the organization if the right people are a part of the team and if they are allowed to generate and implement new ideas. Expecting people to not only perform their tasks but also to optimize the way their function fits in with the business will provide value to the organization and provide meaningful career development for employees. Personnel should be allowed to isolate all business needs and drivers, determine the impact of these on the organization, and be rewarded for the business strategy/planning that results.

■ *Technology.* Nothing is more important than providing people with the right tools for the job. This means appropriately configured computers, communication devices, and planning tools. Simply buying the best technology may not always be the answer. A mistake repeated every day by executives and business owners is falling prey to a vendor's claim that if the smartest or best machine is purchased, the users' objectives will be met. The nature of the tasks to be performed must be taken into account before staff are outfitted with technology. Will desktop computers suffice or will staff need laptops instead? Will finance staff need cell phones or other types of communication linkage? How about planning devices—do staff need personal digital assistants or other wireless devices to share documents and information remotely? Knowing whether staff will be performing tasks in one central location or performing tasks "on the road" will drive decisions for technology.

INFORMATION SYSTEMS   The term *information systems* refers to the backbone technology—servers, switches, operating systems, protocols, and software applications that will drive the finance function. Distinguished from *technology* defined earlier, information systems have a broader impact on the entire platform of the organization's technological capability. This term is used more on a macro-level as opposed to the term *technology.* Information systems give organizations the ability to gather data in the business environment and translate it to knowledge. They also provide the ability to communicate information and data within and outside the organization. Information systems provide a basis for evaluating customers while allowing them to provide feedback to the organization. This aspect of infrastructure also allows the organization to link with information systems of customers and companies in the same industry to achieve synergies in buying, forecasting, billing, and collecting customer payments.

PROCESSES   Processes are the protocols and procedures that envelop information systems. They leverage the impact of information systems and bridge the gap between raw systems capability and company specific needs. Processes cannot be generic but must be customized and suited for a particular organization's needs. To develop processes, the business owner/manager must have an acute knowledge of the organization and what it is trying to accomplish. To succeed in process development, knowledge of employee capability, thresholds of technology, and limits of systems also must be firmly grasped. Chapter 6, "Data Flow Processes," outlines in greater detail the dynamics of process development in the finance function.

Soft Components

Soft components of the finance function are the more advanced considerations of the function itself. Policies, standards, strategies, and analysis paradigms are examples of soft components. These components cannot be bought or replicated necessarily from an outside source; rather they are developed internally. It is management's responsibility to develop the soft components of the finance function and maintain them as the company grows and adapts to its environment. The existence and relevance of soft components are good litmus tests for the strength of management. Companies that are lacking in this area put the organization at risk and leave development of the finance area to chance. Allowing the finance function to evolve on its own without a vision driven by strategies and formed with standards could create more problems than it solves.

Developing finance strategies, standards, and policies may be a luxury for the small and emerging business owner when compared to the day-to-day necessities of keeping the organization running. It is important to note, however, that most soft components of the finance function are not developed overnight. In fact, rarely are they complete or relevant for very long. Soft components are always developing and changing as the business organization changes. Developing them should be embraced as an aspect of organizational culture. Although an organization may be able to enjoy success in its early years without attending to these components of the finance function, eventually issues in the business itself or business environment will demand them. For example, infrastructure may suit a small and emerging business in the short run, but increasing demands for information and new ways to serve customers may necessitate change in this area. Absent the vision for development or the strategy for addressing future data needs, the finance function always will be a step behind, which will result in perpetual short-term decision mode. This may be costly in the long run as managers purchase unscalable technology to solve an immediate need, only to find themselves repurchasing more technology a short time later to accommodate evolving needs.

Well-thought-out soft components will make development of all aspects of the finance function second nature. For example, developing financial analysis paradigms that are relevant to the organization's business fundamentals will drive IS needs. These paradigms will in turn drive the level of qualifications of personnel. Strategies then can be developed that implement relevant software applications, technological tools, communication devices, and so on. This "web of impact" illustrates how all aspects of the finance function cascade off the soft components.

Practically speaking, the small and emerging business owner may not be focused on the mid- and long-term time horizon. Therefore, codifying areas of vision, strategy, and policy in the finance area may not be practical. It is important to note, however, that being aware of developing soft components at the early stage of the organization will greatly benefit the business owner/manager as the business matures. The high rate of change in the business in its early years may render soft components irrelevant overnight. Laying a foundation of thought and intent to develop this aspect of the finance function will become that much easier as the business owner/manager matures with the business and becomes more savvy in developing strategy.

TRADITIONAL PERCEPTION OF THE FINANCE FUNCTION

For the small and emerging business owner, the greatest barrier to developing a sound finance function may be the traditional perception of finance and accounting. The erroneous perception of the finance function as the meticulously slow and detailed process that yields soberingly bad news of past performance must be addressed. The reality is that the finance function *must* be up to the task of steward of the most valuable data the enterprise will encounter. The responsibility of this stewardship requires that the finance function excel in its role as communicator, educator, and visionary. Success in developing a sound finance function will hinge on the ability to deal with these (mis)perceptions:

- Accounting and finance people should be effective, detail-oriented number crunchers.
- When it comes to finance structure, one-size fits all.
- Finance should trail operations.
- Finance is separate from the rest of the organization.
- Rules of accounting are cut and dried.
- Accounting is for taxes last.

Accounting and Finance People Should Be Effective, Detail-Oriented Number Crunchers

Accounting and finance people must step up to their role as communicators who are accessible for all aspects of decision making in the organization. Whether decisions are related to acquisitions, product expansion, or market penetration, the finance organization has an obligation to interpret historical data as well as forecast and budget data and to articulate the practical aspect of any proposed business initiative. The number-crunching and detail-oriented aspects of the accounting world are being addressed more and more by technology and third-party vendors. This has enabled the finance and accounting person's role to become more big picture oriented and business focused. As an educator, the accounting/finance person has an obligation to interpret complex and changing rules and laws that impact the business, especially if the company is publicly traded. As a visionary, the accounting/finance person has the capacity to determine the capability of technology and processes that harness information in the business environment, to create meaningful analyses that will suit the company's business needs. The accounting/finance person must put a premium on networking with peers to understand best practices and alternative solutions to challenges. This potential can be realized only if expectations from management and business owners are consistent with this shifting focus.

When It Comes to Finance Structure, One Size Fits All

What works for one company will not necessarily work for others. While benchmarking and employing best practices are crucial to getting the finance function on track, integrating all tasks smoothly and efficiently with operations is the key to long-term success. Such integration means focusing on the relevance of all components of the finance function, whether they are best practices or not, and determining if they are consistent with the vision of the company. Although they may have success initially, organizations that get caught up in best practices *in spite* of strategy will achieve mediocrity at best with their finance function in the mid and long term.

Finance Should Trail Operations

When strolling through the hallways of larger organizations, it is not uncommon to see the coveted corner offices occupied by operations people, while the finance people dwell on the fringe. This occupancy scheme is indicative of the relative perceived value of the finance organization. The prevailing opinion of finance is that it is not a value-added function but rather a necessary evil that all organizations must endure to stay in compliance with reporting requirements. In reality, major strategic operational decisions should be made with strong influence from the finance organization. Whether the decisions relate to acquisitions, market expansions, product divestitures, or customer retention, the finance organization must be poised to provide input on all relevant facts, particularly those related to synergies and cash flow advantages/disadvantages of decisions.

The small and emerging business owner should understand that every decision must have a positive, long-term financial impact on the organization, whether it is increasing revenue, decreasing expenses, or altering the capital structure. Entering into decisions without input from the finance organization could lead to actions that hurt the organization from a fiscal standpoint. Calling on the finance organization to be a part of overall decision making is a formidable challenge for the business owner/manager. This expanded, operational role of finance includes (where possible) leading the organization by anticipating information needs and providing access to crucial metrics and models that allow for nonfinance people to make well-informed decisions.

Finance Is Separate from the Rest of the Organization

The finance function should be considered a platform or common denominator to all parts of the organization. Whether it is marketing, sales, manufacturing, or Human Resources (HR), all aspects of the organization need to make a reasonable contribution to its financial health. To this end, the finance function must provide access and practical guidance to all aspects of business operations. Making nonfinance aspects of the business a regular part of the budgeting process or a part of the normal data dissemination chain will foster acceptance of the finance organization into the mainstream operational areas of the business. Only through acceptance of the finance organization as a relevant, valuable tool can the nonfinance part of the business organization be optimized. The traditional perception of finance as a detached non–value-added function will degrade the value of financial analysis and breed a culture of recklessness when it comes to making decisions throughout the organization. Finance initiatives should be considered a shared value and be a critical aspect of all decisions throughout the organization.

Rules of Accounting Are Cut and Dried

According to conventional thought, the rules for interpreting transactions and environmental factors in the businessplace are codified in a comprehensive, complete form. The body of guidance, however, used by the accounting profession is a *conceptual framework* better described as generally accepted accounting principles, not accounting *laws*. For many transactions, GAAP is straightforward, leaving little room for interpretation. Much of the guidance, however, in this conceptual framework is not so straightforward. Because many events and transactions come with their own specific set of facts and circumstances, the business world has the latitude to interpret GAAP in different ways for certain transactions. This fact qualifies the practice of accounting as more an art than a science.

The small and emerging business owner's focus is on growth and stability for the fledgling organization, so why would matters of interpreting accounting guidance be an issue? A new slate of stakeholders (debt holders or outside shareholders) may be introduced to the organization as the company grows and looks to financing alternatives. Requirements to maintain financial ratios and certain levels of earnings can become a distraction to the operations of the business. Additionally, management in mature companies may seek creative accounting alternatives in reaction to unreasonable shareholder demand to create value. Viewing the conceptual framework of accounting as a buffet table of solutions is never appropriate, however, especially when it comes to strategizing the finance function. Regardless, business owners and management need to be aware that putting the company's best foot forward in financial statements may mean investigating the continuum of aggressive and conservative accounting, especially when it comes to business combinations (acquisitions), the path of choice for executives seeking value for shareholders.

Accounting Is for Taxes Last

Dealing with the tax needs of the company often gets lost in the shuffle when it comes to prioritizing the needs of the finance function. The prevailing opinion of business owners/managers is that it does not make sense to let the tax tail wag the corporate dog. This *tax tail* consists of managing the company's effective tax rate, maximizing cash flow, tax deferral, tax compliance, and audit defense. Unlike other aspects of the finance function, ignoring these areas can seriously damage the business. Paralyzing tax levies, liens, and audits may demand more resources than the organization can spare and in some cases can shut down the business.

Record keeping and documentation for tax needs must be an integral part of the finance function from the start. Having the ability to respond to taxing authorities quickly and accurately allows the organization to do business without distractions. The practice of paying tax levies promptly as opposed to pulling accurate data together and responding thoughtfully yields millions in overpaid taxes each year. Working a tax strategy into the finance function inoculates the organization from unreasonable and unnecessary tax demands.

NEED FOR INTEGRATION INTO OPERATIONS

Getting in Sync with the Organization

In defining the finance function, it is not enough to identify component parts and how the finance function (as a whole) should be viewed by management. If the finance function does not contribute to operations, then it fails as a viable component of the corporate body. The role of the finance function as steward of financial information requires that it add value to any aspect of the business that relies on finance data by aligning itself with the organization. Characteristics that underscore a finance function that is synchronized with the organization are relevance, accessibility, and agility.

RELEVANCE   The finance function must gather data that is useful to the organization. Data that is neither timely nor appropriate for the organization cannot be converted to knowledge for the purpose of decision making. For example, an airline that can gather revenue data per flight cannot truly analyze its business unless it understands how ticket revenue is broken down by seat. Which seats were booked at $299? Which seats were booked at $2,999? Knowing the total revenue per flight does not provide insight into customer behavior and varying pricing models. Decisions related to ticket pricing would be impossible unless the company understood the impact of pricing models on its customers. Additionally, analyzing data that is weeks or months old does not provide management with the ability to set pricing policies in response to seasonal or competitive factors. The key to growing a relevant finance function is to be *in tune* with the users or data customers within the organization when developing the finance function.

ACCESSIBILITY   Information is useless if those who need it don't have access to it. The finance function must be technologically accessible by all aspects of the business without being overly complex. Retailers that rely on the Internet as a storefront for their products avail themselves of faster, paperless ordering systems. The Internet also provides a tool that is able to mine a treasure trove of demographic data on customers. What good will this information do if the marketing arm of the organization cannot access the data? The mistake many companies make in setting up E-enabled storefronts is that they fail to link them to legacy (old, existing) and peripheral, nonfinance systems.

Similarly, can users *easily* tap into the bank of information gathered by the finance function? Enterprise resource planning (ERP) tools create the ability to gather large amounts of financial and statistical data on customers, vendors, and the business environment. If the process of creating reports that access the data is overly complex, however, potential users may not rely on it as a regular data source. If the end user does not have the knowledge base to interact with central repositories of financial data, then the finance function has failed them.

AGILITY   The finance function must be able to change as the business changes. A business that reorganizes the way it manages products, people, or geographies relies on the finance function to do the same. Can the finance function gather and process data along new geographic lines? Can it change the way it captures data on products and services? The finance function must change and adapt to remain relevant.

The agile finance function is also quick to implement new tools and new solutions. How open is finance infrastructure to proposed E-business solutions? Can they be integrated quickly and cheaply into legacy systems? Can data gathered in these systems be stored in new systems? The small and emerging business owner must be sensitive to the fact that the business is always growing and changing. Addressing this means that the finance function must be easy to upgrade with new tools and more powerful technology. Powerful technological platforms are a sure way to preserve *scalability* of the finance function—that is, to make expansion and upgrades easy and inexpensive to implement. Implementing solutions quickly is one of the key benefits of a solid finance function. Viable solutions include outsourcing business processes and subscribing to application service providers.

Outsourcing

Quick infrastructure solutions for an organization that is changing frequently may lie in outsourcing certain aspects of the finance function. Outsourcing equates to farming out key processes and tasks that the organization would otherwise have to handle on its own. Whether it is billing, accounts payable, accounts receivable, or external/internal reporting, an organization that is growing too quickly to focus on these functions may take advantage of someone else's infrastructure and know-how to perform them.

Outsourcing capability is becoming larger in scope due in part to the Internet and the availability of high bandwidth (robust phone lines that can handle high volumes of data), which have opened up the outsourcing solution to the small business owner who would otherwise have to enter into expensive, lengthy service contracts to enjoy these benefits. The traditional view of outsourcing—using temporary employees to perform tasks—has evolved into the full-scale availability of accounting and finance applications as well as the know-how from people who can optimize their power and functionality. Outsourcing can serve as an alternative solution for the small and emerging business owner/manager who has neither the time to focus on growing a finance organization nor the money to invest in expensive technological platforms on which to build finance systems. A type of quasi-outsourcing that involves the outsourcing of technology and software only is the application service provider (ASP).

Although outsourcing offers a lot of upside to the small and emerging business owner, it does not come without risks. Trusting an outsider to manage the company's financial data makes some business owners nervous. Outsourcing processes subject the company to the same changing business environment that the service provider must handle. What if the service provider changes management, shifts its focus, or, worse, goes out of business? This may leave the company in a void until it can find another service provider. Conceding control of the billing and collections cycle can also put a third party uncomfortably close to the business's customers. What if the dynamics of the outsourced service sours customers on the whole sales experience? Trusting a third party to pay vendors on time and in full bears a level of risk as well. What if vendors don't get paid on time, resulting in credit holds and other red tape?

One of the subtlest disadvantages of outsourcing the finance function is the lack of knowledge retention in the organization bred over time. The finance organization should be an integral part of the decision making and strategic process of the company. Outsourcing the finance function may deny the small and emerging business the development of a key decision maker in the organization. Outsourcing may have tangible, measurable benefits in the short term, but in the mid- to long term the company forfeits valuable learning curves that would be afforded to members of its own organization. Outsourcing arrangements compel a business to surrender esoteric and highly specialized knowledge of customers and the business environment.

Application Service Providers

Outsourcing in its pure technological form is embodied in ASPs. ASPs are third-party vendors that rent software and information system capability. Enabled by the Internet, an ASP can provide the functionality of an enterprise resource planning tool (ERP), E-Commerce tools, customer relationship management (CRM) tools, or other accounting/tax software via web browser. For a flat fee the ASP takes care of implementing, operating, upgrading, and maintaining software for businesses. The benefits to the small and emerging business are obvious. An ASP dispenses with the need for expensive IS staff to implement and maintain complicated software and hardware. Software upgrades are made in a timely manner by qualified professionals. Subscribers to the ASP can avail themselves of the latest and most effective software without having to engage in a large outlay of cash. More important, *renting* it means *not owning* it. ASPs allow for subscribers to position themselves to enjoy the benefits of functionality without being saddled with the responsibility of installation, maintenance, and, worse, dealing with an outdated piece of software or hardware over time. Having to stick with a software package long past its useful life is the painful byproduct of software ownership.

There are, however, drawbacks to relying on ASPs that must be considered. In the long run, ASPs may cost just as much as investing in infrastructure straight-away. ASP contracts may lock a business into a long-term relationship it might not want to stay in as the company matures. Another drawback involves the ownership of the software. Customizations to software for certain businesses will be forfeited if the business decides to end an ASP contract or change service providers. The level of support for users may vary as well. Help-desk operators may have extremely limited experience. Often, help for acute issues may be available only through consulting arrangements that exceed the ASP support model purchased. Support at odd hours may be limited as well—a particular challenge for companies with operations in overseas locations. Integration with the ASP could be difficult and costly or outright impossible for companies that have legacy systems and software. Forgoing the lack of know-how developed in-house is an expensive trade-off, albeit a subtle one.

The small and emerging business owner/manager must understand that relying on ASPs is a viable *short-term* solution to issues of infrastructure. Mid- to long-term goals for the organization must include migrating this function in-house, thus allowing for the development of the finance function in a way that is consistent with the needs of the growing business.

Managing Business Knowledge

If the finance function is adequately integrated into the business organization, it will be adept at extracting, filtering, and delivering information to users that reinforce strategic and vision-oriented decision making. This capability differentiates businesses that must make decisions based on data that is within arm's reach of their information systems from those that base their decisions on relevant data that is sought out and filtered from the business environment. The dynamic of generating knowledge from data does not happen by accident; it is a by-product of careful planning. The usefulness of the finance function lies in its ability to create and manage business knowledge rather than generate data. The essence of understanding this dynamic and how the finance function accommodates it comes with the knowledge of where data will be generated, who the data customers are, and how the data will be delivered to them.

DATA SOURCES   The fully integrated finance function will be able to combine data gathered from all the various input sources within the organization. Whether it is ERP, CRM, or HR applications, the finance function must be poised to manage all data generated from the business environment. To do so means having powerful platforms that support these applications and the capability to run data queries that combine, compare, and filter through data records.

DATA CUSTOMERS   Understanding users of this data and their needs will help in strategizing the finance function. The object is not to generate data from the business environment per se but rather to extract the relevant data, which will guide business decisions. Doing this may mean making data customers an integral part of the strategizing effort.

KNOWLEDGE DELIVERY   How will the filtered data be delivered to key decision makers? The issue of knowledge delivery translates into the need for a well-defined data flow process around which decision makers can build company performance expectations. Users should understand the data flow process, specifically where data is coming from and how often it is mined from the business environment. This will ensure cooperation from the organization regarding finance function initiatives—particularly the creation of a sense of ownership as it relates to infrastructure.

Areas of Impact

Integrating the finance function into the organization means streamlining the process of generating knowledge for all aspects of the organization. What aspects of the organization will be touched by the finance function? If the finance function is strategized properly, no part of the organization will be denied access to the valuable cache of data it manages. Making decisions and setting policies for the organization will cut across all business functions, not the least of which are human resources, marketing, product development, manufacturing, and advertising. Whether access is assured over the Internet via ASPs or through outsourcing arrangements, all aspects of the organization must expect and demand a stake in the finance function.

STRENGTH AND SCALABILITY

The finance function must be considered a living organism that grows, changes, and evolves with the business. It must be strong enough to support the organization's needs while being dynamic and scalable in its structure and functionality. This means it will embrace new technologies, concepts, and needs when and where it is appropriate. Although being flexible and attentive to the needs of data customers, the finance function must maintain the integrity of data and reporting standards—which means ensuring that the organization is complying with external rules and regulations and that the data fairly reflects the state of the company.

Maintaining Integrity

The role of the finance function is more than that of keeper of the organization's financial data. The finance function also serves as the organization's conscience on matters of reporting and interpreting data. The solid finance function is positioned to interpret the needs of the financial data customers, whether internal or external. The value in this role is to ensure the organization does not misuse or misinterpret financial data, willfully or otherwise.

The small and emerging business has a responsibility to represent itself honestly to external stakeholders. This means interpreting rules and laws of disclosure and preparing documents and disclosures honestly for shareholders, debt holders, regulators, and tax authorities. It is up to the finance function to communicate the need for integrity in interpreting financial data. Doing this may pose the biggest challenge for the finance function, especially if business owners/management are under pressure to meet certain expectations of the external community.

The finance function also must evaluate the integrity and viability of financial data when interpreting results for management (internal reporting). Doing so may mean using data to ensure the interests of the entire organization are winning out over those of individuals. For example, if the sales organization is awarded commissions for making sales rather than serving customers, it is the finance function that is positioned to discover this. If salespeople are motivated to make sales, then that is what they will do. However, satisfied customers yield repeat sales in the long run; if salespeople are not following up on sales, ensuring that customers are satisfied with the purchase experience (from point of sale to delivery of products and services), the whole company loses. The finance function is positioned to recognize red flags in situations like these. Sales revenue that is written off as bad debt or that which erodes with excessive purchase returns could be symptoms of an ill-conceived commission system. Statistics on purchasing activity and cash collections from customers also may provide insight. If commissions instead are based on cash collections from customers or direct customer feedback/surveys, the organization is sure to cultivate long-term customers and preserve a steady revenue base into the extended future.

Scalability

The small and emerging business is in a constant state of change. Because it is evolving and shifting, information needs will shift as well. The finance function must be equipped to deal with changing needs, whether the informational requirements are for internal or external data customers. The success of the finance function in accommodating shifting needs lies in its scalability. Scalability in this context refers to the capacity to handle new users, new functionality requirements, or new peripheral applications. Scalability translates to both the concrete and soft components of the finance function.

Scalability hinges on the use of powerful, expandable platforms, from a concrete component (infrastructure) standpoint. How well do servers handle multiple applications? How well do core applications interface with other applications? How easily can processes have additional tasks worked into them? Can processes be reworked, reordered, or overhauled quickly without degrading the desired end result? How easily are processes translated to new users? Will an upward spike in the user population degrade the effectiveness of the overall process? The key to being able to react to new requirements in a changing business environment lies in part with the malleability of processes in the finance function.

Scalability means embracing innovations in technology and thought. A strong finance function will incorporate technology upgrades when necessary. Not only must current technology be factored into the equation, but future technology as well. Success here hinges on the progressive nature of management and its willingness to embrace change. Staying on top of server and E-technology may not be enough. It is predicted that a number of new technological innovations will have a drastic impact on the finance function in coming years. These technologies will redefine the way concrete components (infrastructure) and soft components of the finance function are defined. Finance strategies will have to adopt these innovative technologies to keep the company on par with data and security needs. Seven of these technologies include:

1. *Biometrics.* This enables a computer to confirm a user's identity based on a stable physical trait, such as a fingerprint, face shape, or iris.[1] This technology will add a whole new dimension to computer and network security. The volume and type of data managed by organizations will increase markedly as consumers become more secure about sharing information about themselves (as customers) with those they do business with. Soft components of the finance function that require users to interact with data on a constant basis will be impacted as biometrics redefines the structure of system firewalls.

2. *Fiberless optical networks.*[2] The problem of wiring the last mile—the short distance between fast cable and phone lines that carry digital signals across land and space and the computer in the office space—will become a thing of the past. A job once reserved for malleable but inefficient copper cable will soon be taken over by tiny optical transmission devices. This technology will enable greater speed and data capacity in the workplace, as workstations for personnel are connected to outside networks with what equates to a beam of light. Concrete components of the finance function will enjoy the greatest benefit of this technology.

3. *Wireless application protocols.*[3] This technology enables data to be transmitted to small handheld devices, such as cell phones and personal digital assistants. Wireless application protocols will free data customers from the office when it comes to accessing data. Allowing data customers in the field who were traditionally cut off from data sources to freely access data will extend decision making to when and where it matters most—now and on the front lines. Thus soft components—(analysis paradigms and management strategies)—will be impacted greatly by this technology breakthrough.

4. *Software agents.* These are mini-programs that free users from routine tasks by automating certain computing functions.[4] The greatest contribution software agents will have to make relate to finding and filtering data. Users will be freed from tedious data mining exercises by setting certain parameters, then letting the software agent run in the background. Software agents functioning in this way will make analysis models (soft component of finance infrastructure) more powerful. This technology also will improve processes and perform mundane network tasks and diagnostics, serving as quasi-network administrators, addressing concrete components of infrastructure.

5. *Speech recognition.*[5]   Not only will this technology prompt traditional hardware and software applications through perfunctory tasks, but it also will mine data from caches of voice (as opposed to digital) data. The ultimate application of speech recognition technology is speech-to-speech functionality—processing data in foreign languages electronically. This capability will allow companies to tap into new markets in foreign countries while expanding their finance organization across borders—eliminating language barriers from processes and systems. Most important, it will expand analysis and data-sharing paradigms (soft components of the finance function).

6. *Holographic data storage.*[6]   The business world's struggle with data is partially due to limitations in present-day storage devices. The capacity of magnetic and optical storage devices is becoming inadequate as demand for storage increases with the need to store graphics, video, and sound. Using laser technology to store data in three dimensions via holograms pushes the capacity of defined storage spaces to "hyper" levels. This technology has the potential to ramp up traditional hard drive capacities to hundreds of gigabytes, even terabytes in the near future, creating a huge potential for development of this aspect of concrete finance function components.

7. *Human computer interaction.*[7]   In addition to voice interaction, technology is being developed that will track nonverbal cues, such as eye patterns, body temperature, and body language. Matching these cues with current tasks the computer user is undertaking will allow the computer itself to dictate a course of action in achieving a desired task. This will create a total computer experience rather than a session in front of the screen.

How eager and willing are business owners/managers to embrace this technology? How would these innovations translate into synergies for the finance function? Scalability does not refer to technology alone but to the attitude and point of view of those who control the finance function.

FINAL THOUGHTS

Understanding what the finance function is and how it will help the organization grow is critical. Coming to terms with traditional perceptions and misconceptions about the accounting/finance world is paramount if the small and emerging business owner is to create an adequate finance function for the business. A powerful finance function will handle current business needs and have the capacity to expand and address future ones. Realizing the need for a finance function will give way to the necessity to begin strategizing one.

NOTES

1. Adam Lincoln, "10 × 5," *eCFO*, Fall 2000, p. 46.
2. *Ibid*, p. 49.
3. *Ibid.*
4. *Ibid*, p. 50.
5. *Ibid*, p. 53.
6. *Ibid*, p. 54.
7. *Ibid.*

3

WHY STRATEGIZE?

KEY TAKEAWAYS

■ Understanding what strategizing the finance function means.
■ Realizing the value of strategizing the finance function.
■ Realizing how *not* having a finance strategy will impact the organization.
■ Knowing the scope of impact of a finance strategy.
■ Knowing at what point in a company's life cycle a finance strategy is important.
■ Understanding the key dependencies impacting a finance strategy.
■ Recognizing strategy-avoidance behavior.
■ Gaining a glimpse of the future and how it will impact finance strategies.

STRATEGIZING IN ALL THE RIGHT PLACES

The term *strategy* fits well in many business contexts. Most agree the areas of marketing, sales, and mergers and acquisitions are paced by strategies of sometimes significant depth and breadth. Strategizing the *finance function,* however, seems awkward. The culture of business implies that the accounting/reporting function is far too objective to allow for *strategies.* The numbers *are* what they *are,* and putting them on paper is simply a perfunctory, administrative task.

Business owners and executives are focused on growing the business and achieving success. Because decisions are only as good as the information on which they are based, establishing a reliable pipeline of financial data from the business environment is crucial. Unfortunately, neglecting administrative functions (like the finance function) is common when companies are experiencing success. Who needs answers and analysis if everything is going well? This seems logical until the organization faces challenges. The seasoned executive will attest to the fact that many seek solutions/answers only when problems arise. It is imperative at this point that accurate information be readily available. Many businesses, however, accept mediocrity when it comes to the quality of data and their decision support system. They deal with the here and now and worry about problems only when they arise, resorting to knee-jerk or ill-fated short-term fixes. This is often the case with public companies when they are faced with a crisis of earnings. The next example illustrates this point:

> Sentec is a multinational manufacturer of electronic components whose stock is traded on a major exchange. Its success lies in its ability to utilize low-cost foreign manufacturing sites to produce electronic components for the high-tech computer industry. Although its business is sound, its data flow dynamic is weak, relying on outdated software packages and manual processes to gather and process actual results as well as budget and forecast data.
>
> Sentec's warm relationship with Wall Street hinges on its uncanny ability to achieve earnings expectations, which are consistently set at a growth rate of 20% each quarter, a target it has hit for 21 straight quarters. The atrophy in its budget and forecasting capability has been brought on by this simple, easily articulated goal. The arduous, error-prone closing process is shored up by regularly *truing up* the actual results with small, seemingly immaterial adjustments to get them in line with the forecasted expectations.
>
> When Sentec's major customers experienced a bump in the road due to a softening economy, an interesting thing happened. Customers began releasing data to the Street indicating lower-than-predicted earnings for the next few quarters. Sentec, having no evidence to the contrary, saw no reason to adjust its own earnings estimates. Management felt that unless lowered results could be quantified *in detail,* there was no sense in putting out lowered earnings expectations. They felt that at the least they would be misleading the public; at worst they would be derelict in their duties by putting out inexact information that could damage the upward momentum in stock price they worked so hard to establish. In spite of the sympathetic mood of the analyst and investor community, Sentec stood its ground and passively sent the message to the Street that the 20% growth would continue.
>
> As predicted, Sentec's customers experienced the soft quarters they had predicted, some with more accuracy than others. The first quarter subsequent to their customers' initial soft quarter resulted in dismal results, and the auditors would not sign off on any adjustments linking actual results to forecasted results. This left management with the unenviable task of packaging the bad news and presenting it to the Street. Sentec executives insisted that they would have to enact a plan that included permanent reduction in the job force and plant closings. They knew that the poor earnings would be hard enough to communicate, but poor earnings with no plan of action would be worse.
>
> When the news was announced, the stock price dropped almost 40%. The executive team, however, was lauded for its plan to reduce the company's global workforce by 20%. A year later Sentec's customers recovered along with the economy. Unfortunately for Sentec, though, the year saw a steady decline in its customer base as the workforce reduction and plant clos-

ings curtailed its ability to meet the heightened demand of customers it could easily address in the past. A slow erosion of the stock price and an eventual delisting from the exchange on which it had been traded for years resulted.

Executive teams throughout the business community face challenges like these all too often. Without the benefit of hindsight, business leaders are forced to balance the demands of stakeholders (shareholders, customers, employees, etc.) in a dynamic business environment. Could Sentec's management have prevented the large slide in stock price? Should the drastic cuts in workforce have been avoided? No one knows for sure how a different approach to management's course of action would have impacted the company. Key areas of note, however, are:

- *Why couldn't Sentec's actual results be released as accumulated?* The fact that Sentec's management was adjusting the actual results to meet Street expectations exposed two areas of concern: (1) the propensity of management to meet unrealistic expectations at any cost and (2) a weak finance function. Should management be focused more on the well-being of the organization or how it is perceived? No doubt both, and in that order. In this case, though, Sentec's management seemed comfortable with a *form-over-substance* finance model. The consistent gap between Sentec's forecast and actual results is indicative of a weak finance function. The fact that the company relied on forecast data as the actual results when the two differed implies that management was preoccupied with the needs of the Street over those of the finance organization. These are manifestations of the quarter-to-quarter thinking that is predominant in many public companies.

- *Why did Sentec have a poor or nonexistent forecast process?* Why was the company consistently off the mark when it came to hitting the forecast? Even though the closing process was poor, the fact that the company regularly missed its forecasts was more a function of a weak *forecasting process* rather than a poor *closing process*. Growth models that show steadily climbing earnings may be realistic in the short term or very long term, but rigidly consistent growth models are unrealistic. Not experiencing a spike in either direction as it relates to earnings for 21 quarters is suspicious if not outright impossible. Did Sentec have a real forecast that predicted the future with relative accuracy (that management chose to ignore), or did the forecast and budgeting process consist of applying a 20% growth rate to the *actual* results of the prior period?

- *Why didn't Sentec foresee the decline in customer demand?* Why was management so oblivious to the environment, in particular the state of the economy and the disposition of its major customers? Forward-thinking companies employ business models that address the impact of softening demand, including the unlikely event of losing major customers. Had Sentec ever considered how it would react to a sudden drop in demand for its products? The finance organization must have a handle on events that could lead up to volume demand shifts and dips in cash flow as well as a plan to counteract them.

■ *Why did Sentec not build contingencies into the business model?* Did the company adequately protect itself against poorly performing customers? Doing so may be as simple as seeking a diversification in customer base or booking adequate reserves on the balance sheet. Companies often become complacent when they have a steady flow of revenue from a small number of "big" customers. This is frequently the case with businesses that rely on government contracts. Getting a little business from a lot of customers is more often than not safer than relying on a lot of business from a few customers. Although this business model takes more work to cultivate, it lends more security to the business in the mid to long term.

■ *How could Sentec not have known what plant closures and headcount reductions would mean in the long term?* Taking a swipe at infrastructure is gratifying at first and looks good to the analyst community, but what does it mean in the long run? How would this impact capacity and quality of production in the future? A company must understand the ramifications if operations are pared back. Sentec may have been able to mitigate the challenges of meeting future, increased customer needs by *temporarily* reducing the workforce. This would have given the company a good story to tell the Street while leaving its options open for the future. Another alternative would have been to leave everything as is and weather the storm for a time until the economy recovered. Because the company acted rashly, it sacrificed the future for instant gratification.

■ *Why did Sentec rely on a quick fix?* It is debatable whether Sentec's management chose headcount reductions and plant closings as a proactive approach to managing earnings or as a *knee-jerk* reaction to the marketplace. One could make a reasonable argument either way. It is clear, however, that Sentec had no grasp on the effect plant closings would have on future operations. The health of operations took a backseat to the expectations of the Street. Management was feeling the pressure to dampen the impact of poor earnings on the stock price. This is an example of how short-term solutions can create long-term difficulties.

■ *Why did Sentec let the environment dictate circumstances?* The fact that Sentec's management reacted in knee-jerk fashion to its poor earnings is indicative of a reactive management style. Although no one can predict the future with certainty, Sentec was lulled into a false sense of security with its 21-quarter string of 20% growth. The company slumped into an *if-it-ain't-broke-don't-fix-it* posture and failed to enhance the finance function during this 21-quarter period when demand for information was light. Whether it was shortsightedness, overconfidence, or presumption that created the problem, management's actions doomed the company. The reality is that if businesses are not in a state of continuous improvement, they are moving backward.

■ *Did Sentec lose confidence in its ability to analyze?* Although speculative, it appears that Sentec's management had no confidence in the finance function's ability to analyze data. This seeming lack of confidence could have precipitated the reactive decision to reduce headcount and close factories. Was lack of confidence due to a prevailing opinion that the finance function was weak? Perhaps the organization minimized the finance function, seeing it as a strictly non–value-added function. Regardless, management must have confidence in the ability of the finance function to provide input on operational decisions. An attitude of inclusion regarding the finance function ultimately begets the need to build it up. This is a healthy approach by management that forces the organization to focus its resources toward its lifeblood—information flow.

The myopic thinking that prevailed at the executive level of Sentec ultimately destroyed it. No company makes short-term thinking a matter of policy; however, a lack of awareness of certain aspects of the business—in this case the finance area—can force management into a reactive and short-term posture. To gain an appreciation for how strategizing the finance function can protect the organization from short-sightedness, the benefits of strategy must be understood.

BENEFITS OF STRATEGIZING

Strategy Defined

What is meant by the term *strategy* in the context of the finance function? A strategy could mean any of the following:

- Employing best practices in business processes
- Seeking out and employing innovative technologies
- Developing new paradigms for analyzing or managing data
- Achieving economies of scale in the data flow dynamic
- Seeking out and employing the best minds in the business

Although many executives/business owners may employ any one or combination of these as their finance strategy, the term itself has a broader application. *Strategy* in this context involves the choices and perspectives that best suit the circumstances or tasks at hand. Determining an appropriate strategy means understanding the desired end result, then aligning all core competencies (unique strengths of the business itself) and tools to achieve this end as quickly and effectively as possible. Success in employing a strategy lies in the effectiveness of trade-offs or decisions to mix certain core competencies to achieve certain benefits. Strategizing has no absolutes. Because the finance area typically has limited resources at its disposal, a commitment must be made to developing only specific, relevant aspects of the finance function. Having a strategy in which a company wishes to create a *world-class* finance function is not practical. Employing parameters is as much a part of strategizing as being forward looking. Being world class at closing the books or budgeting and forecasting are concrete and practical objective statements for strategies. Because developing a sound strategy for the finance function will take time, the small and emerging business owner will be best served by staying focused on critical aspects of the finance area in the short term rather than being all things to all people as it relates to the numbers—the ultimate long-term objective.

Why Does Having a Strategy Count?

As discussed in Chapter 1, "Doing Business in Today's Environment," maximizing shareholder wealth or the wealth of business owners is the purpose of the organization. This being the prime objective of the enterprise, the small and emerging business owner is obligated to make sound decisions that move the organization forward. Positioning the management team in a way that they can handle challenges optimally is the best way to achieve forward momentum. Putting this objective in the context of the finance function means anticipating informational needs, laying the groundwork of infrastructure, and conceptualizing the adequate soft components (analysis paradigms, policies, and models). Setting the stage for such initiatives and tasks means dealing with mid- to long-term time horizons. Balancing these goals with the short-term needs of a small and emerging business is a challenge—hence, the need to strategize.

Business does not stop even though the owner is devoting time to planning for the future. Knowing this, small and emerging business owners must focus on the areas of the finance function that count most. They may struggle with relinquishing the focus on current operations to pursue long-term strategy development. The following questions must be asked to better grasp the need for finance strategy development and balance short-term needs with long-term goals:

- *Who are the key stakeholders in the business?* Stakeholders are those who have an interest in the success or failure of the business. Major stakeholders, in most cases, are shareholders (absentee owners in the case of publicly traded companies) or debt holders (bankers). Stakeholders also can be employees, a local municipality (in which the business is located), or other businesses that depend on the company's products, services, or presence. The company also is dependent on stakeholders to perform their function. How sensitive to the needs of stakeholders is the company? What are their needs? Is the company satisfying shareholders, debt holders, and employees? Could their needs change? If so, how would this impact the company? Anticipating the needs of stakeholders can be key to continuing the symbiotic relationship that exists between them and the company.

- *Who are the key people who make the business run?* Every business has its key circle of employees. Whether it is the person who drives product development or the one skilled at garnering customers, the small and emerging business will always have a few employees who are critical. How is the business motivating them? Have thoughtful bonus or compensation schemes been put in place to retain employees? Does the business rely on cash-only incentive schemes, or does it use ownership (stock and options)? Are all key employees incentivized in a way that is not counter to the organization's objectives? How is the business evaluating the options available in this area? Retaining key employees is a particular priority in the finance area since knowing the company's fiscal history will be key to garnering financing and expansion. What would the company do if it had to deal with a lost generation of knowledge when and if key employees exit both in and outside of the finance area?

- *What is the key competency or competitive advantage of the business?* Determining what makes the organization uniquely suited to do business is another challenge of the small and emerging business owner. Is the company's key to success ownership of a certain patent or copyright, a location, or access to business and community leaders? Merely identifying the key is not enough, however. How are these aspects of the organization quantified for business valuation purposes? How will the business preserve these key competencies and advantages, and at what cost? Letting them exist without thinking about how and to what extent to preserve them may create difficulties for the company in the future.

- *What is the history of the industry/business?* How have past and present players fared in the industry? Understanding what survivors have done right may be just as important as knowing what the nonsurvivors did wrong. How will the business avoid the pitfalls that contributed to the demise of other businesses? Defining an objective and getting there as quickly as possible are often the most widely employed strategies when it comes to business. The numbers rarely lie—how did they look for the businesses that made it and those that did not? What inherent dangers in the business world exist that can derail the enterprise? How is the business going to avoid them? Waiting to deal with a crisis situation is not the preferred way to deal with a challenge. Can the business anticipate potential trouble in advance? How does information management fit into this aspect of anticipating and heading off trouble? Incorporating the success track that other businesses have employed makes the job of the small and emerging business owner easier.

■ *How well is the company balancing what it does best with what customers want?* The business cannot be based solely on producing a widget in the most efficient way possible. Continuous improvement and best practices are necessary but not the ultimate objective of business. Just as generating customers alone is not the secret to success in a business, real success is balancing the mix of goals and objectives with core competencies. The company may be able to produce widgets quickly and cheaply, but who will buy them? Do customers want a variation of the widget? Assuming that a variation of the widget degrades production time and heightens costs, will demand and pricing make it worthwhile? The ability to decipher the business environment and customer needs may lie in the company's capacity to anticipate needs and fulfill them. How will the finance function help the company do this?

What Not Having a Strategy Means

Positioning the company for success means understanding the business environment and the limitations of the company. Strengthening the company may mean diversifying the customer base or evaluating the mix of products and services offered to the public. Addressing the finance function and its capacity to serve the organization is key to strengthening the organization as well. Focusing on the data flow dynamic and analysis models can be just as important as assessing customers and products. Nowhere can this be better illustrated than the case of Daewoo Motor Corporation:

> In July 2000, Daewoo Motor Corporation, a Korean car manufacturer, was poised for the pending acquisition by U.S. car giant Ford Motor Corporation. During the due diligence process, Ford executives found that Daewoo's accounting and information systems were dangerously substandard. Among other things, they found that their multinational target was collecting data from its local operations in differing versions of GAAP. Daewoo's financial data had been accumulated from its various operations across Europe and Asia, with no consistent use of Korean or other GAAP for that matter. Additionally, Daewoo's capital structure included debts in India, Poland, and Uzbekistan that were unacceptable to Ford. All told, Ford executives spent 90 days foraging through a difficult maze of financial data. What began as a $7 billion bid for the company ended with Ford briskly walking away, in spite of Daewoo's willingness to reduce the asking price to less than half of the original bid. Daewoo soon after filed bankruptcy, in spite of the host of suitors that Ford originally outbid.[1]

Daewoo was struggling with managing multinational finance data generated by its organization. Ignoring the deficiencies in its data flow dynamic proved fatal when Ford executives began reviewing their data. No doubt these were ongoing issues for Daewoo, which was relying on the same data that Ford used to make major policy decisions. Why had Daewoo forsaken its finance function? Was it a matter of passive or active neglect?

Interestingly, Ford had the opportunity to purchase Daewoo at a deep discount after its examination, an opportunity it chose to decline. What was it that made Ford retreat? Reviewing the numbers may not have been an exercise in determining whether the debits and credits were within their threshold of acceptance so much as it was an examination of the quality of Daewoo's management. As a multibillion-dollar company, Ford could have absorbed Daewoo easily, warts and all. The substandard state of the finance function, however, may have fueled doubt regarding the quality of competencies it believed it was acquiring from Daewoo. Because the finance function is the life-blood of the company, Ford may have interpreted Daewoo's financial disarray as indicative of the rest of the organization.

INITIATIVES SHAPING THE FINANCE ORGANIZATION

Unstructured Growth

Growing the finance function must be an orderly, well-thought-out process. Many organizations (both small and large), however, allow varying levels of motivation to shape the finance function. These motivational levels have a direct impact on all aspects of the finance function, from the accuracy and timeliness of the historical reporting, to the timeliness and relevance of budgeting and forecasting. As a business grows, pockets of unstructured infrastructure sprout up to accommodate growing data and reporting needs inherent in a burgeoning organization. Reporting and informational needs inevitably evolve into initiatives that, in some cases, span large periods of time and employ more and more people. These initiatives in their raw, disconnected form shape the finance function. For example, the need for performance measurement and Street expectations spawns a budget and forecast department. The need for federal tax compliance and planning gives rise to a tax group, which yields offshoots for various state and local tax groups. The need for SEC filings yields an external reporting department and the need for an internal business unit, and/or product evaluation gives rise to a management-reporting department. The organization's need to communicate financial information to the Street (if publicly traded) may have yielded another organization altogether that liaises with analysts and shareholders.

Achieving Harmony in Finance Tasks

Vision-oriented business owners and executives do not grow the organization in this random, reactionary manner. Although the organization may be willing to live with such a growth paradigm in the short term, the real problem in letting reporting and data needs dictate the structure of the finance function over the long term lies in the resulting patchwork of tasks. Is the finance organization doubling efforts? Do staff in the external reporting group compile the same data as the management reporting group? Worse, are they getting different results from the same data? Do operating sites spend hours providing the same data to these disconnected finance groups? Does anyone at the corporate level reconcile all the information compiled and analyzed across groups? Do these mutually exclusive groups employ their own finance systems and processes? Do the leaders of these disparate finance groups have a big picture of the entire company finance effort? Can economies of scale be achieved with systems, processes, and people with a big picture view? All too often the genesis of a finance organization is based on the haphazard reaction to a deluge of confusing, albeit necessary data and reporting requirements.

Although a random approach to growing the finance function may be working for the small and emerging business owner now, especially when the focus is on growing operations, pulling together the information-gathering and reporting efforts under one umbrella is necessary. Small and emerging business owners with ambitious goals for the growth of the company must address this area in order to keep decision support systems in top shape. What challenges face management/executives of organizations that enable the random development of the finance function? Over time the satisfaction derived from the finance organization that has evolved—or mutated—by happenstance may be as short-lived as the sigh breathed as executives drop the tax return in the mail or hit the send button to EDGAR. As that momentary joy and relief fades, subsequent sleepless nights are spent pondering why the finance organization seems to reinvent the wheel every time a filing deadline arrives or an information request is encountered. In the ensuing restless slumber, business owners/executives may ponder whether the information pulled together was complete. Adding to the anxiety, questions may arise regarding the interpretation of transactions and events in applying generally accepted accounting principals or the tax law. The reality is that *legally* it is the business owner, not members of the finance function per se, who is responsible for ensuring that complete and accurate data is in official documents, such as tax returns and SEC filings. Is the finance function generating good historical and prospective information? If the company has an external reporting requirement (for debt compliance or the SEC), is it representing itself fairly when it comes to preparing financials? Are positions too aggressive? Is the company interpreting GAAP too conservatively, hence selling the company short to shareholders and analysts? Assuming things are right from a reporting standpoint may be dangerous, especially if the company operates in a dynamic growing industry where it must grow to survive. Reflecting on these issues may compel the small and emerging business owner to take stock and harness all available resources, going beyond mere compliance and ad hoc reporting and tying finance initiatives into the growth of the company.

SCOPE OF STRATEGIZING

Gaining a better understanding of the need to strategize the finance function will require defining the scope of finance needs. Doing this involves understanding the company's capacity to meet obligations and handle the day-to-day challenges of being in business. Such an analysis will bear different results for different companies. Small and emerging business owners may find that certain aspects of the finance area are more in need of attention than others. They must understand that an overall finance strategy will benefit the organization most. The following items should be priorities:

- *Assessing capital structure.* How is the company financed, and how will it be bankrolled in the future? Is the company more comfortable with debt on its books or additional owners? These decisions must be carefully thought out. The question of financing is paramount for the small and emerging business owner as the need to grow is omnipresent. Some of the things to consider if an organization opts for debt financing are debt covenants and cash flow. What types of financial ratios will have to be maintained? Is the finance function adequately suited to monitor these requirements? Will the organization be able to remit debt payments in a timely manner? What are run rates (expense patterns over a given period of time) on expenses and other obligations? The finance function must play an important role in evaluating the ability of the organization to take on debt and the responsibilities associated with it. If the company chooses equity financing, what reporting requirements will it have? Will the organization be subject to audits? If so, how often—quarterly, annually? What are the expectations of shareholders? Will they be met? What if expectations are not met?

- *Managing expenses.* How well is the organization controlling costs? Companies focus on minimizing expenses as a function of earnings management and cash flow. So how do they do it? Analyzing expenses is a skill that must be mastered by the finance arm of the organization. Can the finance function chart run rates and analyze them for reasonableness? Does the finance organization employ reliable expense ratio (e.g., expense to revenue) analysis? Making decisions about costs in the company are contingent on employing adequate tools to analyze them. When adequate tools are in place and analysis is optimized, setting goals for this aspect of P&L management becomes easy.

- *Employing best practices.* Does the company know what it is doing right and what it is doing wrong? Employing best practices is more a function of culture than a cookbook, algorithmic process of replacing old ways of doing things with new ways of doing things. It is an ongoing process of evaluating and reevaluating the way a company does business in hopes of always improving. Management takes the lead on this culture or state of mind. If management expects the finance function to improve on what it does now, then the finance function will respond. Maintaining best-in-class closing, budgeting, and data processing is key to an organization girding itself for the changing business environment.

- *Measuring performance.* For the small and emerging business owner, growth is inevitable for the business to survive. How will the organization monitor growth? Part of the growth strategy is developing and monitoring key measurements (metrics) in the organization. Do these performance measures exist? Are they meaningful? Many times organizations struggle with metrics that are too shortsighted or that work against overall long-term growth of the company. Strong, sensible metrics must be a part of the finance function.

- *Planning process.* A logical extension of monitoring growth, the budget and the forecasting process must be accurate and easily maintained. The finance function must be adept at dealing with historical as well as forward-looking information. This aspect of finance must be reliable in the near *and* the extended future in order to develop and maintain a sound overall business strategy. The company must go beyond one-year goal setting and position itself to look three to five years into the future and set reasonable goals. Because strategy impacts the future, the planning process must be at the forefront of all finance-oriented strategizing efforts.

- *Analyzing revenue growth.* The only thing more important than managing expenses is managing revenues. Although the term *managing revenues* connotes using less than legitimate accounting practices, the goal is to make the company's revenue streams as predictable as possible. This is crucial when planning future resource allocations or communicating performance to stakeholders. Can the organization analyze revenue quickly and accurately by geographic region and product type? Can revenue be tracked by salesperson or territory? Can recurring revenue be tracked by customer? Should the company stick with organic (internally generated) revenue growth models or seek acquisitions? The finance function should be equipped to analyze and consult management on the status of revenue growth in the company. Strategies must be in place that facilitate the examination of revenue.

- *Maintaining a strong finance team.* The preoccupation with maintaining information systems, upgrading processes, and meeting prescribed deadlines can make it easy to lose sight of the *people* aspect of finance. Technology and best practices will never eliminate the need for the human element. The skills of finance staff must meet the needs of the business, needs that may stay static or change over time. For example, in the early years, when the business is small and money is in short supply, the need may be for accountant-type staff to simply "pull" the numbers together each month and report them to management. As the company evolves, finance staff will need to be more systems savvy as the development of finance applications and sophisticated platforms may be the objective. At a more mature stage of the company's existence, the need for true finance people who are more economic and business oriented may predominate over pure accountant types who sufficed in the early years of the business. Knowing these needs, how is the company positioning its pipeline of talent? What types of programs are in place to not only bring suitable talent in house but to retain and develop it?

Small and emerging business owners must determine those areas of finance on which to leverage growth initiatives. Being aware of strengths will allow them to better construct finance strategies. Note that this is different from merely identifying weak areas of the finance function. An example of building a growth strategy off a particular area of finance is illustrated with Brewco:

Brewco is a publicly traded company that manages a nationwide chain of microbreweries and restaurants. The swiftly moving, brand-oriented restaurant business compelled Brewco to seek out a growth strategy that would appeal to internal (employees) and external (external investment community) stakeholders. Two key components of Brewco's strategy involved methodologies for acquisition accounting and a generous employee stock option compensation plan. High market capitalization (shares outstanding × share price) was the trophy metric in the race to maintain top-dog status with the investor community. Through its use of the pooling method of accounting (recently banned by the accounting industry) for business combinations, the company was able to legitimately put nearly 4 billion shares of its stock into circulation. As a result, small ticks in share value had an exponential effect on market capitalization, making it an in-demand stock by the market community. Brewco also employed a stock option compensation program for employees that enabled it to avoid taking a charge to its financial (book) earnings while taking a charge (deduction) to tax earnings. This action allowed the company to manage wage expenses going forward, minimize the amount of federal taxes paid, and issue more stock.

The versatility in the option program provided an attractive, noncash compensation avenue for the company that provided the best of both worlds from a financial standpoint. This example of researching, conceptualizing, and employing a win/win strategy (born from the finance function) for company shareholders and employees is a testament to the forward-looking prowess of the leadership at Brewco.

WHEN DOES STRATEGIZING BEGIN TO COUNT?

Company Is Never Too Big or Too Small

Companies are never too big or too small to begin strategizing the finance function. Because every stage of the business comes with its own specific challenges, business owners must understand that the company cannot afford not to strategize at any stage of its life cycle. Believing that the business is not complex enough to warrant strategizing is a dangerous position for the small and emerging business owner to take.

Small and emerging businesses have an advantage over their larger brethren. Because these businesses are smaller and (for the most part) lack complexity in size and structure, they are more suited to instituting change quickly. Small and emerging business owners and executives are, in most cases, more open to innovation and change than management in larger, established businesses. Larger organizations often must deal with slow-moving bureaucracies and culture issues when implementing finance strategies. This situation is further exacerbated by the fact that finance does not typically connote progressive thinking. Laying the groundwork and culture of strategic thinking in the early years will serve the organization best.

Stage of the Business

Although strategizing the finance function is crucial at all stages of the organization, at no time is it more important than when the organization is posturing for a major business life-cycle event. Life-cycle events or milestones in a business's life represent major changes in the organization intended to make the company stronger. Events such as going public, seeking financing for the first time, or seeking growth through acquisition are examples of major business life-cycle events dependent on a sound finance function. Posturing for the next stage is crucial. Will the finance function hold the company back or propel it forward? The case of Daewoo Motor Corporation is an example of the former. Ford might have looked past shortcomings in Daewoo's capital structure had the due diligence process gone smoothly. Unfortunately, the window to Daewoo's soul was planted in the finance function, and whether it was through neglect or misaligned priorities, Daewoo's finance organization yielded a less than satisfactory experience for Ford.

KEY DEPENDENCIES

Having a strong finance function will, among other things, help provide alternatives for the company when it is faced with challenges or difficulties. The finance function works best when it is plugged into the overall operations of the business.

Carefully evolving the finance function to serve operations involves identifying key dependencies. These *trigger points* will provoke the small and emerging business owner into action when reassessing the finance function. In turn, the finance function will help insulate the company from exposure as these aspects of the business change. A sound finance strategy will address this co-dependency.

Two major trigger points must be tied to the finance function:

1. *Business model.* The business model will define the overall objectives of the organization and how it will achieve them. The business model addresses internal attributes of the organization, particularly strengths and weaknesses, along with external factors such as opportunities and threats. The landscape of the business model will play an important role in the functionality and effectiveness of the finance function. The small and emerging business owner must understand the relationship between the business environment and the adequacy of the business model. Can the business model be accessed, changed, and redeployed quickly? How often will executives and management have to update the business model? The business model relies on the finance function—both concrete (infrastructure) and soft components. Does a particular model depend more on financial data or nonfinancial data? Is the need for information broad with little depth or deep with little breadth? The finance function can be an integral part of the business model or exist apart from it. Regardless, the small and emerging business owner must carefully assess the business model and what role the finance function will play. Is the business environment changing quickly? Does the business model shift as a result? A business or business environment that changes often puts the onus on the finance function either to keep pace or to anticipate change and adjust accordingly.

2. *Economy.* How recession proof is the business? No business is completely resistant to economic downturns. The small and emerging business owner must position the business to survive in a soft economy. When business is good, the need for information is less urgent; however, when the business is experiencing difficulties, the need for data becomes imperative. This is the case whether the change is due to internal or external factors. The finance function should be equipped to handle informational needs adequately whether the business is doing well or not. In other words, the finance function—both hard and soft components—should be designed to handle the most difficult and demanding times. Consider what data is not being gathered when times are good that may be imperative when times are bad. Built into this basic level of readiness is the ability to analyze or identify customers of the business that are not recession proof. Who are these customers? What would it mean to the business if the economy paralyzed

them? The finance function may not be able to inoculate the business completely from a soft economy; however, creating a level of readiness that will suit a challenging economic environment will lessen the effect of an economic downturn. Because leaders are judged on how they excel or fail in bad times, the finance function will attest to the quality of management when the organization needs leadership the most.

INITIATING THE CULTURE OF STRATEGY

Seeking strategy in the finance area means turning over rocks that would normally be left alone. While this may seem painful in the short term, the benefit lies in setting a predictable and stable course for the company. The small and emerging business owner sets a dangerous course for the business by not seeking to examine the road ahead but instead allowing the future to unfold on its own. Creating a strong finance organization via sound, all-encompassing strategies will be difficult at times, as old paradigms and comfort zones are challenged.

Because developing a culture of strategy is so crucial, it is incumbent on the small and emerging business owner to establish this type of thinking where it does not exist, while at the same time altering counterstrategic tendencies in the finance function. The greatest enemy in strategizing the finance function is resistance and indifference to forward thinking. Management that does not aggressively seek to be prospective puts all stakeholders at risk. The organization may be in a strategy-avoidance mode regarding the finance function and not be aware of it. The following are symptoms of strategy avoidance in the finance area:

- *Having a bloated finance organization.* A bloated finance organization is people heavy. Mechanizing finance tasks takes time and effort. The high-velocity business environment, however, often denies management the luxury of time. As a result, reliance on *quick fixes* becomes common. This demand for immediate results too often equates to individuals being called on to perform manual workarounds or odd, nonstandard tasks. This may not be a major issue for small and emerging businesses as finance tasks may be relatively simple and few in number. However, as needs change and tasks become more voluminous and complex, these one-time tasks accumulate, rendering even the best-intentioned finance person ineffectual. Letting recurring tasks accumulate and fall into the hands of finance staff eventually will lead to inefficiencies and gaps in effectiveness as employees change roles or leave the company. The small and emerging business owner must reflect on the last few finance hires. Were they hired to manage a process or perform a task? If the answer is the latter, chances are the finance organization is fraught with task-oriented jobs filled by underemployed people.

- *Having exception-oriented management.* Another symptom of ineffective, shortsighted finance functions is exception-oriented management. This is the tendency for management to create (in a reactive manner) unique solutions to even the most fundamental and repetitive business issues. Exception-oriented management involves reinventing the wheel when it is not necessary. While this particular characteristic is born of good intentions and teamwork, the lack of uniform processes puts the finance function in a precarious position when it comes to managing or troubleshooting finance issues. Variables that compound this issue include employee turnover, process enhancement, and the demand for more functionality/output by data customers. Because exceptions to business processes hinder scalability, expanding needs of the organization become difficult or impossible to address.

- *Pushing software applications rather than letting needs "pull" them.* A problem common to midsize and large companies, this scenario is played out all too often in small and emerging organizations. Although finance should drive the purchase and development of finance-related applications, the rationale for seeking new applications should be rooted in need. Finance people often initiate software purchases on the basis of "Everyone else uses it." Rather, soft components (see Chapter 2's, "Soft Components") of the finance function should drive all infrastructure needs in the organization. Analysis paradigms, business/finance models, and key ratios/metrics promulgated by the executive level and codified in the finance strategy will yield certain informational needs. This need for information should dictate the need for hardware and software applications. Purchasing these tools for any other reason may result in underbuying or overbuying for the tasks at hand—two costly scenarios.

- *Doing what was done last year.* Many finance organizations have reduced the sum total of their process documentation to "Do what was done last year." As a general starting point for transaction management, closing the books, or analyzing account balances, finance often relies on this methodology in the absence of comprehensive documentation or uniform processes. Excessive reliance on doing the same thing as last year is symptomatic of processes that are incomplete, ineffective, or not thought through. Relying on what was done last year leaves the finance organization ill prepared for a fast-moving business environment. How has the business changed in the last year? How will it change in the future? Are information needs accelerating? Reorganizations and changing business models will require the finance function constantly to rethink its business processes. Strategizing the finance function will provide for appropriate changes to business processes and information systems and yield perspectives that articulate how to accommodate changing information needs.

- *Getting used to being slammed.* Dealing with an inadequate finance function is bad enough; tolerating its shortcomings day in and day out is unacceptable.

Symptomatic of this passive act of negligence is tolerating difficult working conditions brought about by a weak finance function. For instance, requiring finance staff members to clear their weekends or prepare to work late in normal anticipation of the close hints at a broken closing process. Although any given finance/business process (monthly close, budgeting process, or provision analysis) can have extraordinary circumstances, the routine of following through should be just that: *routine*. The finance function should be geared toward making recurring business processes nonevents. The overall finance strategy must focus on making the processes strong enough to easily handle the normal tasks that define them. The finance strategy also must be poised to adjust these processes as the business changes and needs evolve.

- *Being unable to reorganize quickly.* When the business changes, how difficult is it to reconfigure the data flow process? Is the right data being gathered? Is the organization living with outdated remnants of the old structure and processes? Change due to new products, new territories, or different management directives should result in a need for changes in how data is gathered and/or reported. Many companies live with outdated data flow schemes simply because reconfiguring systems and processes is too disruptive to the organization. Excessive downtime that may result from adjusting systems can make users depend on the old, incorrect data rather than tolerating temporary information blackouts. Systems and processes should be scalable and agile enough to adapt to changes in the business environment. Finance strategies should take this capacity for adjustment into account and provide for the ability to change the finance function in a timely and effective manner.
- *Being unable to point out weaknesses in the finance area.* No process or system is bulletproof. With this in mind, the finance strategy should focus on constantly evaluating and reevaluating tasks, processes, and systems. The culture of continuous improvement is essential to ensure that the finance function serves the needs of external and internal users. The absence of an urgency to improve continuously is, more often than not, indicative of the absence of strategy in the finance function. If members of the finance organization are unable or unwilling to identify and improve weak points in the finance function, processes and systems will not change, evolve, and improve. Assessing the finance function and improving it must be a part of the finance strategy.

The case of Microstrategy Inc., a maker of data mining software, brings up some provocative points related to the need to focus on strategizing the finance function.

Microstrategy announced on March 20, 2000, that it would restate revenue and earnings for 1998 and 1999. Officially, the restatement was due to the company's historic use of aggressive revenue recognition policies that allowed it to recognize revenue on sales contracts up front in the year of sale as opposed to ratably over the life of the contract. The effect of the restatement brought results from earnings of $.15/share (before the restatement) to a loss of $.44/share (after the restatement). The share price dropped nearly 50% immediately after the announcement. Within two hours after the press release, the stock plunged over 122 points, wiping out almost $9 billion in market value. In the end, the share price slid from a high of $300/share to a low of $18/share. President and CEO Michael Saylor noted that the restatement rendered a more accurate depiction of Microstrategy's business.

The question remains: Why did Microstrategy's management team wait so long to employ the more appropriate, albeit conservative, methodology? Was it due to poor information systems employed in 1999 and 1998? Could it have been due to poor processes? Were they compelled by auditors or the SEC to make the change? No one knows for sure except Microstrategy's management. Many laud the management team for coming forward and taking responsibility for the accounting change. However, excusing a one-time mistake causing a restatement is one thing, but systematically employing the wrong accounting methods over a sustained period is another. What is clear is that Microstrategy might have steered clear of this predicament from the outset if it had employed a finance strategy that addressed the decision support system as well as information systems and the processes that comprised them.

Each year thousands of executives face the same challenges as Microstrategy. It's possible that the aggressive business model that put them in the fore led to Microstrategy's demise. Although this change at Microstrategy was an accounting change and not operational, the Street was very unforgiving. It would be speculative to say that the company should have seen this coming early on. However, the culture of aggressive growth and rapid expansion that predominates in small and emerging businesses seemed to sweep away any remnant of conservatism, especially as it applied to financial reporting. This restatement came about as a response to a statement of position put out by the accounting profession. Would a forward-looking, strategic culture have weighed a circumstance like this and positioned the organization to avoid such a debacle?

THE FUTURE: READY OR NOT, HERE IT COMES

If the small and emerging business owner is still skeptical about the need to strategize the finance function, a glimpse into the future may provide perspective. The business environment will demand more from organizations and executives, which in turn will drive a heightened need for data. Waiting to address the finance function may decrease the number of executive decisions in the short term; however, the business world will keep changing and evolving, demanding more and better decision making. Even though no one can predict the future with certainty, the following facts will impact the finance function:

■ *Round-the-clock accessibility and technology will make finance a 24/7 operation 52 weeks a year.* Technology is making the world smaller while extending the workday and workplace. Wireless technology, cell phones, personal digital assistants, and the like have extended the decision-making environment beyond the office, standard workday (nine to five), and standard workweek (Monday through Friday). This means accessibility to data 24 hours a day, seven days a week, 52 weeks a year. Around-the-clock support, powerful technology, and sound processes must be in place to accommodate the needs of a multiple time zone organization. Critical events happening overnight—acquisitions, geopolitical, and economic changes—will demand that executives and business owners have access to financial data in a moment's notice, at all times. Strong strategies will have to be in place not only to create an adequate finance function but to maintain its functionality at all times.

■ *A premium will be placed on timing.* If one word can sum up the future of the finance environment, it will be *speed,* as the rate of change in the business world will continue to accelerate. What does this mean for the finance function in the small and emerging business? Positioning the business to seek out new strategies, drive profitability (where it does not exist), enhance profitability (where it already exists), and chart a course for rapid growth will be the major role of the finance function. The demand for more frequent looks at historical data—exit rate reports, budget to actual comparisons— will push the finance function into perpetual and virtual closes. Forward-looking data needs will force forecasting processes to be more robust and accessible on a weekly or daily basis. Data delivery itself will have to be swifter. Overall, the ability to realign data gathering, processing, and analysis functions quickly will coincide with the need to evaluate and codify new strategies.

■ *The finance function will become less manual.* If the small and emerging business chooses not to embrace the new Internet-centric, digital world, it risks coming up short when it comes to meeting the needs of customers and suppliers. Not only will suppliers and customers be entering into the digital age, but competitors will be also, leaving the small and emerging business that is slow to embrace this technology desperately behind. Sophisticated systems and Business-to-Business applications will become mainstream in reaction to demand from customers and vendors, shrinking the traditional finance organization while heightening the capacity to handle information quickly and efficiently. This result will enable operational areas to manage their financial house in a self-serve manner. Additionally, manual, non–value-added finance tasks that the organization is unable to digitize will be outsourced. Headcount will become less of an issue as the finance function will be measured based on its win/loss record in making enterprise-wide decisions. Strategizing the finance function will become more and more about technology and its impact on the business model.

■ *Demand for overall business efficiencies will put the responsibility on finance to be more operations oriented.* As the world shrinks under the influence of the Internet, businesses will be forced to be more aggressive with their growth models. Growth and hyperexpansion will mean increasing market shares, moving into untapped global markets, and engaging in business combinations. The finance function will face an increased burden in regard to advising on day-to-day operations. Researching and implementing financing arrangements and performing due diligence analysis on strategic ventures will no longer be extraordinary activities but a part of normal activity. The finance function will no longer exist in a vacuum but rather will move with and anticipate operations. Because operational initiatives will be aggressive, the decentralization of certain components of the finance function will be necessary to allow managers in the field to actively use finance tools to leverage these initiatives.

■ *The demand for performance will be more comprehensive.* The advanced capability for stakeholders to access data coupled with the enhanced ability of businesses to gather, process, and analyze data will lead to a heightened demand for more data (volumes and types). The new challenge for the small and emerging business will be filtering out superfluous data as opposed to gathering it. Systems and processes that gather data will be simple to implement; however, discerning relevant data will become the challenge. The enterprise will be more transparent, which means analysis that was difficult or impossible in the past will be easier and faster. The down side, however, is that stakeholders also will demand the management view. As backseat drivers, stakeholders will demand access to metrics (financial and nonfinancial) traditionally reserved for management alone. Management's challenge will be to fine-tune the development of relevant metrics and the data gathering processes that feed them. These acute expectations will demand a finance strategy that focuses on traditional needs of infrastructure and analysis while catering to the expanding need for ad hoc information needs.

■ *The finance function will become increasingly less about finance.* The small and emerging business, like midsize and large organizations, will find itself saddled with the need to create value for shareholders and owners. Doing this will mean stretching beyond the traditional *manage operations* business model and seeking out strategic acquisitions, joint ventures, and other expansion-oriented strategies as a matter of routine. The finance function must provide the foundation for evaluating and measuring the viability of such endeavors. Finance's role as "keeper-of-historical-and-strategic-information" will expand to include customer relations, technology stewardship, business unit consultant, and global partner. The traditional separation between finance and operations will blur as the finance function becomes a toolbox for the Chief Executive Officer (CEO) and Chief Operating Officer (COO), as well as for business unit directors and managers.

FINAL THOUGHTS

Regardless of the nature of the high-level strategies of the overall business, a sound finance function will address the most basic dependency of the enterprise's success—accurate and timely information. The challenge of the small and emerging business owner is to take advantage of the relatively small size and simple structure of the organization and align key items of infrastructure to suit the current and future needs of the enterprise before it gets too large and complex to manage. The small and emerging business owner must seize the opportunity to establish a culture of continuous improvement and forward thinking at the early stages of organization development. The organization must make a commitment to dedicating decisions and resources to:

- Enhancing finance decision making
- Interpreting events and transactions accurately
- Optimizing data flow
- Maximizing quality of data
- Securing data from outsiders and insiders

Focusing on the concrete and soft components of the finance function will, at best, optimize strategizing and decision making and, at least, make the data flow dynamic predictable. Effective finance strategies will parlay the company's data needs into customized finance solutions.

NOTE

1. Tom Leander, "The Great Debate," *CFO*, December 2000, p. 43–44.

4

MULTILEVEL APPROACH

KEY TAKEAWAYS

- Understanding the need to rely on more than instincts to make decisions.
- Understanding the evolving nature of finance strategies.
- Realizing that most issues affecting finance are not mutually exclusive.
- Knowing where to begin the strategizing effort.
- Understanding the need to gather all finance needs and identify all issues before strategizing.
- Understanding the need to prioritize all needs and issues before strategizing.
- Understanding the multilevel model for strategizing.
- Understanding the need to analyze the business life cycle.
- Understanding the need to evaluate financial data customers.
- Understanding the need to analyze the finance organization, information systems, and finance/business processes.
- Appreciating the role of data flow processes.
- Distinguishing between upper-tier considerations and lower-tier considerations of the multilevel model.
- Recognizing the need to manage cash flow.
- Knowing the importance of setting balance sheet policies.
- Knowing the importance of setting profit and loss (P&L) policies.

INITIATING THE FINANCE STRATEGY

Where to Look First

The health and well-being of the organization is the number-one priority of the small and emerging business owner. Leadership must focus on both the operational and the nonoperational (back-office) aspects of the business to keep the organization healthy. One of the greatest challenges for any business leader is balancing time and resources between front-line and back-office issues. Typically, the small and emerging business owner is, because of the life cycle of the enterprise, more oriented toward operations. Identifying and dealing with nonoperational issues, specifically the finance function, can be a particular problem in this phase of business development.

Many small and emerging business owners feel that it takes a certain level of experience to address the finance function properly. These owners can be proactive in maintaining a healthy finance area without having to be finance/accounting experts. The best place to start is with a positive attitude and two key realizations. First and foremost, they must appreciate the finance function—knowing what it is and how it will help the business. Second, they must recognize that they exist within a continuum of finance knowledge. No business owner knows everything there is to know about finance. The same goes for the other extreme—no business owner is totally devoid of knowledge. The fact that a viable business has been started in the first place implies that there is fiscal value in the enterprise (i.e., the enterprise yields benefits that exceed the amount of resources used). The business owner has already made decisions with a fiscal grounding—usually attributed to instinct. The danger is, however, taking comfort in the belief that the small amount of knowledge accumulated in the finance area is sufficient to run the business indefinitely. Business owners can never have enough knowledge to deal with every challenge the enterprise will face. They must recognize this fact as they mature and delegate duties and responsibilities.

The need to strategize becomes logical as business owners become aware of this continuum of knowledge. Recognizing and recording business needs and acknowledging the organization's capacity to meet those needs will help business owners approach the finance area, either for the first time or to improve it.

There is no one way to develop a finance strategy. Fraught with subjectivity, this task has numerous dependencies and variables—elements that change and evolve as the business grows. A further complication lies in the different strategies needed for small and emerging, midsize, and large businesses. The differences lie in the demographics of management and the life cycle (level of maturity) of the business:

- *Small and emerging businesses.* In such organizations, business owners typically wear many hats—operations, finance, human resources, and so on. Staff is typically small, and business owners must rely on their own instincts to make operational and nonoperational decisions. The lack of finance expertise may put the organization at risk, as sound decision making requires multidimensional thinking. When the business is in its infant stage, it often lacks overall infrastructure, particularly in the finance area (concrete components). The need for soft components of the finance function is less a priority as the urgency to grow and yield cash is great.
- *Midsize businesses.* More stable than their smaller or younger brethren, these businesses typically have dedicated finance staff focusing exclusively on finance issues. The finance area usually is good at accumulating histori-

cal data but not as adroit at being forward looking. Infrastructure exists, though it may or may not be adequate. The business itself is typically stable enough to begin looking ahead at opportunities to grow or threats it wants to avoid. Addressing hard components of the finance function may take the form of continuous improvement as infrastructure may already have been conceptualized and implemented. Soft components of the finance function begin to be more of a priority as the business has the luxury of setting its own course.

- *Large businesses.* These organizations have ample resources to dedicate to the finance area. Headed by seasoned, sophisticated executives, these organizations have the manpower and experience to handle major business issues. Improvements in infrastructure are addressed on an ongoing basis and set the stage for future business initiatives. The focus in these businesses is on the soft components of the finance function. A premium is placed on the finance function's ability to set policy and initiate strategies that will lead the organization in a prosperous direction, resulting in increased value for stakeholders.

Developing a finance strategy can be intimidating for the small and emerging business owner. When beginning the process of strategy development, these questions must be asked:

- *How long will it take?* If the enterprise is examining the finance function for the first time, it may take weeks or months to construct a sound finance strategy on which everyone agrees. Once a consensus is reached, it may take another period of months to put the strategy in motion.
- *Will it endure?* Once the finance strategy is codified and put in place, it will take on a life of its own. If done properly, this process becomes part of the corporate culture. Particular strategies will come and go as the business evolves; however, the process by which strategies are developed and maintained must be embraced by business owners/executives.
- *Once complete, is it immutable?* Nothing in the business world is certain. The finance strategy must become a living organism within the organization that changes and evolves with the business. The only thing more damaging than not having a finance strategy is clinging to one that is no longer relevant.
- *How hard is it to maintain?* Maintenance of the finance strategy is a function of the myriad of issues that affect the business. The finance function must be the basis of all aspects of operations. Maintaining the finance strategy depends on the changing needs of the organization, which depend on the business environment and overall strategy. If the industry in which the organization operates changes frequently, maintenance may be an ongoing process, while maintenance in a stable industry may not be.

■ *How will the strategy be formed?* Like any other challenge in the business, careful research and determination will be two key aspects of strategy development and implementation. Uncovering all current and prospective finance issues is the logical starting point. Subinitiatives then can be developed that put the overall strategy in motion. The key will be identifying and arranging all issues in a way that well-informed, practical decisions can be made.

Evolution

The finance function must evolve and change with the organization. Because most businesses are in a constant state of flux, the finance function must be flexible enough to evolve in both growth (organic and acquisitive) and contraction cycles. The finance function must be nimble enough to deal with environmental factors quickly and decisively in both cases. Faced with a cycle of growth, scalability will be necessary. Being nimble refers to the ability to refocus the finance function quickly if a new direction is taken by the business, while scalability refers to the ability to incorporate the impact of an additional initiative or business objective of the company. A strong finance function will exert control over a changing environment and temper the chaos associated with change in both instances. This controlled evolution will serve the small and emerging business well as it faces the challenges of the high-velocity business world. The only way to control this evolution is to continually update, review, and evaluate the strategy that governs the finance function.

ASSESSING NEEDS

Getting Started

Where to start may be the most difficult question to answer. The inclination is to investigate the finance areas that are most familiar. Doing this may or may not be effective, as the finance knowledge relied on may be inadequate or exist in odd combinations. The ideal starting point lies within the business—in particular, analyzing inherent resources and assessing needs. Every business is different, however, with needs and resources that vary from situation to situation. It is worthwhile to begin this exercise by examining the case of Palmer Products Inc.:

> Palmer Products Inc. is a purveyor of collegiate candles. Started by two brothers, Mark and Andrew Palmer, the company owns the right to create candles in the form of over 50 college mascots. They also own the right to the respective fight songs, which play as the candles are lit. The two entrepreneurs have established a relationship with a manufacturer in Asia that can produce the candles and ship them to the United States at a very low cost. Having attended a university in which the culture of sports is very prominent, the brothers saw a market for these candles in university alumni, students,

and others. The demand for their product is rooted in the intrinsic allegiance to the universities themselves and not so much the success of the sports programs, though success helps.

The collegiate product market is challenging in that colleges and universities are extremely protective of their likenesses and demand annual renewals of the licenses based on fiscal success and the quality of the management team (measured by a required quarterly financial report). Mark and Andrew recognized that they cannot patent their product, so quick market penetration would be key to their success as they developed brand recognition before other larger companies got the same idea. The two relied on money from relatives to get the company started; these funds financed the first round of shipments from the Asian manufacturer. The manufacturer required large minimum orders to make it worth his while. Unfortunately, the brothers could not find a domestic manufacturer to produce the quality of candle they need at the price they can afford. Their relatives did not interfere with the business at this stage; however, they did insist on periodic updates to ensure the two stay on track.

The brothers have not thought much into the future; however, they share dreams of becoming successful, high-level executives some day. They want to expand the business into a public company and eventually scale back their involvement, sitting on the nest egg they have built up in company value. They are realistic, however, and know that anything can happen between now and then.

Parcel post is the chief mode of distribution as they get responses to their magazine ads. Their principal mode of advertisement is through campus magazines and bookstores. They also sell a significant number of candles outside of stadiums and arenas at football and basketball games, where they employ students to man small kiosks.

They have incorporated for liability purposes, on advice of an attorney friend of theirs. The liability inherent in the product and the legal requirements of the colleges and universities to create the candles require very expensive insurance coverage. The brothers sold $50,000 worth of candles in their first year, and they plan on doubling that in each of the next 10 years. Eventually they want to consider taking the company public.

Palmer Products Inc. is typical of most small and emerging businesses in that its leadership consists of innovative individuals with a keen insight for an unexploited market. This demographic usually lacks practical experience in the business world and is ignorant of the administrative area, particularly finance. Mark and Andrew seem to have made the right decisions for Palmer Products so far; however, issues they will be forced to address soon include:

- *Expansion/financing.* Survival of the company may be based on the ability to acquire adequate financing to fund organic growth and/or strategic acquisitions.

■ *Data customers.* The management team (consisting of Mark and Andrew for now) must make decisions every day. They will need quick, reliable finance information to keep them in the know at all times. Indirectly, the universities and colleges are consumers of sales and royalty data while the IRS will be the recipient of the financial results on the company's first tax return.

■ *Process limits.* No business processes address the finance function at this stage of the company. Mark and Andrew prepare the quarterly reports for the universities by hand and remit the royalty payments based on these reports. They are seeking help from a tax professional to help them prepare Palmer Products' first tax return. They are aware that they may have sales tax issues in multiple states but have no idea where or how to gather data to address this issue.

■ *Systems/technology.* The only technology the two brothers possess are two personal computers from their college years. They use basic spreadsheet and word processing software to handle all the tasks demanded of them to date. They want to expand their distribution capability to the World Wide Web but have not gotten around to completing a website, though they have been working on one for several months.

■ *Environmental factors.* Mark and Andrew recognize that they can be put out of business by any large company with expansive distribution capabilities. Their manufacturer seems accommodating, but they realize that he will produce for any organization that orders in large quantities—something a large retailer could do. The brothers have been advised that an exclusive distribution agreement would be difficult if not impossible to enforce in an international setting. Another consideration is that the universities and colleges have no obligation to renew the licensing agreements from year to year, a fact that impels the brothers to focus only on the short term.

■ *Accounting/reporting requirements.* Palmer Products has two reporting obligations right now—a quarterly report of sales and royalties to be prepared for the colleges and universities and the federal tax return. They gather invoices and rely on memory when it comes to filling out the quarterly remittance reports. They are in the midst of having the company's first federal tax return prepared. They provided a shoebox full of receipts and invoices to the accountant and have been responding from memory when answering his questions. They are aware that they may owe sales tax in the state they are incorporated (Florida) and possibly in other states in which they have sold candles via mail order and their 800 number. They provide informal reports to their financiers (family) but nothing concrete or comprehensive. (They know this will have to change if they are to expand quickly.) They do not generate any sort of financial data to help them run the company, relying instead on their gut instincts.

Need for the Multilevel Model

All of the relevant issues are not exclusive of one another, although Mark and Andrew would like to evaluate them individually. The ability to acquire financing for expansion will depend on the nature of prospective data customers, which could be bankers, venture capital companies, or a consortium of friends, family, and acquaintances. The sophistication of the financial data demanded by customers will drive the quality of reporting processes as Mark and Andrew seek to generate accurate data in a timely manner. Meanwhile the limitations of their reporting processes will be dictated in part by the sophistication of systems and technology, which may be hampered by their ability to get financing. These interdependencies must be dealt with in a logical manner when conceptualizing, formalizing, and executing a finance strategy. Rather than isolating each of the issues and attempting to prioritize them, arranging the issues and letting them build on each other will allow the brothers to conceptualize a more stable strategic plan. Small and emerging business owners need to take this approach in developing a finance strategy. Addressing the overall objectives of the business and building upward toward the more accounting/finance issues works best. This approach can be easily understood in a pyramidlike diagram (Exhibit 4.1) with fundamental (concrete components) issues relating to infrastructure and the business plan appearing at the base and the more malleable (soft components) initiatives appearing at the top.

The essence of this schematic is the alignment of vital business and nonbusiness issues that have financial implications. The base of the pyramid represents the fundamentals of the business. The issues become more specific to the finance and accounting area as the base rises to the apex. The premise of this model is that certain topics have more of an overall impact on the organization than others—and that no one issue stands alone or is mutually exclusive of another. For example, anticipated watershed events in the business life cycle (e.g., seeking a bank loan or taking on new partners in an expansion) will dictate the type and timing of the financial data customers encountered, which in turn will dictate the sophistication of the finance infrastructure, which drives the ability to optimize the P&L and balance sheet presentation. Generally, concrete components of the finance function are more apt to be addressed in issues nearer the base of the pyramid while soft components are dealt with at the top of the pyramid. The challenge is to position the finance organization not only to address environmental and internal changes effectively but to bolster decision making as well.

The multilevel model serves two purposes: as a working blueprint for the finance function and as a reference to develop and maintain overall business strategies. Small and emerging business owners typically are more focused on the former, as the finance function is usually underdeveloped or nonexistent. The multilevel model will allow management to isolate and assess the needs of the business and determine how the finance function will address them as the company

Exhibit 4.1   **Multilevel Approach in Pyramid Form**

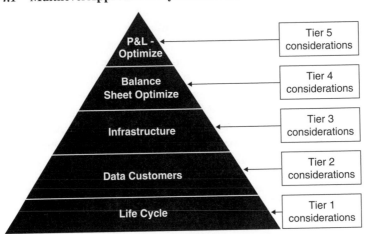

matures. Thus, the multilevel model is one that evolves and changes with the business. In both cases, though, the layering of issues is key, determining how particular needs will be addressed and assessing the trade-offs and costs involved in doing so. The goal is to address a need without degrading other areas of the finance function. An adjustment at the top or mid-level of the model can be evaluated for impact or relevance before the proposed initiative is put in motion.

The small and emerging business should be focused on establishing a relevant finance function. The objective is to properly arrange the company's current profile and identify areas of improvement or development. The levels of this model must be defined to gain an understanding of how it lends itself to finance function development.

TIER 1 CONSIDERATIONS: LIFE CYCLE

What Is the Life Cycle?

The life cycle of a business represents all events from inception forward. Small and emerging business owners may find visualizing the end of their business absurd given their current focus on building it. A more practical way of thinking about company life cycle is to conceive the *exit strategy* (no matter how far into the future this may be) and all events leading up to it. If a business plan was prepared for the enterprise, chances are an exit strategy was considered or at least mentioned in some form.

In the context of the business plan, an exit strategy defines the point in time and/or circumstances in which the business owner will leave the business or significantly reduce his or her role. Exit strategies outline such events as taking on venture equity, selling the company to a third party (or partners), and final liquidation. It is important to understand that an exit strategy not only defines the end point but outlines the events leading up to it. Events or milestones contributing to an exit may include due diligence related to financing arrangements such as venture equity/debt, a private offering, or bank debt. It also may involve the plan for marketing the business to potential buyers.

The exit strategy is the culmination of the business life cycle. The establishment of milestones in a logical sequence will bridge the gap between present-day operations and future exit strategies. While initially conceptualizing the business, an exit strategy may have already been defined via business plan. Many business owners and executives, however, may not have considered an exit strategy, or if they have, the nature of the business may have changed to a point where the original exit strategy and milestones have become obsolete. Small and emerging business owners must examine the life cycle for the first time (if they haven't already done so) and revisit it periodically.

Thinking Long Term

Long-term planning may not be a priority now, but it is worthwhile for small and emerging business owners to at least conceptualize major milestones and the prospective steps to achieve them, regardless of the time horizons. Major events such as going public, selling the company, or transferring the company to children are a few examples of major life-cycle milestones. Prioritizing these events and establishing how these milestones will bridge to the exit strategy will take some thought. These questions will help in documenting the milestones the small and emerging business owner will want to achieve:

- At what age will the owner or significant executive retire?
- Is there a succession plan in place?
- Is an expansion planned?
- Do the expansion plans involve growing from within (organic growth) or acquiring other companies?
- How much financing is needed to fit expansion plans?
- What kind of financing would be preferred?
- What burdens will taking on debt create?
- Will it be necessary to refocus the business on other markets and/or other products?
- Is taking on other equity partners beneficial to the business owners?
- Is the small and emerging business owner prepared for the scrutiny involved in taking the company public?

- What would it cost to participate in the equity markets?
- How is the business positioned from a cash perspective to achieve any of the above?

This list of questions is not exhaustive. Because some entrepreneurs are so close to day-to-day operations, taking a step back and looking at the big picture is imperative. When this self-examination is complete, the small and emerging business owner should have an understanding of:

- *Firm* company succession over the next year, laid out in a step format.
- *Rough* company succession over the next five years (10 years if possible), laid out in a step format. (Succession plans should include market and/or product development goals as well as revenue or asset thresholds.)
- A schematic of the need for financing including the details addressing how much, why, and when it is needed.
- The level of involvement by the business owner.
- Whether the owner wants to continue with a significant role or whether he or she will accept a lesser role.

The ultimate goal of this exercise is to create a rough time line of significant events. The basic premise is that major events do not unfold randomly but rather in a well-thought-out, controlled way. The early years of a business may seem like a struggle for the small and emerging business owner, but the leadership is best served to position the company for the next significant event as opposed to surviving day to day. Approaching the business in this manner will create a strategic culture that will carry it through the short, medium, *and* long term. Each milestone event should build on the preceding one, creating a succession that leads to each exit event, whether they occur in one or 20 years.

Getting Personal

The line between personal life goals and those of the business may be blurred for the small and emerging business owner. This lack of clarity becomes more complicated when the personal goals of other partners/owners are considered. A cursory understanding of personal goals and the trade-offs owners are willing to endure in order to grow the business will help the strategic vision of the company and prevent conflict between owners as the business matures and the challenges become more complicated. This reasoning suggests that Mark and Andrew Palmer should understand each other's level of commitment to the growth of the company and the sacrifices needed to achieve it.

It is imperative that Mark and Andrew share and ultimately agree on their intentions for the company's future. They may find it necessary to discuss:

- *How long will they want to stick with this?* Their lives are similar from a socioeconomic perspective for now, but what happens as they grow older and family or other personal interests take precedence? Their current commitment to the organization may be undying and equal, but there is no guarantee this will last. The extent to which Palmer Products makes their lives better may not be in proportion to the sacrifices they make in time and attention. They may be motivated to grow as quickly as possible and then sell out, recognizing the temporary nature of the business and their potential waning commitment.

- *Is there an industry peer that they can model their organization after?* They may have to rely on more than gut instinct to manage the company as business issues become more complex and the two have more at stake. Issues from inventory management, shipping, support staff, and tax compliance are areas in which they need professional consulting. Companies in similar industries may be the best to mimic in this regard. Establishing some sort of relationship with owners/executives of companies they do not compete with can be worthwhile. Doing so also may allow for a mentor/mentee relationship with more experienced executives.

- *What do they have to gain by growing?* This may be the most important question for them to address as individuals and collectively. Is the reward they seek financial? Social? Life experience? The answer will provide an understanding of whether they want to continue growing the organization indefinitely or use it as a stepping-stone for other endeavors.

- *What are the immediate needs of the business?* Vital needs of the business must be addressed with urgency. What are the business needs in the next one, three, and six months? If the company can't make it to the next year, strategizing will be moot. Immediate concerns may focus on customer acquisition and retention, maintaining good relationships with vendors and suppliers, and financing. Strategizing will build on the initiatives they put in place to handle these issues.

- *How recession proof is the business?* Depending on how oriented toward the long term the brothers are, external circumstances beyond their control must be acknowledged. Most small and emerging business owners do not waste time thinking about circumstances beyond their control when it comes to active policies. It is important, however, to understand what options or contingencies are in place to address such events. Since no business owner can control the economy, viewing the business in light of a shifting economy is helpful. Is their product a necessity or a

Exhibit 4.2   **Life-cycle Time Line for Palmer Products Inc.**

$10,000 loan from parents to buy first shipment of candles.	Double first year revenues to $100,000. Have website in place.	Push revenues to $1.6 million. Hire staff to manage orders/ shipping.	Top the $6.4 million revenue mark. Borrow money to finance storage/office space.	Top the $25 million revenue mark and go public.

Inception	Year 2	Year 6	Year 8	Year 10

nonessential? Does the pricing scheme define their product as a luxury good or an inferior good? Understanding their products will give the Palmers a good indication of what will happen when things are not as good as they are now.

■ *Can they evaluate the intangibles?* What makes the company unique? What aspects of the business can no one else replicate? How will the two preserve this? Can Mark and Andrew value these unique components? If they plan to sell the company, these unique aspects of the business will be considered *goodwill* and play a major factor in the price they would receive for their life's work.

■ *What is the succession plan?* What happens if Mark or Andrew leaves the company? Can the necessary duties be carried on in the short and midterm? How much goodwill will be lost if one leaves? Can this be quantified? If so, can a mechanism be put in place that replaces this?

Exhibit 4.2 is a sample of a simple life-cycle time line for Palmer Products. This example illustrates Mark and Andrew Palmer's intention to grow the initial investment of $10,000 into a $25 million public company over 10 years. The brothers are long on enthusiasm, but they have yet to conceive a solid strategy for the company. Typical of most small and emerging businesses, they have neither a business plan nor a model company to mimic or refer to as they encounter more decision crossroads. It is possible they are surprised they took the business this far. The sum total of their strategic goals lies with revenue targets (doubling growth each year for 10 years) that they have casually articulated to each other. These goals are illustrated in linear form in the exhibit. It is important to note that external factors will play a large role in this succession of events, possibly pushing the business in a different direction altogether. Documenting the landmarks in the business life cycle as it is predicted now creates a goal-oriented day-to-day routine that will allow Mark and Andrew to flesh out initiatives and position the business for positive growth.

Establishing the business life cycle will be the most fundamental step needed to strategize not only the finance function but the whole business and its component parts (marketing, production, and research functions). The caveat is that any watershed event will be subject to change and must be adjusted when necessary. Although this 30,000-foot view is very high level for Palmer Products, it will serve as a starting point for their forward-thinking endeavors. The business owner must identify what needs to be done and when—offering a rough schematic of the life-cycle time line. The process of fleshing out will ensue—in which the data customers most likely to be encountered in achieving these milestones are identified.

TIER 2 CONSIDERATIONS: DATA CUSTOMERS

What Are Data Customers?

Business owners (large or small) must understand to whom financial results will be communicated. The parties to whom this information is provided are referred to as *data customers*. The most important data customers at the early stage of a small and emerging business are the owners. Being responsible for all decision making and strategy makes those managing the business the number-one customer. The base of data customers will expand as the company matures and takes on third-party financing, whether it is bank debt or equity financing from a public offering or private placement. Data customer requirements will grow from the need to see the rudimentary aspects of operations to the more complicated statutory needs of banks or the Securities and Exchange Commission.

The small and emerging business owner's needs for data are easy to define. Managers of small organizations usually are focused on customer needs and the important metrics that drive the business. What about the needs of other potential data customers? Will the finance function be positioned to serve these needs? Who are those customers and what do they want? Is there anything that can be done now to lay the groundwork for meeting their needs? It may help to ask these questions:

■ What are the owners' requirements as data customer?
■ What is the turn-around time for a typical data request?
■ Which data customers need summary data?
■ Which data customers need detail data?

- Are the internal data customers (those within the organization) financial or nonfinancial personnel?
- Do internal data customers have ready access to company data?
- Can the company's top five external data customers be named?
- Does the company have a standard suite of reports or formulas that management references regularly?

Tying in to Life-cycle Considerations (Tier 1)

At this stage of strategy development, a rough time line or expected sequence of events should be in place outlining identifiable company milestones from inception to exit. The time line will identify all significant events in the planned life cycle of the business and their expected time of occurrence. If any of these significant events entail financing, business combinations, or a public offering, due diligence must be performed on company financial statements. Depending on the milestone events identified in Tier 1, the company may be forced to produce complex, legally defined financial statements. These financial statements and related disclosures will be reviewed, questioned, and adjusted throughout the due diligence process that will precede most relevant milestone events. This means the company will be subject to a new, perhaps unprecedented level of scrutiny.

Understanding the characteristics and level of sophistication of data customers is crucial at this stage of finance strategy development. Understanding the different types of data customers and their motives will be crucial as the company matures. An important consideration is to understand the distinction between sophisticated and unsophisticated data customers. More often than not, a particular data customer is standing between the business and a particular milestone objective. Giving the data customer what is wanted in a timely manner may mean the difference between success and failure when encountering a life cycle event. The finance function must recognize this and be poised at all times to deliver timely and accurate information for all financial data requests. Ensuring this aspect of data delivery involves planning all infrastructure and financial statement presentation policies in advance of need. Waiting until the need is imminent is too late to begin conceptualizing follow-through.

Exhibit 4.2 illustrates Palmer Products' high-level growth goals for the next 10 years. Are Mark and Andrew aware of what is required to achieve these goals? Doubling revenue in Year 2 may not be difficult, but doubling revenue in Years 3 and 4 may require an infusion of cash to fund the storage of product while they wait for customer payments. How much will they need? What about their website and advertising campaigns—how much will they need to finance these endeavors? If they need less than $1 million, chances are a local bank loan will cover it. Producing the volume to break the $1 million mark in Year 6 will require Palmer Products to hire help to handle order processing, shipping, and inventory management.

The company will need more funds to finance the burgeoning business. At some point Mark and Andrew will have to go beyond what a bank is willing to lend. Doing this may mean taking on equity partners or making some sort of advanced debt arrangement. Eventually they will want to take the company public and surrender control of the business.

Somewhere along the way, a level of examination (audit or formal review) will be required for Palmer Products' financial statements. If the company takes on financing from outside the company, whether it is bank debt or equity financing from the capital markets, some sort of limited review procedures will need to be performed periodically on their financial statements. Securing bank financing at this early stage of the business may require a local or regional audit firm to perform this service, with the financier (bank or financial institution) seeking comfort in compliance with debt covenants and review procedures. If the brothers choose to go public, a comprehensive audit is required and a host of detailed filings will need to be made with the SEC.

If Palmer Products goes public, its future will depend on its ability to present itself to the world via financial statements. Is the company prepared to generate financial statements that conform to generally accepted accounting principles? Do proper controls exist in the finance organization to ensure the proper handling of cash receipts and cash payments? Are processes and information systems strong enough to generate the proper analysis schedules required by examiners (auditors)? Can they be generated in a timely manner? These issues will be addressed in detail farther up the finance strategy pyramid. At this stage it is essential to evaluate the milestones listed in the Tier 1 analysis and determine:

- The need for generating financial data (statements)
- For whom the financial data (statements) will be generated
- The level of sophistication of the financial statement audience (data customers)

Combining Tier 1 and Tier 2 considerations provides more insight into the needs of the company. Strategy can take form as these levels of consideration are put into proper context. In the case of Palmer Products, the milestones noted in Exhibit 4.2 are combined with Tier 2 considerations and illustrated in Exhibit 4.3.

Exhibit 4.3 provides detail on the requirements for achieving the company milestones in the business life cycle illustrated in Exhibit 4.2. Mark and Andrew Palmer will now have an idea of the kind of finance decisions needed in the next two to 10 years, specifically as they relate to data customer needs. An analysis such as this provides insight into the conceptual groundwork that must be established for finance strategy development. When this analysis is complete, the company can confidently progress to Tier 3.

Exhibit 4.3 **Tier 2 Considerations on Proposed Company Milestones for Palmer Products**

Event/Milestone (Tier 1 consideration)	Requirement	Financial Statements required?	Most Likely Data Customer (Tier 2 consideration)	Data Customer Sophistication (Tier 2 consideration)
Begin business	$10,000 loan from parents	No	N/A	N/A
Double first year revenue to $100,000. Put website in place.	None	N/A	N/A	N/A
Push revenues to $1.6 million. Hire staff to manage orders/ shipping.	$100,000 loan from bank	Yes	Bank, Local CPA	Low to Moderate
Top the $6.4 million revenue mark. Borrow money to finance storage/ office space.	$1,000,000 loan or private placement	Yes	Larger Financial Institution, Regional CPA firm	Moderate to High
Top the $25 million revenue mark and go public.	Audit, SEC filings	Yes	Large National CPA Firm, Attorneys, SEC, Analysts	High

TIER 3 CONSIDERATIONS: INFRASTRUCTURE

Objective

Tier 3 of finance strategy development is the point at which the small and emerging business owner can begin to define infrastructure (concrete components of the finance function) issues. The finance infrastructure will need to support decision making (for internal data customers) and financial data queries (for external data customers) for all milestone events. While keeping immediate needs in mind, the objective is to outline the conceptual considerations that will support short-, mid, and long-term decision making as it relates to infrastructure. The implication is that the finance infrastructure will evolve as the business develops. The objective in approaching this topic strategically is to engineer a controlled evolution that serves the company's needs and pocketbook. The four areas to be addressed at Tier 3 of the multilevel model include: finance organization, Information Systems, data flow processes, and a policies and procedures manual.

Finance Organization

The *finance organization* refers to employees and the tools (technology) they need to do their jobs. This aspect of the finance structure will grow with the company, like it or not. It is the challenge of the small and emerging business owner to make sure this growth is *controlled* and well thought out. Doing so can be a daunting task, given the potentially chaotic environment the emerging company is probably experiencing. Are the right people in place to handle the tasks at hand? Do staff members have the right tools to get the job done? Answering these questions at a static point in time is difficult enough; in the context of a dynamic, growing business, these questions become a challenge to address. Some management teams are successful in getting the right people in the right places with appropriate technology at a given point in time. Where they fail is in keeping up with future needs. If the needs of the finance organization are put on the back burner until a crisis arises, management could handicap the organization and miss or nullify a key growth/development opportunity. At the other extreme, stocking up on unnecessary personnel and technology will burden the company with inflated administrative costs. So how does a company gauge the appropriate level of development for its finance organization?

Continuing with the case of Palmer Products, milestones were identified and put in a time line format in Exhibit 4.2. The need for producing financial statements and proposed data customers were matched up with each milestone event in Exhibit 4.3. Exhibit 4.4 clarifies the need to produce financial statements with the minimum financial reporting requirements listed. It also outlines general finance organization characteristics necessary to address the milestone financial reporting requirements.

The characteristics outlined define in general terms the appropriate finance organization components for Palmer Products that are necessary to accommodate each critical milestone event date. Using this template will enable Mark and Andrew Palmer to conceptualize the needs of the finance organization—keeping up with the company's milestones while controlling the amount of capital dedicated to this function in the spawning years of the business. Key issues in coordinating the finance organization will center on people, technology, and the proper mix of the two.

PEOPLE Assessing finance personnel needs and translating them to an effective team is a subjective process. Interviewing and evaluating candidates with varied backgrounds and knowledge levels can be challenging—with no guarantees. The

Exhibit 4.4   **Finance Organization Characteristics**

Milestone/ Timeline (Tier 1 consideration)	Minimum Financial Reporting Requirements	Finance Organization Characteristics (Tier 3 considerations)
Inception	Keep company checkbook and make customer deposits	Mark and Andrew
Year 2	Keep company checkbooks and make customer deposits. Minimal pro forma financial statements prepared to facilitate product orders.	Mark and Andrew
Year 6	Minimal financial statements prepared for external reporting and internal (management) reporting; liaise with bankers and reviewers (auditors).	Full-time finance team; defined data flow processes
Year 8	Full set of financial statements prepared for external reporting; detailed financial statements for management reporting.	Sophisticated full-time finance team; streamlined data flow processes
Year 10	Full set of financial statements prepared for external reporting; detailed SEC disclosures and filings; detailed financial statements for management reporting.	Robust finance team; streamlined processes and strong information systems technology

small and emerging business owner should consider the following in attempting to objectify this process:

- *Education level.* Can the finance function live with clerical-level personnel, or will there be a need for degreed individuals? Will the finance organization need professionals with graduate degrees? This question must be weighed when evaluating the need for a simple, sophisticated, or highly sophisticated staff. The business owner must consider employing a mix of these educational backgrounds.
- *Experience level.* Is there a need for seasoned professionals, freshly minted college graduates, or paraprofessionals? Depending on milestone needs, both the level and the mix of talent must be considered closely. Small and emerging business owners may need employees with industry-specific specialties.

■ *Certifications.* This will apply in more sophisticated finance teams. Certified Public Accountants, Certified Financial Analysts, and Certified Management Accountants are examples of finance-specific certifications. The small and emerging business owner might consider a mix of certifications to balance out staff. Some peripheral certifications that will ensure a well-rounded organization include Microsoft Certified Systems Engineers and Certified Project Managers.

■ *Accounting and finance mix.* Measuring the appropriate level of education and experience may not be enough. Managing the *mix* of disciplines may be just as important. What type of analysis paradigms will the organization employ? What tasks will the finance organization be charged with? If the tasks at hand are numbers oriented, someone with a pure accounting background may suffice. If the position is more operations oriented, a finance person may fit the bill. Technicians who really understand the finer points of generally accepted accounting principles would be an example of the former. They are equipped to translate data to financial statements; they may not be as well suited for interpreting data and parlaying it to good business decisions. Finance people may not be as well versed in employing GAAP as they are in advising management on operational decisions. Both areas require a fair amount of education and experience in their respective tracks. Juggling this mix may suit different stages of the organization—the accounting person early on when the organization is applying GAAP for the first time, and the finance person when the organization is looking for an operational strategist.

■ *Talented professionals.* Does the small and emerging business have ready access to qualified finance people (access to the collegiate ranks and/or an experienced pool)? Being located in the Northeast or Silicon Valley is ideal for accessing both. If the business is not close to collegiate talent, how will it recruit them? If no pool of experienced professionals is close, how will the company avail itself of talent? Will relocation be a standard part of the employment process?

■ *Employee retention.* How will the small and emerging business keep the talent it hires? Will the company rely on financial incentives? What type of advancement track will the company offer—promotions, titles, and so on? How willing is the company to invest in its people? This investment refers to training, education, and performance enhancement programs. What type of tools and amenities is the company willing to offer? Will computers and software be top of the line and updated frequently? Will employee services and flexible time schedules be available? All of these should be considered a part of the total employment package. The company should be prepared to address this issue in the employment contract.

TECHNOLOGY   Arming staff with the appropriate tools will be imperative. The most important constraint may be the availability of cash to bankroll technology or to maintain current technology. Some considerations in this area are:

- *What is the need for computers?* Do all members of the finance team need a computer? If so, do they need a workstation or laptop? It is wise to avoid disparities in technology within the group.
- *What types of operating systems and applications will be needed?* What applications are *needed* and what applications are *wanted?* It is important to remember that games and Internet access use up memory and distract workers. Sorting this out will take some homework and policing on the part of the management team.
- *How frequently will upgrades be performed?* It's easy to revamp technology every six months. Doing so does, however, get expensive after a while. Understanding the processing, random access memory (RAM), and hard drive capacity needed and making sure everyone is outfitted equally throughout the organization is important. It is imperative to avoid getting sucked into individual preferences and wants.
- *How will the system be configured?* How sophisticated is the standard suite of tools for users? Does a network exist? Some may dismiss this as "techie details"; however, understanding that downtime of servers and machines costs money in underutilized staff will add to the strategizing effort. Having only one staff member handle computer issues will get old after a while, resulting in frustrated users and a frustrated expert. The small and emerging business owner may want to consider a full-time IS person or outsource the function if necessary.

MANAGING THE MIX OF STAFF AND TECHNOLOGY   Carefully thinking through personnel needs and equipping staff members with the right tools to do their jobs will pay dividends for the small and emerging business as it matures. Pegging the sophistication level of finance personnel in a manner similar to that in Exhibit 4.4, the small and emerging business owner will be able to gauge both the short- and long-term growth needs of the finance organization. Getting the right tools in the hands of the right people will maximize output. Knowing personnel needs well in advance will be advantageous to ordering and maintaining the right technological tools. Other considerations in strategizing the finance organization at Tier 3 of the finance strategy development pyramid are:

- *Cost.* Buying the best computer technology and hiring the brightest people can be expensive. Just as a gas station does not buy all the gas it will sell for the year on January 1, neither should the small and emerging business owner purchase or hire more staff than is needed to address the tasks at hand. Exhibit 4.4 provides a menu of needs for Mark and Andrew Palmer at Palmer Products, illustrating the particulars of what, who, and when. This guide will be particularly helpful when it is time to hire high-ticket finance people. Getting a handle on the size of the finance staff six months, two years, even five years down the road will give the small and emerging business owner an understanding of how many computers and printers to buy and the volume of office space needed to accommodate them.

- *Timing.* Just as a business owner would use *just-in-time* methodologies or on-demand methods in business processes, bringing in the appropriate professionals to help when they are needed (not too soon, not too late) is crucial. Although this issue has a cost element, the timing concern may have more of an impact on the initiatives and challenges faced by the company. Using a schematic similar to Exhibit 4.4 will allow management to measure personnel and technology needs appropriately. The goal is to cede over the day-to-day and strategic decision making to a qualified finance person who has the foresight to grow the finance organization to fit the small and emerging company's needs.

- *Consultants.* Consultants are a good resource to help a company get through difficult initiatives and bridge the gap between growth plateaus and turnover. It is important to keep in mind that some consultants (not all) may be more motivated to keep management happy so they are asked back for repeat engagements than to provide lasting solutions to problems. While outsourcing will always be a consideration, the small and emerging business owner must be wary of handing over key areas of the business to outsiders who have no true stake in the company's long-term success. One major down side to using consultants is the potential for developing a dependency on their expertise— expertise that exits the building every time the consultant leaves.

  The key strategy for avoiding dependencies on consultants is to grow and retain as much company-specific knowledge internally as possible. The opportunity for this development is great in the early years of the business as infrastructure decisions are made on a daily basis. Managing consultants wisely should be a priority for the small and emerging business owner. Managing consultants means setting milestones, conveying clear expectations, and asking for or creating work plans that can be evaluated. A permanent member of the organization should be driving all initiatives. To use the age-old axiom, it is best to have the consultants teach the organization to fish as opposed to having them provide the fish.

- *Imminent and future needs.* The small and emerging business owner will face the inevitable circumstances of change due to growth. Finance personnel capabilities will have to change as the company grows and faces new challenges. The need for accounting people, for example, will be important in the early years to focus on the initial translation of the company's activity to GAAP. The organization will inevitably evolve and change, yielding a dependence on staff members who are more systems and/or business savvy. Knowing what skills will be needed and when will give an indication of the kind and level of talent demanded. Is a wider palate of skills worth paying for now rather than waiting until later? Will the company be stuck with someone hired to respond to current needs without considering the experience or educational level needed for future needs?

Information Systems

Tier 3 focuses on the relationship between personnel and IS. The role of technology in any finance organization is to automate as many low-level tasks as possible. Human capital is best used for discernment and judgment. The goal is to isolate these two roles and maximize the role of personnel (making decisions and drawing conclusions) and technology (gathering and processing data). Chapter 7, "Investigating Information Systems," addresses certain information system issues more specifically. For now the basic premise will be discussed.

The need for financial data, whether it is for internal or external purposes, will drive the need for efficient, reliable data flow processes. Small and emerging businesses typically are focused on immediate information/data needs. Regardless of the long- or short-term nature of data needs, the foundation of data flow processes is the capability of information systems technology including canned or off-the-shelf applications. Exhibit 4.4 illustrates that, for Palmer Products, Year 6 will require something beyond manual processes. Year 8 will demand that processes be fine-tuned, as the need for financial data for external and internal data customers heightens. The milestones in Year 10 will dictate the need for robust data flow processes with best practice capability. The successful evolution of these processes over this 10-year period will be due in part to the ability to automate as many tasks as possible. Years 2 to 6 will allow for the books to be closed using spreadsheets. Beyond Year 6, the transition to something more sophisticated for financial reporting, such as Hyperion, Oracle, or Cognos, should be under way. The company should have in place a powerful enterprise resource planning tool (e.g., SAP, JD Edwards) to gather and process financial data and a data warehouse to manage and convert data to knowledge by Years eight through 10. The one constant here is the waning role of "people" in data handling. The time line in Exhibit 4.4 will aid in keeping proper perspective during this evolution.

Processes

Data flow processes are outlined in greater detail in later chapters. Tier 3 of the finance strategy development pyramid indicates the importance of data flow processes. Process considerations must work in concert with information systems considerations. Because processes are integrated with systems and systems serve as the core for processes, changing one will have an impact on the other.

The term *processes* refers to the entire data flow dynamic—data gathering, data processing, and data analysis. Data flow processes manage data related to tax, external, and management reporting as well as budgeting and forecasting. Processes include all actions and tasks of people and technology throughout the data flow dynamic. Process development may not seem to be an issue if the small and emerging business has easily accessible data. The challenge will begin as the business grows to remote areas and products or as services change or expand. Getting data quickly and accurately as well as keeping track of the correct buckets in which to classify data will become more difficult as the business matures. The small and emerging business owner must focus on honing the data flow dynamic to a razor-sharp edge. The goal is to minimize manual intervention in the gathering and processing phases and maximize the focus on analysis. An optimal mix of systems and people will have to be established within reasonable budgetary constraints. The speed and quality of analysis will be dictated by the sophistication level of data customers. Decisions can be made on capital expenditures or investment in staff only after customer data requirements are understood. Major considerations in process evaluation include:

- *Benchmarking.* What are peers (competitors and noncompetitors) in the industry doing? Small and emerging business owners need to know if they are maximizing the people/technology mix. One way to benchmark is to pay for consultants to evaluate processes and discuss what others are doing. Subscribing to industry publications that provide guidance on these matters is another avenue. Finally, it is acceptable simply to pick up the phone and talk to professionals in other organizations. Chances are they are dealing with the same challenges and may welcome the dialog. Networking with peers may be the best investment in benchmarking the small and emerging business owner will ever make.

    What if the business and industry are too young for benchmarking data to exist? A company benchmarking against its own performance may be the only option. Comparing activity across geographic regions or management areas may be helpful. Comparisons between products and services or management teams to one another also may be options.

- *Improving discipline.* It is equally important to keep those in the trenches in line as it is to ensure that certain protocols are observed at the executive level. Keeping chains of command intact, especially for requests for data, serves all parties the best. Key considerations center on sticking to processes, adhering to time schedules, and establishing accountability.

- *Maximizing communication.* Having intact information chains throughout the organization will help push key initiatives. Doing this may be easy in small and emerging organizations at the beginning. The goal, though, is for businesses to grow at a rapid (but manageable) pace. Holding periodic information *cascade* sessions with key individuals throughout the business may help in disseminating key information in larger or geographically spread out organizations. Product or information champions dispersed throughout the company also may serve as information resources at the extremities of the organization.

One component of evaluating processes that deserves consideration includes the development of *common data standards,* one of which is a Standard Chart of Accounts. Swiftly moving organizations, regardless of size, must have a common platform to communicate company results. Complications involve complying with local statutory reporting requirements (which may dictate keeping certain accounts), maintenance and updates, and monitoring compliance. A more detailed discussion of processes is presented in Chapter 6, "Data Flow Process."

Policies and Procedures Manual

A policies and procedures manual is not considered part of infrastructure in a traditional sense. Finance policies and procedures are less fundamental to the business than understanding the exit strategy and developing processes and information systems, yet they underscore the management of the P&L and balance sheet (the premier responsibilities of finance). The small and emerging business owner may have resorted to implied policies or used procedures that have simply evolved without structure. In the beginning, when the business is not complex, laying the foundation for a finance policies and procedures manual may be as simple as documenting what is currently being done.

Policies and procedures should outline the basics of the finance function. Issues like handling cash receipts and disbursements or handling the checkbook may be the only relevant policies and procedures to document. Large, mature companies will need to document their accounting treatment methodologies and certain internal controls. Sensitive areas, such as revenue recognition, reserve bookings, and expense accruals, are a few examples of policies and procedures that need documentation in large organizations. General topical areas include: accounting, finance and credit, purchasing and shipping, information systems, business continuity, and manufacturing.

Whether the organization is small or large, a careful examination of the business is important when constructing or refining policies and procedures. Outlining policies that do not fit the business will be a waste of time and weaken the credibility of the policies and procedures manual. Making a habit of updating policies and procedures is a good discipline. Doing so will add to the culture of uniformity and discipline.

UPPER-TIER CONSIDERATIONS

Purpose

The top two levels of the strategy development process involve topics and issues that are more strategic in nature in relation to the accounting and finance area. These issues focus on specific areas of financial statement preparation, business modeling, and statutory compliance. The small and emerging business owner's position on these issues impacts the core strategies of the entire organization, thereby defining the business from an accounting standpoint. Decisions and policies that come about from upper-tier considerations are also long term in nature, although the small and emerging business owner must be prepared to alter them at a moment's notice to ensure they are still relevant. Using the computer as a metaphor for the relationship between the upper-tier consideration (soft components of finance function) and infrastructure (concrete components), the hardware (monitor and central processing unit) is analogous to infrastructure while the operating system makes up these upper-tier considerations.

Narrowing the Focus

Upper-tier considerations for small and emerging businesses are different from those of midsize to larger organizations. Issues also vary among small and emerging businesses due to industry and/or geographic differences. While the issues may vary, the one that should receive the highest priority for business leaders is cash management. If any one issue dictates the short-, mid-, and long-term viability of the organization, it is the company's ability to generate and retain cash. The upper tier of this strategy model can address a myriad of issues; however, the focus of this text is on maximizing cash flow.

Managing cash goes beyond monitoring the check and deposit book. Keeping a close eye on both of these may be effective in the beginning, but as the organization becomes more complex, the business owner will have to rely on data generated by the business itself to make good decisions. Working capital may be the best area on which to focus. The generic definition of working capital is the current assets and current liabilities of the organization. These areas of the business represent liquid resources that are readily available (current assets) as well as the immediate obligations (current liabilities). Examples of current assets are cash, accounts receivable, inventory, and other resources that are accessible by the organization within one year. Examples of current liabilities are accounts payable, short-term debt obligations, mortgage obligations, and lease obligations. Companies that have a handle on working capital have a greater amount of stability in the short term, which provides more options for directing the business.

In setting an overall finance strategy, the upper tier focuses on managing the three major areas of working capital that directly impact cash: accounts receivable, inventory, and accounts payable. If a small and emerging business owner minimizes the amount of working capital tied up in the combination of these three, cash flow will be maximized. The primary concern is to keep accounts receivable and inventory levels low (without disturbing the business) while allowing for accounts payable to hover at a level that is comfortable for both the company and vendors.

Policies related to working capital may make or break Palmer Products, especially if Mark and Andrew have a difficult time finding someone to lend them money or provide them equity financing. Palmer Products will have to be keenly aware of the inventory levels needed to feed customer demand. The company also must be cognizant of excess or *leftover* inventory. Excess product that was overordered or simply not sold at the end of the selling season will leave the company with a cache of inventory that it cannot sell (convert to cash), thereby denying the company cash it needs. The company must focus on accounts receivable, especially the payment terms it gives its business customers. Selling big blocks of merchandise to large retail chains benefits the company little if it has to wait 60 to 90 days for payment. Based on past experience, Mark and Andrew prefer to pay vendors immediately upon receipt of the bills. This may be a sound practice ideologically, but they should consider exercising terms to the extent they are available. If a vendor freely grants payment terms of 30 days, paying a bill the day it is received denies the company the use of that cash for 30 days. This does not mean that a company should make a policy of paying bills late, but rather it should hold onto cash as long as possible.

Tying Upper-Tier Considerations to Lower-Tier Considerations

It is important for small and emerging business owners to understand the relationship between upper- and lower-tier considerations as they employ the multilevel approach and begin sketching out the finance strategy. As mentioned earlier, the whole model must be conceptualized before action can be taken or initiatives put in motion. Analysis models or management paradigms conceptualized at the upper tier will have to be compatible with lower-tier considerations. Infrastructure or concrete components of the finance function in particular will have to support these upper-tier components. Employing a powerful cash flow or ratio analysis model for all levels of the organization will be of little value if the Information Systems and processes cannot gather the data or process it in an acceptable manner. All aspects of the multilevel pyramid must be in harmony for the total strategizing effort to be worthwhile. This harmonization will mean addressing and reviewing various levels of the multilevel pyramid on an ongoing basis. Examples of the impact upper-tier considerations will have on the lower tier of the model include:

- Needs of data customers
- Suitability of systems and processes

- Suitability of professional finance staff
- Suitability of technology tools
- Ability to dictate life-cycle milestones

NEEDS OF DATA CUSTOMERS (TIER 2 CONSIDERATIONS) Internal and external data customers can either benefit or suffer from the policies and initiatives established in the upper tier of the multilevel model. If a company is publicly traded, analysts and shareholders will have specific informational needs. Depending on the industry or business sector in which the company operates, performance expectations related to revenue, earnings per share (EPS), or cash flow may be demanded. Understanding these expectations and cultivating a finance function that accommodates them will serve the organization well. The same goes for data customers within the organization. The leadership will be positioned to make good decisions by making analysis of key financial areas of the business a priority.

SUITABILITY OF SYSTEMS AND PROCESSES (TIER 3 CONSIDERATIONS) Putting analysis paradigms and models in place serves no purpose if the finance function cannot translate data into relevant information. For example, analyzing margins by customer may be pegged as a key analysis tool to help the organization groom its customer base. If the general ledger or financial consolidation tool captures revenue and cost of sales by sales territory only, this analysis paradigm is useless. The finance systems and processes must be able to accommodate the upper-tier considerations. One could turn this around and note that finance infrastructure must be developed to suit upper-tier considerations. Both perspectives are valid and lend credence to the idea that the multilevel model itself is a living, evolving depiction of the financial aspect of the business and should be maintained and changed as necessary.

SUITABILITY OF PROFESSIONAL FINANCE STAFF (TIER 3 CONSIDERATIONS) Depending on the stage of the business, the finance staff may have an accounting orientation, finance slant, or a mixture of both. Upper-tier considerations may dictate the complexion of staff in this regard. The organization may be focused on accommodating external customers only in the early stages of its life cycle. The result may be that finance priorities focus on tax returns, SEC filings, and standard financial reporting. If this is the case, finance staff should be technical and GAAP oriented. Robust upper-tier initiatives may demand that the finance function be actively involved in business decisions. If comprehensive growth modeling and mergers and acquisitions (M&A) are priorities of the organization, professionals with a finance or business orientation may be more appropriate. These professionals have a broader base of skills, although they may lack the depth of knowledge in applying GAAP.

SUITABILITY OF TECHNOLOGY TOOLS As a follow-up to the last section, certain analysis policies or business models may require finance staff to be armed with powerful, real-time tools to carry out their duties. Business models that demand daily or weekly forecast predictions from the field will require finance staff to respond to the information-gathering, processing, and analysis needs that underlie these models. Powerful laptops with remote and/or wireless connectivity may be necessary to facilitate such an upper-tier model. Companies that are less aggressive with their data models may not require such tools for their staff.

ABILITY TO DICTATE FUTURE LIFE-CYCLE MILESTONES   If the entire model is working, the small and emerging business should position itself and plan for business life cycle milestones by dictating appropriate upper-tier policies. Setting high expectations in the finance function is one way for the business to optimize overall business strategies. Understanding the business and information needs will give management the knowledge to conceptualize and implement business models via upper-tier considerations that will not only streamline the data flow dynamic but prepare the organization for the next logical life cycle milestone. Palmer Products (for example) eventually will need to access financing for future growth. Finance institutions will require, among other things, that the company maintain certain financial ratios and report on them quarterly. Realizing that Palmer Products' finance function is not suited for this *after* the papers have been signed is too late. Mark and Andrew would risk the lender calling in the debt if they failed to accurately report the data in question in a timely manner. The ongoing challenge for Palmer Products' finance function will be to analyze and monitor these ratios in the interim. Knowing in advance that these reporting capabilities are a real part of the financing equation, Mark and Andrew can factor in these requirements in the upper-tier considerations area of their strategy model and let them filter down through the lower-tier considerations well in advance of the need to seek financing.

Putting the Upper Tiers (Tier 4 and Tier 5) into Effect

The considerations addressed at this part of the multilevel model cue the small and emerging business owner to define the way in which it characterizes the data gathered from the external environment. Optimizing the upper tier involves knowing the ultimate information needs and the company's capacity to capture, process, and analyze data. Sound policies and strategies that stem from analyzing upper-tier considerations will provide a solid platform for the small and emerging business to navigate burdensome due diligence exercises and enable precision analysis. This will instill confidence in the small and emerging business owner to tackle major company life-cycle milestones. Carefully analyzing upper-tier considerations will yield:

- *Analysis paradigms.* Analysis tools and models that provide input on the company's performance and well-being are key to managing the business. The challenge is to ensure they are relevant and accurate.
- *Revenue recognition policies.* Sound methodologies for recognizing revenue must be in place for the company to properly reflect its activity on fi-

nancial statements, both internal and external. The organization must be poised to address the expectations of external stakeholders. The credibility of management is at stake when it comes to recording results and issuing them to the public.

- *Capital structure strategies.* The company must be positioned to make decisions about financing. Discerning financing options will require an understanding of the advantage of debt over equity financing and/or vice versa. Most important, the trade-offs involved in employing one over the other or a mixture of both must be understood. The finance function must be prepared to provide input into these decisions.

- *Margin and operating expense goals.* It is critical for the small and emerging business owner to analyze outflows of cash. Having a sound methodology for capturing and classifying expenditures will pave the way for sound decision making. Such tools for evaluating the business will give management the opportunity to segregate product/service decisions from general operating decisions.

- *Company valuation metrics.* The organization must have an understanding of how well the individual components of finance are performing. The key is establishing fair and accurate measures of company performance relative to other companies in the industry. These metrics may be narrow (inventory turns or operating expense run rates) or less specific (value of assets or revenue size).

Even though the small and emerging business owner may not be prepared to predict medium- and long-term company milestones (Tier 1 considerations) or develop a robust finance organization (Tier 3 considerations), there will always be a need to translate environmental data into meaningful and consistent financial tools to feed the decision support system. Cash flow must be at the top of the list of finance areas addressed by the small and emerging business. Considerations are classified into two categories: *Tier 4—Optimizing the Balance Sheet* and *Tier 5— Optimizing the P&L.* Balance sheet considerations have a long-term impact on the financial state of the company, hence these considerations will underscore P&L considerations. It is important to note that agility in decision making in the upper tier is dependent on solid planning in the lower tier.

TIER 4 CONSIDERATIONS: OPTIMIZING THE BALANCE SHEET

During the spawning stages of the company life cycle, the small and emerging business owner must focus on survival and *flash* (hyper, high-impact) growth. Managing cash flow and working capital is imperative. Throughout the company's evolution it will be forced to deal with capital management strategies (equity and debt) and other aspects of the balance sheet that will dictate its success. The small and emerging business owner must become accustomed to developing and implementing balance sheet strategies and initiatives to position the company to handle the challenges of future life-cycle milestones. The task of fine-tuning the company's balance sheet is never ending, especially when the business environment and the business itself continue to change.

One temptation for the small and emerging business owner is to focus exclusively on the P&L, maximizing revenue and minimizing costs. The balance sheet speaks volumes about the health of the company, although it does not receive as much attention as the P&L. Balance sheet policies yield more subtle results that, if implemented properly, will sustain the organization indefinitely. Novices may feel that balance sheet policies/issues seem too esoteric to manage. The executive/business owner skilled at evaluating the company's health, however, will attest to the fact that the balance sheet never lies. Some argue that balance sheet strategies tend to be more defensive and less proactive in nature than P&L strategies. Balance sheet strategies typically have a mid- to long-term time horizon when it comes to payback. For this reason balance sheet strategies must be prospective to be of any use. The impact of the balance sheet on cash flow and earnings prompts attention to two areas that must be handled proactively—working capital (current assets and current liabilities) and debt.

Knowing how the balance sheet will serve analysis needs is essential in keeping up with a balance sheet maintenance plan. A good place to start balance sheet management is by focusing on working capital. The goal is to optimize certain elements of working capital and, in turn, maximize cash flow. Optimizing the dollars tied up in receivables, inventory, and payables means more cash available for investing in the business.

The company's ability to manage cash flow is the true indicator of short-, medium-, and long-term survival. The short term is the most critical time frame for the small and emerging business; therefore, establishing discipline in cash flow management via working capital models now will benefit the company as it grows. Knowing this, managing these areas of the balance sheet is critical:

- ■ *Accounts receivable.* Are customers paying? If so, how long does it take to collect? Days-Sales-Outstanding (DSO) is a frequently used metric for evaluating overall collection efforts. The DSO calculation (dividing the receivables balance by a daily average revenue number) will give small and emerging business owners an idea of how long, on average, they are waiting for customer payments. Making this analysis meaningful depends on the company's understanding of cash flow needs. It may be able to budget revenue to some degree, but how about predicting cash flow? The company needs to understand how long it can reasonably go without customers paying. Management also must understand the averages for this metric in the industry. Perhaps cash needs trump that of industry averages. The industry may be so new that no averages exist. If this is the case, the company will need to analyze liquidity needs (i.e., payroll, vendors, debt service) along with projected revenue targets and develop time horizons for receiving cash payments on sales. Depending on the industry, 30 to 60 days is a fair collection period. If collection efforts go into the 90- to 120-day range, red flags begin to go up; anything over 180 days is generally unacceptable.

■ *Inventory.* Managing inventory is crucial to good cash management, especially for the retail and manufacturing sector. Idle inventory sitting in warehouses or storerooms could be cash used for paying bills, funding expansion, and the like. The inventory turnover ratio (i.e., inventory turns) is a strong metric for evaluating effectiveness in inventory management. Inventory turns (i.e., dividing total cost of sales by the inventory balance) will yield the number of times the company turns its stock of inventory. Slow-moving inventory (i.e., a low number) indicates excessive inventory levels. Managing inventory in a retail environment is fairly straightforward (the company has either overordered/undersold, or oversold/underordered); however, inventory issues in manufacturing environments can be more vexing. Supply chain issues, purchase price, and manufacturing variances all have an impact on inventory balances. How about customers; are they flexible with inventory delivery terms? Do they take delivery in a reasonable amount of time? Devising sound guidelines for inventory management and accounting will help control inventory and its impact on cash balances. The first step in managing inventory is to perform reliable analysis. Capturing, valuing, and analyzing inventory balances will position the organization to maximize cash flow and liquidity.

■ *Accounts payable.* How quickly is the company paying bills? One might think paying bills as quickly as possible is good from a discipline standpoint, but a company needs to hold on to cash as long as it can. This is especially true for a small and emerging business that needs to have as much cash available as possible to fund growth. Working out terms with vendors is standard. A window of 15 to 30 days to pay bills is standard. Depending on the clout the business has with vendors, this may stretch to 30 to 60 days. Pushing for payment terms, however, has its down side. Vendors get wise to customers who push the envelope in this area and often increase the price of the product to offset the risk they experience in waiting for payments. It is important to note that the company's payable to the vendor is the vendor's receivable from the company. Just as the company is trying to shorten the time period that receivables are outstanding, so is the vendor. A firm but reasonable payment policy works best when it comes to managing accounts payable.

■ *Liquidity ratios.* Measuring liquidity is an ongoing concern for growing businesses. Keeping tabs on liquidity ratios and debt-to-equity ratios is important especially when complying with loan covenants. Monitoring these ratios will help management assess immediate needs for running the business or predict future needs in the case of expansion or divestiture. The organization is best served to understand liquidity ratio benchmarks for companies in the same industry and measure itself against them.

TIER 5 CONSIDERATIONS: OPTIMIZING PROFIT AND LOSS

The small and emerging business owner's primary focus is on the P&L statement. It is hard to refute that growing revenue and minimizing expenses is the key to staying in business. However, success for the small and emerging business owner demands more than generating more sales and keeping costs down. The business environment demands strategies that address a wide spectrum of issues from financial statement presentation to solid operational business strategies—areas dependent on P&L policies. If the small and emerging business is publicly traded, for instance, the need to maximize shareholder wealth (keeping the stock price high) will be a major priority. Initiatives related to pleasing shareholders and laying the foundation for solid growth often conflict. Private, closely held companies do not face pressure from absentee stakeholders; however, making good decisions will depend on an understanding of the dynamics of revenue and expenses in the business.

The small and emerging business owner must view the business as a cash machine. Revenue represents *cash in* and expenses represent *cash out*. Employing accrual accounting, however, distorts this paradigm. Sometimes complicated devices are used to translate activity or expected future activity to revenue. Acceptable methods for accruing revenue are often employed in questionable ways, resulting in a distorted financial picture of the enterprise. Methods used in percentage of completion accounting, sales-type lease accounting, and accounting for long-term subscription revenue are examples of methodologies that create a gap between the P&L (revenue) and the balance sheet (cash). Accrual methods for recording expenses—depreciation, deferred taxes, and restructuring charges applied arbitrarily can paint a confusing if not deceptive picture of the organization. This dilemma drove the accounting profession to develop the parameters for the statement of cash flows—which is now a standard part of any formal financial statement package.

The small and emerging business owner eventually will have to apply GAAP properly to the enterprise. Strategies that focus on minimizing the pitfalls of recording revenue and expenses are a must if external data customers are relying on GAAP financial statements. Meeting this need will mean developing strategies that focus on generating, analyzing, and recording revenue in a way that benefits the company and stakeholders. Additionally, initiatives will have to be developed that focus on the recording and analysis of expenses.

Frenetic day-to-day activities of the small and emerging business may prevent owners/executives from crafting mid- and long-term strategies. Immediate needs can be accommodated by optimizing reporting and analysis initiatives as they relate to the P&L. Understanding the dynamics of the two major P&L classifications—revenue and expenses—and how they take shape in operations will provide a head start in creating a solid foundation for analysis and decision making.

Revenue

The recording and analysis of revenue is a challenge for any organization. A complete understanding of the business is the first step in translating events and transactions to revenue. Revenue issues can be broken down into two groups: presentation issues and operational issues.

PRESENTATION ISSUES   These issues relate strictly to the recognition and recording of revenue. They are particularly acute for public companies or those that have some sort of reporting requirement as a result of financing or absentee ownership. The need to employ GAAP is the primary motivation for examining presentation issues. Considerations in this regard are:

- *Applying uniform revenue recognition policies.* A good indicator of the suitability of revenue recognition policies is the disposition of the receivables created by the sales. Are they being paid in a timely manner? Are they recorded in a way that allows them to be aged properly? Monitoring a natural offshoot to revenue such as receivables provides an indication of whether the company is recording revenue events properly. The ability to budget and forecast revenue also will require intimate knowledge of the business. Knowing whether to ramp up inventory in anticipation of customer needs and vice versa depends on the organization's skill at prospective reporting.
- *Applying accurate revenue recognition policies.* The small and emerging business owner must determine if, from a GAAP perspective, the methodology for revenue recognition fits actual events and/or transactions. Nothing creates angst for business owners more than auditors or examiners paring back revenue because of a methodology that doesn't fit the revenue event. This occurs if the revenue is not characterized correctly from the start. Basing budgets and forecasts on inaccurate revenue recognition methodologies will create a ripple that will affect inventory ordering and capital expenditures. To avoid problems, guidance from accounting professionals or industry experts is key. Basing internal analysis on numbers that are derived in the same way externally reported numbers are recorded also will cut down on confusion in decision making.
- *Using aggressive versus conservative revenue recognition.* In many cases GAAP allows for a spectrum of treatments for events and transactions.

Nowhere is this continuum abused more than in the revenue recognition area. The temptation for small and emerging business owners is to rely on the judgment of auditors to determine whether revenue recognition is fair. Auditors, however, rely on management representations in forming their opinions— representations that business owners agree to (unwittingly or not) when they sign the letter of representation at the end of the audit engagement. Aggressive revenue recognition policies are used all too often when a company seeks to meet or exceed the expectations of the analyst community. Again, consulting a qualified professional who understands the company's business will serve the small and emerging business owner's best interests.

OPERATIONAL ISSUES   These issues are the practical aspect of revenue policy. All high-level executives agree that the presentation of results to outside parties is important, but small and emerging business owners have a greater need to set sound policies for evaluating the business and charting a course to prosperity. This need can be addressed by tackling the following operational issues:

- *Positioning for recurring revenue.* Businesses approach their markets in two ways: making the sale and cultivating more sales. The nature of some services and products, however, may allow for quick saturation of the market. This is the case with businesses that sell systems or solutions that may be good for the life of the company. An example is a home security system or antitheft system for businesses. These products represent large one-time outlays of cash for the customer but offer little room for future revenue streams for the selling company.

   High-ticket items like these often work against the businesses selling them as they fall victim to the allure of big one-time sales while failing to cultivate their market in a way that allows for future revenue streams. The business must be able to evaluate future products and services that augment such offerings. Revenue strategies may be put in place that offer less expensive one-time outlays of cash from customers but require a steady recurring revenue stream in the future. The business may adjust the pricing on a security system so that while it receives revenue up front on the initial sale of the system, they also can lock customers into long-term commitments to buy monitoring or maintenance services. In this way the finance function should be on the point in providing data and a platform to analyze all potential alternatives.
- *Recognizing volume versus quality of revenue.* The pressure to make sales and increase revenue may force the small and emerging business owner into short-term decisions that may not be in the company's best interest. Chief among these dilemmas is the question of quality versus quantity of revenue. Does producing and selling a lot of products with a lower selling price (and inferior margin) make more sense than selling less of a higher-priced

(higher-margin) product? Although a sale is a sale, what will pursuing one type mean compared to pursuing the other? Business owners often get sucked into alluring revenue patterns that hurt the organization in the long run. The organization should be looking hard at the impact of high-volume, low-quality sales versus lower-volume, high-quality sales. The finance function must be positioned to support decision making in this regard. A well-informed policy will not only enhance the prospects for profitability over time but build a more stable, reliable base of customers.

■ *Negotiating the sale effectively.* The small and emerging business owner must be aware of variables in pricing schemes and know how a negotiation will impact the resulting revenue. High-end (priced) products or services typically demand a face-to-face negotiation with customers. The salesperson must be educated on the impact of trade-offs on the deal before going into negotiation. Will it be necessary to cut product/service prices to generate sales? Should add-ons, freebies, or give-aways be used to induce sales? Should the company demand cash for sales or give generous terms? The intent of the sales experience is to create satisfied customers. Contrary to conventional thought, the customer is *not* always right. The finance function must play a significant role in developing sales contracts and sell sheets to prevent salespeople from turning a good sale into a long-term burden for the company. Similarly, it should yield information on all aspects of product and service pricing that should be a part of training programs for salespeople.

■ *Interpreting analysis and results.* The finance function must lie at the center of evaluation and measurement of products and people. Policies that are used to motivate sales organizations or determine the viability of the product/service mix should rely on input from the finance function. Challenges in comparing sales activity across geographical areas for the purpose of bonus structures and incentive plans should also be controlled by the finance function. Does generating $1 million in sales in Racine, Wisconsin, require the same amount of effort as generating the same in New York City? To what degree do demographic and economic factors alter this comparison? The same goes for evaluating the pricing of products and services. Policies impacting these areas must be developed based on accurate and timely information.

Costs/Expenses

Preservation of capital is imperative at the early stage of the business. Therefore, it is important to be aware of expenditures and their purpose. What is the nature of expenditures? Are they capital expenditures, for furniture and computer equipment? Or periodic expenditures, for payroll and utilities? Unlike revenue, expense considerations and strategies often trail expense events. Sound policies related to expenditures will address many cash flow and working capital considerations as well as earnings goals and expectations.

Approaching expense policies is similar to establishing revenue policies, in that a complete understanding of the business is necessary. The need to establish presentation-oriented policies is key if the company is publicly traded; however, the organization has a greater need to analyze (and alter) expense patterns and/or manage the circumstances that give rise to expenses. The development of expense-oriented policies will fall more into the operational/analysis realm than the financial reporting area for the company to receive true success in this area of strategizing. The next topics provide guidance for the small and emerging business owner to start the development of expense policies:

- *Striving for meaningful analysis.* How good is the organization at interpreting costs and expenses? Are tools in place that can interpret expense activity over time? How will the organization be able to interpret cash outflows that are detrimental to it? The finance function will have to be equipped to classify expenditures properly and to develop meaningful analysis tools. Developing analysis tools that track run rates (the results of specific expenses over an extended period of time) or provide comparisons between current- and prior-year activity (bilevel variance analysis) or current, prior-year, and budget analysis (trilevel variance analysis) will go a long way toward managing events that give rise to expenditures. Having the capacity to segregate expenses and compare them to different parts of the P&L is also important. Examples include capping operating expenses at 20% of revenue or pegging Research and Development (R&D) expenses at 15% of revenue. Expense goals like these are powerful measures that are easy to communicate to the organization and easily understood. Such policies are heavily dependent on the finance function for development and maintenance.
- *Managing the timetable for paying vendors.* The organization as a whole must make a commitment toward treating vendors in a consistent manner. Doing this includes managing payment terms. The challenge for most businesses when paying bills is deciding whether to pay early and enjoy discounts or to exercise terms and preserve cash. The business must balance its vendor relationships with its own cash flow needs. For the business to develop policies in this area, the finance function must provide information on its cash needs. Holding back on cash outlays as much as possible may seem like a sure solution, but the organization must know whether vendors are charging it higher prices based on that payment history.
- *Distinguishing between one-time and recurring costs/expenses.* When evaluating and analyzing expenditures, it is important to make a distinction between one-time expenditures of cash versus periodic expenses. Considering one-time or nonrecurring expenditures for things like capital improvements or real estate is different from evaluating and analyzing periodic expenses for payroll and utilities. Periodic expenses are easier to analyze; run rates or percentage analysis can be employed to determine operational trends or

anomalies. One-time expenditures, however, are more difficult to put into an analytical context. Contributing to the difficulties of analyzing one-time expenditures is that often these cash outlays do not make it to the P&L but rather get capitalized on the balance sheet and amortized over time. The small and emerging business must understand the difference between these two types of cash outlays and have the capacity to analyze them.

- *Classifying operating expenses and cost of sales properly.* Analysis in this area will rely on discipline in the finance area. Are expenses being classified properly? For example, classifying an expenditure as cost of sales versus operating expenses may have a huge impact on decision making. How important is managing margins (revenue versus cost of sales)? Do external shareholders have an expectation for the company's margins? Is certain expense activity related to general business activity (operating expense) or the production of a specific product or service (margin)? Understanding how expenditures will impact the business is the key to decision making. The finance function must be able to interpret data properly and provide input to management to facilitate this kind of decision making.

- *Understanding nonoperating expenses.* Non-op expenses are those that do not result from day-to-day or recurring business decisions. These are typically items that result from events in the business environment or nonrecurring business decisions. Examples include interest expense or foreign exchange gain/loss from currency fluctuations. The key to managing nonop expenses is knowing the events that give rise to them. Taking on debt, for instance, will require the company to endure the interest expense impact on its financial statements for the life of the loan. This may not be a problem if the company is privately held, but for those that have external reporting requirements it may be an issue. What is the per-share impact of interest expense? How will interest expense impact the statement of cash flows? Regarding foreign currency translation gain/loss, the company must understand that economic events in foreign countries can have a major impact on its financial presentation. Allowing receivables, payables, or debt to remain denominated in foreign currencies may expose the company to potentially radical fluctuations in currencies that are beyond its control. Relying on the finance function to provide input on this matter gives management the ability to fairly evaluate the merits of expanding into overseas markets.

FINAL THOUGHTS

Although no scheme for strategizing the finance function is foolproof, the multitier approach will provide some context for considering the relevant issues of business growth. Every business is unique. The accelerated pace of today's business environment makes strategizing at any level a challenge. The multitier schematic will lend order and structure to strategizing efforts. The overall objective is to build an agile decision-making infrastructure that can anticipate and effect change where and when necessary. The fundamental formula for success is rooted in understanding the business and the industry in which it exists. Enlisting input from experts in finance and accounting is recommended when ascending the pyramid in Exhibit 4.1. Mastering this ordered approach to strategizing will spawn a culture of strategic mindedness in the organization.

5

ANALYZING DATA CUSTOMERS

KEY TAKEAWAYS

- Understanding the need to be customer-centric when developing finance strategies.
- Understanding the drawbacks/pitfalls of not being customer-centric.
- Knowing how to classify data customers as external/internal and sophisticated/unsophisticated.
- Knowing which data customers will be encountered and when.
- Understanding how to anticipate data customers needs.
- Understanding how to link Tier 2 considerations to all other tiers of the multilevel approach.

WHY ANALYZE DATA CUSTOMERS?

Understanding Tier 2 of the Multilevel Approach

The need for financial data will become more prominent as the business grows, resulting in a heightened focus on providing financial data to those inside and outside the company. Success in serving data customers will hinge on the finance organization's ability to give data customers *what* they want, *when* they want it. The challenge is to understand the nature of data customers—specifically, what they want and how they will use it. Additionally, the finance strategist must anticipate when these audiences will be encountered and have the proper infrastructure in place to serve their informational needs. Translating this analysis to the multitier model, understanding how Tier 2 considerations relate to the business life cycle (Tier 1), infrastructure (Tier 3), and upper-tier considerations will be critical as the finance strategy is conceptualized, implemented, and maintained.

Data customers may be internal or external to the organization and at varying levels of sophistication. This chapter provides background on understanding the nature of various data customers and how to fulfill their informational needs. This discussion stresses, among other things, anticipating certain data customer types at various stages of company growth.

Being Customer-centric

The small and emerging business owner must position the finance function to be *customer-centric*. Focusing on finance as an entity and function in and of itself may not serve this purpose. The myriad of complex issues involved in strategizing can breed a shortsighted approach toward finance and its relationship with the rest of the business. Will finance dictate the capacity of the business to move forward or vice versa? The finance strategist may find it easy to shift from one extreme of this continuum to the other; however, the ideal position is somewhere in between. The business must dictate the development of the finance function, and the finance function must enable the business to move forward. One will be ahead of the other at any given time, but over time they must be in sync.

What determines or drives the development of the finance strategy? The answer to this question lies in the same criteria that measure its success—customer satisfaction. Finance strategy development must focus on meeting the data needs of customers. Moving a finance strategy forward without considering customer data needs is akin to building a business without a marketing plan. Without understanding and incorporating into the finance strategy who the data customers are, what they need, and when they need it, the strategy will be incomplete and/or ineffectual.

The most effective way to articulate the benefits of developing finance to suit data customers is to understand what *not* being customer-centric means. A weak finance function will create havoc in the short term and the long term. A finance function that does not accommodate data customers will yield:

- *Redundant databases and processes.* Data customers will not wait to be served by a finance function that is either lacking or nonexistent. This is certainly the case when it comes to internal data customers who must make daily operational decisions. Although they may be patient and supportive of the central efforts of a unified finance strategy, these data customers will have no choice but to develop their own methodologies when faced with untimely or irrelevant strategy initiatives (to the extent they are enacted) for generating finance data. The result could be a cache of data separate and apart from the rest of the organization that bears no relation to the company's actual results. The same goes for processes, as redundancies put a strain on company-wide resources. The goal of the finance function is to create a central database that is maintained with minimal effort and on which all aspects of the organization rely.
- *Development of inappropriate infrastructure.* Not clearly understanding the needs of data customers will hinder the development of relevant components of the finance function. How robust must systems and processes be to be con-

sidered effective? What is the risk of overbuying systems? Forsaking the needs of data customers by assuming that the finance function will suit all of their needs may prove costly in more ways than one. Developing a palette of technology that is too complex and overdone will burden the small and emerging business financially and result in underutilized technology. If systems are not strong enough to handle the needs of data customers, the strategizing effort will be useless and require another round of investment and development to bring it to a level acceptable to the organization. This will result in unnecessary financial costs and lost credibility of the finance function.

- *Lost credibility.* Creating systems and processes for data customers but shutting them out of the development process will leave them feeling disenfranchised and frustrated. Evolving the finance function will be a constant initiative. The continual ebb and flow of needs and the capacity to serve them will require a spirit of patience and cooperation between the strategists and data customers. Excluding data customers from the development and implementation of strategy will damage this relationship and hurt the long-term development of the finance ecosystem.

- *No stake from data users.* Similar to inadvertently or actively excluding data customers from strategy development is allowing them to remove themselves from the process altogether. Data customers who are given the impression that their input is not necessary or unimportant could degrade the entire strategizing effort. Soliciting input from data customers, incorporating the input, and holding them accountable for the result will optimize the strategizing effort. Ensuring that these users have a stake in a successful finance strategy will add to the effectiveness of the development of the finance function itself.

Putting Tier 2 into Practice

Most finance functions evolve naturally (in absence of a true strategy) in reaction to the needs of data customers. This effect represents a reactionary model that suits many businesses in the short term. The disadvantage to this evolutionary model is that it adheres to the squeaky-wheel axiom and accommodates data customers who make the most noise, rather than those who are most critical from a strategic standpoint. This may result in the development of a finance function that expends too many resources for certain data customers and not enough for others. Many times a company will get only one chance to achieve its objective with a data customer. Squandering that chance because the finance function was ill prepared to accommodate the customer's needs may mean the difference between prosperity and failure. Strategic mindedness regarding the finance function means understanding the nature of data customers and anticipating when their needs must be met. The following example illustrates a company encountering certain business life-cycle events that require an understanding of data customers and their needs:

> Chaban's Magic Carpets is an importer of fine Oriental rugs. The company's founder and principal owner, Amanda Chaban, imported rugs for a small select group of upscale customers for 10 years before she decided to expand her customer base to retail distributors and design firms. Her semiannual visits to the bazaars and markets in the Middle and Far East have produced a reliable source of suppliers that give her access to the finest silk and antique rugs. The expansion entailed a $2 million bank loan that enabled her to establish regional sales offices throughout the United States and build a secure warehouse to store the valuable antique rugs she imports. She has four equity partners who matched the funding that the bank provided in addition to the bank loan she secured in the past year. Amanda enacted an incentive program for the sales regions, which has led to a steady increase in revenue and a heavier demand for rugs. Revenue for Chaban's Magic Carpets has doubled over the past year from $2.5 million to just over $5 million. The import process and unconventional business culture Amanda must endure to bring rugs into the United States makes frequent ordering difficult; hence she must carefully anticipate customer needs over a four- to six-month time period. Amanda has historically handled the ordering and stored inventory in her home; however, volume demands are dictating that she store inventory exclusively in the new facility. Amanda hired a full-time order person/inventory manager who has slowly taken on the growing finance responsibilities in the organization. Amanda has yet to focus on any kind of formal reporting mechanism for internal or external purposes. Internally, she is feeling pressure from her regional sales reps for a periodic report on their results. Additionally, the heightened demand for product is requiring that she focus more intently on budgeting, a process that is currently highly subjective and driven by her gut feel. Externally, the bank is requiring that quarterly financial statements be prepared and reviewed by a local CPA. Amanda's equity funding has come from a group of four business associates who have asked for annual financial statements to review her operations (and their investments). She realizes that she will have to put thought into some mechanism that will enable her to corral the data she needs to run the business; however, she is uncertain whether to start with something small to expand or jump right in with a powerful financial reporting tool.

Amanda Chaban, like many other small and emerging business owners, is standing at an important crossroad in expanding her company. Moving the company to the next level will entail harnessing financial data in the business environment and applying it to the company's decision making process. Although Amanda is in need of a comprehensive finance strategy before she invests in any type of infrastructure, she will be best served understanding the data needs that will drive decision making in the company. She must consider the following areas to grasp the data needs of the company:

- *Equity owners.* Although Amanda's equity partners are silent, they undoubtedly want to see the company succeed. Reporting the results of operations may not be an issue if the business is doing well and there is adequate liquidity for them to access. If the business begins to decline, however, equity partners will want to be reassured that the challenges are identified and addressed. Poor reporting in this case may undermine the confidence of these investors and become a distraction for Chaban's Magic Carpets. How prepared is the company to meet this group's needs? Amanda must establish a dialogue with these investors and understand their expectations for financial results and accompanying information as soon as possible.
- *Debt owners.* The bank will have their eye on the debt covenants that focus on liquidity of the enterprise. Chaban's Magic Carpets must be positioned to prepare accurate and timely financial statements each quarter. More important, Amanda must monitor her cash position on an ongoing basis and understand well in advance of the quarter how the organization will translate to financial statements, particularly the working capital accounts on the balance sheet. Has she fashioned a finance strategy that will address the needs of the bank?
- *Suppliers.* Amanda hired a professional to manage the supply chain and accounting function. Handling issues related to carrying slow-turning inventory and high storage costs will require accurate and timely data. This information along with sales forecasts should play a prominent role in ordering new product. Her new supply chain/accounting manager will undoubtedly be the most prominent internal data customer. Will having one person to manage this function be enough? At what point will Amanda need to expand her finance organization? Absent a finance strategy, the finance function at Chaban's Magic Carpets will be shaped by the needs of her sole accounting manager.
- *Area sales managers.* The incentive program established by Amanda has created a class of data consumers with a vested interest in the financial results of the company. These sales area managers will be compelled to create reasonable budgets and track results throughout the quarter as they measure themselves for performance bonuses. The challenge for Amanda will be to create a finance function that provides access to accurate sales data in a timely manner. Ignoring this need will result in the sales managers developing their own data repositories, which may or may not be accurate. Amanda must avoid relying on renegade data from these separate data repositories to pay out bonuses; however, in the absence of an alternative she may not have

a choice. Her finance strategy must be in tune with these data customers and the potential for abuse.

- *Tax authorities.* Reporting data for federal tax purposes is an annual exercise to which Amanda has become accustomed. Even though this reporting requirement is (for the most part) predictable, reporting to state and local tax authorities may not be so predictable. Chaban's Magic Carpets is particularly exposed to state and local reporting requirements as it expands its scope and sells in more states and municipalities. Is the organization suited to meet the needs of these data customers? Should Amanda wait for tax notices to come in from these tax authorities or preempt them and self-report? How detailed are these data customers when it comes to filing requirements? Amanda will have to understand this class of data customers, who may vary in sophistication and aggressiveness from state to state and municipality to municipality.

The small and emerging business owner will always be challenged with making the best of limited resources. This challenge translates into the need to prioritize initiatives and objectives in such a way that allows the business owner/manager to do the most with the least. Similarly, when strategizing the finance function, data customers must be prioritized in such a way that those who are the most critical to the company's well-being are accommodated first. Doing this means identifying these critical data customers and understanding their needs. Understanding the different types of data customers who could be encountered is the first step to exploring this area.

DEFINING DATA CUSTOMERS

Classifying Data Customers

The small and emerging business must deal with a myriad of data customers throughout its life cycle. Although every data customer is unique in its circumstances of encounter and resulting needs, certain general classifications are common. Translating Tier 2 considerations of the multilevel approach into actionable strategies requires identifying these common characteristics in hopes of classifying data customers appropriately.

While generalizations are dangerous, data customers usually are classified along two general axes. The first of these axes involves characterizing them as either internal or external. The second is focused on their level of sophistication. Depending on the reasons for encountering a particular data customer, the data sought will vary from general information at a high level of the organization to narrow, detailed information at lower echelons of the organization. The finance function must be prepared to deal with customers with advanced data needs and those with more basic, fundamental data needs. Additionally, the finance function must be able to handle data needs that are broad with little depth and those that are narrow with considerable depth. Regardless of customer needs, the strategist must be prepared to create and maintain a finance strategy that develops appropriate concrete and soft components of finance that suit all current and prospective data customers.

External versus Internal Customers

Classifying audiences as internal or external is fairly straightforward. Data customers within the organization are internal data customers. These include, for example, management, board members, and executives. Classifying shareholders as internal or external is less obvious. Closely held private companies have shareholders that often are part of the day-to-day management team. These shareholders are obviously internal. Publicly traded companies are, however, for the most part owned by absentee shareholders. Shareholders in some cases are employees, and close to operations. However, most are far removed from day-to-day operations. These nonmanagement shareholders are external data customers. Examples of other external data customers include financiers, governmental authorities, auditors, and attorneys.

Generally speaking, the data needs of internal customers will be more fluid than those of external data customers. Internal customers' data needs may be complex and detailed or simple and straightforward, depending on the stage of the business's life cycle. The role of internal data customers is to analyze company performance and make decisions. Because of their proactive role in the organization, their informational needs must be considered paramount to the organization. External audiences, however, are more concerned with general company performance. Reporting and informational needs may be prescribed or dictated by matters of law or contractual agreement. Examples of the former are needs of shareholders (in public companies), the Securities and Exchange Commission, and tax authorities. Data customers with informational needs dictated by contractual agreement include banks or other financial institutions as well as business partners that result from business combinations. Auditors and attorneys are also external data customers who may have data needs that come from either circumstance. Exhibit 5.1 provides a list of data customers and their designation as external or internal and sophisticated or unsophisticated.

Sophisticated versus Unsophisticated Customers

Understanding the sophistication level of data customers will play a crucial role in the dissemination of financial data. Sophisticated customers are well versed in either the mechanics of packaging financial information or interpreting it, or both. These audiences typically look at a range of financial data and view all financial information from the company in a holistic manner. The unsophisticated data customer is most likely interested in a limited amount of financial data or one narrow part of the company's total financial picture. Either group may have more or less

Exhibit 5.1 **Data Customers with Notations on Sophistication and Type**

Audience	Sophisticated/Unsophisticated	Internal/External
Auditors (public accounting)	Sophisticated	External
Attorney	Sophisticated/Unsophisticated	External
Banks/Financial Institutions	Sophisticated/Unsophisticated	External
Board Members	Sophisticated	Internal
Management	Sophisticated	Internal
Other Executives	Unsophisticated	Internal
Sell-side Analysts	Sophisticated	External
Buy-side Analysts	Sophisticated	External
Shareholders	Unsophisticated	External/Internal
Tax Authorities	Sophisticated/Unsophisticated	External

at stake in the data they are requesting; however, from a finance perspective, sophisticated data customers are generally more in tune with evaluating the integrity of data than unsophisticated ones.

Exhibit 5.1 provides a listing of customers along with a notation of their sophistication level. A look at two frequently encountered data customers illustrates the contrasting needs of sophisticated and unsophisticated data customers.

1. *Auditors/CPAs* (sophisticated data customers). The need for audited financial statements may be precipitated by a public offering of stock or a sophisticated financing arrangement. Auditors in the public accounting arena are governed by a well-defined code of conduct and must adhere to audit and review procedures dictated by the industry. Auditors typically are focused on formal financial statements and the detail that backs them up. They look at the statement of cash flows along with the balance sheet and P&L for overall congruence. Because their audit and review procedures are meant to evaluate financial statements for their overall conformity with GAAP, the finance function must provide accurate and timely information.

2. *Sales manager* (unsophisticated data customer). This data customer may be focused exclusively on financial data that feeds a particular metric or evaluation paradigm. The need in this case may be for revenue, margin, or operating expense data. This data may be required by region, area, or sales rep. Unlike auditors from public accounting, the sales manager may be less concerned with the mechanics of the data and its conformity with complex accounting rules and more focused on timely data for decision making. Their need may be for period-to-period comparison or actual-to-

budget comparison. The sophistication level of these data customers is moderate from a financial perspective as their needs are recurring, predictable, and relatively simple to address.

Most Frequently Encountered Data Customers

Generally, data customers become more sophisticated as a company matures. Life cycle events such as acquisitions and public offerings of stock lead to enhanced scrutiny of company results. Maturity also means the business will become more complex and require enhanced data for the decision support system. The following offers a more detailed discussion on frequently encountered data customers:

- *Auditors (public accounting).* These data customers are the most technically sophisticated and potentially invasive. The auditor community, from a financial reporting standpoint (as opposed to IRS auditors), is made up of Certified Public Accountants licensed by a particular state to perform attestation work. Attestation work involves performing specific procedures that gather evidence and documentation necessary for rendering an opinion regarding whether the financials are stated fairly in terms of GAAP. These professionals are educated and trained to understand GAAP itself and how it is applied in specific industries. Their capacity as auditors requires them to review transactions and bookings as well as the supporting documentation. Auditors also will review and document information systems and data flow processes. They have a stake in the integrity of management and the data generated by the finance function. These state-sanctioned auditors are a necessary data customer for any organization submitting financial statements for bank loans, private placements, or public offerings of stock.
- *Attorneys.* Lawyers are external data customers who play a role in due diligence initiatives. Because of their role in reviewing financial statements for acquisitions and public offerings, they are more sophisticated than most data customers. Their function is to review financial statement disclosures if a public offering is being sought or a business combination (acquisition or disposition) is pending. Unlike auditors, these customers are more focused on disclosures than on the integrity of numbers in financial statements. Disclosures related to future litigation, contracts, and future obligations may be required in various filings with the Securities and Exchange Commission (10K, 10Q, proxy, 8K) or in documents prepared during the due diligence surrounding a business combination. The areas attorneys focus on in this context often require significant judgment; thus professionals well versed in the areas of contracts and disclosures must review all such representations. Attorneys who review disclosures look at content as well as presentation.
- *Banks/financial institutions.* These external data customers are focused on compliance with debt and loan agreements. If debt financing is being

sought, a set of audited (or reviewed) financial statements will be submitted to a lending institution (bank or financial institution). Professionals there will require that a CPA perform some procedures on the financials—either limited review procedures or audit procedures. Once an opinion is rendered by auditors on the fairness with which the financials comply with GAAP, the assumption is that they fairly reflect the company's performance and current financial condition. In granting a loan, the institution will dictate that a series of rules be followed throughout the course of the loan period. These rules, known as covenants, will dictate that the company maintain liquidity ratios, cash balances, and revenue levels. These covenants also may forbid the company from entering into other loan or debt arrangements with other institutions. Not maintaining the prescribed levels of performance at any given time may violate the loan covenants, hence rendering the loan agreement null and void.

These customers may or may not be sophisticated. Their focus will be clearly set on the financial condition of the company as it relates to the resources that have been loaned. Specifically they have a need to understand the company's position and performance as it relates to the loan covenants set forth in the loan document. They will be focused exclusively on the ratios, balances, and conditions laid out in the list of covenants. The reality is that the bank does not want to call the loan any more than the business organization does. An important factor in dealing with these data customers is that policies and procedures are usually cut and dried in banks and other financial institutions. The challenge of the small and emerging business owner will be to provide thorough financial data as it relates to covenant compliance.

■ *Board members.* The company, as it matures, may seek the services of professional board members. Typically these are experienced executives active in the operations of other large and/or successful businesses. Independent board members lend a level of expertise as well as a third-party perspective helpful in providing strategic direction for the business. Their time-tested powers of discernment and decision-making capabilities make them a valuable asset and powerful resource for companies looking to position themselves for long-term success. These internal data customers typically are advanced in their knowledge of the dynamics of financial statement presentation and the interpretation of financial data. Board members are concerned with the big picture of company performance over the long term. They also are motivated to make decisions that contribute to the company's success as they are contracted directly by the shareholders to provide strategic expertise and guidance. These data customers focus on financial data that provides clues to future performance and the external business environment.

■ *Management.* Management's role as consumers of financial data is that of decision makers. This internal data customer is saddled with the responsibility of day-to-day operational decisions. Its informational needs may be recurring or extraordinary depending on the manager's position within the organization and where the company is in its life cycle. Data needs may be as generic as information disseminated to the public or customized to specific aspects of businesses operations. Individual components of management may be sophisticated or unsophisticated, depending on the individual in question and his or her role. Generally, the higher the manager's level, the more sophisticated the audience. Unlike other data customers, management may demand data and analysis on numbers beyond the scope of the financial statements prepared for external purposes. This need for spontaneous reporting makes providing information to management an ongoing challenge for the finance function.

■ *Other executives.* The executive management level of the organization, as opposed to the day-to-day level, is charged with the strategic direction of the company. These include the CEO, Chief Financial Officer (CFO), vice presidents, and directors. Executive data customers will be particular to midsize to larger companies, as opposed to small and emerging companies (where the management team is charged with all aspects of company management). Unlike independent board members, executives are mainstream employees. Their information needs can concern the top level of the organization or focus on narrow areas of operations. Regardless, they are typically the conduit of information to the external business community. These internal data customers are often the most sophisticated of all financial data customers. Their need to make strategic decisions and communicate results to board members and shareholders requires accurate and timely information.

■ *Sell-side analysts.* This external data customer is composed of stock market analysts who work for investment houses on Wall Street and abroad. Small and emerging businesses do not encounter these data customers unless they are publicly traded. These analysts are relatively sophisticated consumers of financial statement data. Being external third parties, they rely on statutory filings and public disclosures made by public companies. Sell-siders work for retail investment houses that dispense strategies to others in the investment industry. They use their research to create these strategies, which advocate certain industries, sectors, or companies. Their sophistication is limited to the dynamics of the marketplace, particularly how the Street will react to data that relates to a target company. Although many are CPAs, the breadth and depth of their knowledge on GAAP is fairly limited. Sell-siders flourish by feeding public information and historic data into internally generated models and making judgments on the market performance of certain stocks—judgments that are published to the general public. While their knowledge of a particular company's financial statements and operations may be limited, their ability to move markets is potentially limitless. Successful public companies navigate the sell-sider community with precision. Company executives make liaising with the sell-side community a high priority. Whether a company has full-time resources dedicated to sell-siders or not, it is beneficial to understand and appreciate their perspectives. The finance strategist must build into the finance function the capacity to establish earnings expectations and performance achievements that satisfy certain players in the sell-side community. Having a reputable advocate in the sell-side community can be a priceless asset to a company as it pushes to develop market capitalization. If a company is public or planning on going public, incorporating the needs of the sell-side community into financial strategies is essential.

■ *Buy-side analysts.* This external data customer is similar in some ways to the sell-side community. Buy-siders are professionals who work for investment houses. They are external third parties who graze from the caches of public information to derive strategies to apply to investment initiatives. The buy-side community keeps its strategies (i.e., recommendations) close to the vest as opposed to sell-siders. Buy-siders manage money and portfolios contractually for customers. Pension fund managers and mutual fund managers are examples of buy-siders. They are more adroit in matters of market dynamics and how a particular company may play a role in them. They are fairly sophisticated interpreters of financial data; however, they are generally not well versed in the finer points of GAAP and how it is applied in producing financial statements. They rely on review mechanisms (i.e., auditors, reviewers) put in place to ensure financials are accurate and complete (i.e., auditors).

■ *Shareholders.* These data customers may be external or internal. Although shareholders who are internal data customers are typically management, external ones may be sophisticated or unsophisticated. Some of these data customers may be large institutional investors. While this group may not be versed in the mechanics of GAAP or the dynamics of the finance function, as market makers and portfolio managers, they have vested interests not only in the results of operations as communicated by financial data but in the quality and integrity of management that produces this data. The burden is on the finance function to generate accurate and timely data for shareholders' reporting needs. The other group of shareholders is made up of at-home investors who do not make their living by navigating the market. These are usually individuals purchasing stock for their individual 401k plans, IRAs, or stand-alone portfolios. These shareholders are not market makers and rarely demand a direct dialog with management. This audience consumes the statutory reporting requirements that companies dispense. Quarterly and annual earnings statements as well as periodic information disclosures (Form 8K) are the diet of financials and disclosures on which this data customer thrives. These data customers also focus on information disseminated by sell-side analysts and market pundits.

■ *Tax authorities.* This external data customer is made up of two major types: federal and state. Federal tax authorities are focused on levying and collecting taxes based on income. Comparing foreign tax authorities and U.S. tax authorities is beyond the scope of this text; in the following discussion, *federal tax* refers to U.S. tax. Reporting to the federal tax authorities comes in the form of filling out the various tax forms that apply to the company's business form—1120, 1120S, 1065, 1040 Schedule C, and so on. Because this tax system is income based, this audience is focused on reporting revenue and expenses as defined by federal tax laws. Month-to-month financial reporting is based on GAAP; however, income tax reporting may be markedly different and happen only once a year. State tax authorities levy and collect taxes based on two platforms: (1) income and (2) sales and use. Each state defines income in its own terms and puts the burden on the business to report income properly.

The rules for reporting vary from state to state, each with its own basis and rates of tax due. Tax authorities on the state and federal level may be either sophisticated or unsophisticated. Depending on the form of the company and the complexion of its business, filings may be simple or highly complex. The finance function, in either case, must be prepared to provide the information necessary to all taxing authorities to avoid business interruption.

EVALUATING DATA CUSTOMERS

Set the Stage for Evaluation

Understanding the types of data customers that may be encountered and understanding how equipped the organization is to accommodate their needs is the first step in excelling at the Tier 2 level of strategizing. Although anticipating data customers and their needs is critical, understanding how to evaluate data customers will enable the strategist to better suit the finance function to serve them when they are encountered. The company must be able to identify the different types of data customers and understand what aspects of the finance function will impact the company's capability to deal with them. What data customer is the company most likely to encounter? Is the finance function suited to handle that customer? If not, what needs to be done to prepare the organization for encountering that customer?

Identify the Growth Stage of the Company

Businesses must maintain their focus at all times. Ideally, small business owners/ managers will be focusing on generating new customers and accommodating old ones. Administrative matters such as finance must be prioritized behind urgent matters of operations in the early stages of business development. Sooner or later, however, certain finance issues will be of major importance to the organization, and data customers will become as important if not more so than standard business customers. The need for financing will force the company to translate itself to financial statements accurately and timely, while the need to reorganize or redirect its sales or product focus will depend on sound, accessible data. The company's growth stage will determine the prominence of finance issues in the business strategy, which in turn will drive the level of focus for the small and emerging business owner on relevant data customers. The following levels of development will demand different levels of focus to meet data needs:

- *Cultivating growth/expansion.* This stage of the business life-cycle demands that the small and emerging business owner focus on growing the customer base and cultivating new ones. It also means increasing capacity to offer more and better products/services. Examining the data customers involved in these two initiatives will reveal internal data customers who demand relevant and accurate data to analyze. Corraling these internal data customers and understanding their needs may be easier for the small and emerging business owner than surveying the landscape of external customers.

- *Seeking financing.* Data customers in this stage may overlap with those in the growth/expansion stage. Particular to this life-cycle event is the need to interface with external data customers. The finance strategist must be prepared to move past the familiarity with internal customers and deal with more sophisticated, savvy data customers with needs that have quality and timing components. The first trip to the bank for financing is often a wake-up call for the small business owner regarding the company's capacity to generate reliable financial information. Unfortunately, many small businesses squander encounters with potential financiers because they have not adequately anticipated their need for data—whether in regard to quality or to timing. Understanding what is involved before the need for financing will enable the finance strategist to prepare the organization's finance function for such an encounter.

- *Holding the line.* The business may find itself in a state of suspension, that is, it is neither growing nor declining. This may be brought on by economic conditions or nonbusiness circumstances of owners. While it is hoped that the circumstances that bring on such a stagnant state are temporary, the finance organization must be prepared to move in and out of these unexpected phases smoothly. Are there data customers specific to this phase of the organization's life cycle? More than likely there are not; however, this is a time where current data customers, particularly internal data customers, can be reassessed and their needs reviewed. The finance strategist can now focus on needs once deemed a lesser priority and address them adequately.

Know the Level of Sophistication in the Organization

Not only do small and emerging business owners have to focus on matters of finance; they must have the capacity to address the demands of maintaining a suitable level of competence in the finance organization. The ability to anticipate data customers is useless if the organization is not suited to address their needs. Even though the components of the finance organization were discussed in greater detail in Chapter 2, "Finance Function Defined," it is worth noting that success at Tier 2 of the multilevel approach to finance strategy development depends on understanding the finance organization's attributes *and* how it will accommodate current and prospective data customers. Taking a quick inventory of the finance organization at any given time will indicate the company's ability to excel at a particular juncture in its life cycle. These areas of attention should be prominent:

- *Dedicated staff.* Is the finance function stocked with specialized employees suited for addressing finance needs, or is it a shared function where anyone and everyone does what they can to muddle through? Having a shared function may be the only solution for the small and emerging business owner in the present; however, the organization must be prepared to take on dedicated, specialized staff when appropriate. It is too late to find out that the finance function is undermanned when a crush of data needs must be met.
- *Owners and finance tasks.* In the early stages of the business, the owner may take on administrative tasks, particularly finance tasks. This may be appropriate as the owner often has the best strategic view of the organization. Sooner or later, though, the jack-of-all-trades mentality will fall short of meeting the specialized needs of data customers. Small and emerging business owners must understand their own limitations and arrange for qualified full-time personnel to take on the finance role or at least rely on consultants and specialized part-time staff.
- *Consultants versus full-time finance employees.* When it comes to transforming the finance function from a shared responsibility environment to that of a dedicated organization, the appropriate middle ground may be the use of consultants. Using consultants to do the heavy lifting when it comes to meeting a reporting deadline or developing an advanced finance model may be the answer if the organization cannot afford to hire full-time qualified finance staff. This works when acute data customer needs are few and far between; however, it should be considered a temporary solution as the company grows and data needs become acute and persistent within and outside the company.

Know What Kinds of Data Are Available or Accessible

Accommodating the disparate needs of data customers may be akin to navigating a minefield of varying perspectives and expectations. The small and emerging business owner/finance strategist will not always have the depth of understanding of each and every data customer and their needs; however, having a clear picture of the *capacity* to serve data customers will make traversing Tier 2 considerations of finance strategy development more predictable. This means having a firm grasp of the finance function's capacity to generate knowledge. Regardless of how sophisticated or suited the finance function is, the small and emerging business owner must be prepared to set realistic expectations with those demanding financial data from the organization. What type of data can the organization generate? How quickly can it deliver results?

The finance function's capacity to generate financial data may depend on the complexity and nature of the business model as much as it depends on the health of the finance function itself. Having multiple sources of revenue may seem like a good business model, but from an analysis standpoint, this data may not be gathered and classified properly. Simple business models often generate clear, intuitive data that is easily accessible and accurate. Can the finance function generate detailed data? If so, how much effort does it take? Is the finance function limited to producing high-level data only? This may not necessarily be a weakness as high-level analysis may be all that is needed for the organization to move forward. How about reporting? Does the organization produce structured financial statements regularly? Is there flexibility in the processes and systems that generate them? Do internal data customers have access to the data that feeds financials to allow for dynamic, ad hoc reporting? Investigating these areas of data dissemination will give the strategist an idea of how much fine-tuning will be necessary for the finance function to serve data customers adequately. Exhibit 5.2 outlines specific types of financial information that the organization may generate and the most likely data customers that may consume it.

Recognize the Need for Good Communication

Key to evaluating and dealing with data customers is the ability to communicate with them. Data customers will reside internally and externally; therefore, the organization must be prepared to understand the customer type and the nature and timing of their needs, and set expectations as quickly as possible. Can the finance strategist quickly gain an understanding of current and changing needs for analysis (internal data customers)? Does the finance function have the capacity to communicate with external customers in an adequate and timely way as it relates to financial results? *Communication* in this context goes beyond determining whom to dialog with and begs the need to speak the language of data customers as they are encountered.

Exhibit 5.2 **Internal and External Data Customer Needs**

Data	Internal Data Customer Needs	External Data Customer Needs
Margins by business unit	Yes	Yes/No
Margins by product	Yes	Yes/No
Expenditures by department	Yes	No
Subsidiary inventory balances	Yes	No
Accounts receivable aging by business unit	Yes	No
Total company days sales outstanding (DSO)	Yes	Yes
Total company margin performance	Yes	Yes
Total company expenditures by type	Yes	Yes
Total company inventory turns	Yes	Yes
Total company cash flow	Yes	Yes
Total effect of currency fluctuation	Yes	Yes
Constant currency performance by subsidiary country	Yes	No
Cash flow by subsidiary	Yes	No
Order backlog	Yes	No
Projected bookings	Yes	No

What mechanisms are in place to handle this crucial communications task? If the finance function's obligations have been historically suited for internal data customers, how will it adjust to the more formal and sophisticated needs of external data customers? Is one person in the organization deemed the owner of the finance data? The small and emerging business owner may be the only individual that has access to financial data on a corporate-wide basis. Is that person sophisticated enough (from a finance perspective) to communicate this data to erudite underwriters or financiers?

The small and emerging business owner may not have the luxury of a dedicated group of financial professionals that keep track of and interpret financial data. Such a group will be a necessity at some time during the company's life cycle. Until that time comes, the organization still may avail itself of professionals who interface with sophisticated data customers, such as governmental authorities or institutional investors. What mechanism is in place for disseminating accurate information to data customers? Companies with no public reporting or disclosure requirements may not need a formal mechanism to release financial data; however, publicly traded companies must be careful that only officially reported and audited data gets released to the public. Laws that govern the release of financial data demand a controlled, uniform distribution of data. These laws, along with the need to communicate with sophisticated data customers, may demand that an investor relations group be established to handle all communications with the public. Having specialized professionals dispense data to the public will keep the organization in conformity with fair disclosure laws and ensure that external data customers' needs are being served.

ANTICIPATING DATA CUSTOMER NEEDS

Need to Anticipate Customer Requirements

The finance strategist must go beyond identifying data customers to understanding their needs well enough to anticipate them before they are critical. Doing so is crucial when it comes to conceptualizing infrastructure and long-range analysis paradigms. The ability to build into the finance strategy scalable infrastructure and relevant soft components depends on knowing what is needed and when. Anticipating data needs may not be difficult when it comes to internal data customers; however, doing so for external data customers may be a challenge. The finance strategist must investigate and understand the strategies of external and internal data customers and must be clear on the current and prospective capability of the finance function to accommodate various needs in various circumstances.

Know the Strategies of Data Customers

Most data customers, like the business itself, are operating in a dynamic environment. Internal data customers are a prime example, as their growth and data needs embody the evolution of the business organization itself. Physical proximity and unity of purpose make keeping in step with growth strategies less taxing for the finance strategist. How about the strategies of external data customers? Companies with external reporting requirements to the Securities and Exchange Commission, for instance, should be in tune with future reporting requirements. Are there particular reporting initiatives on the horizon? How about the Financial Accounting Standards Board (FASB) when it comes to GAAP reporting and disclosure or the federal government when it comes to tax law? Although it may seem difficult to comply with current laws, future rules may represent a greater burden. Understanding these law or rule changes and how they impact the organization in advance will allow for the capability to develop infrastructure, particularly systems and processes that will minimize the impact of change on the organization.

How will the strategist be clear on data customers' future strategies? Simple research may suffice when it comes to external data customers like the FASB, SEC, or federal government. Solid lines of communication, however, must be in place with internal data customers. Teams or task forces that meet periodically to discuss future strategies are great ways to understand the needs and strategies of internal data customers. This avenue allows for the finance strategist to communicate expectations and plans for development while enabling data customers to do the same. Communicating strategies and growth plans will be effective in creating platforms to handle current needs and expand to manage future ones.

What types of data will be demanded of the organization? Reporting financial data will take many forms; however, all reporting, whether it is for internal or external purposes, will focus on a standard slate of financial statements. Generally, the term "financial statements" refers to the balance sheet (a snapshot of the company at a point in time) and the profit and loss statement. The goal of generating financial statements and reporting financial data is twofold: (1) creating an accurate representation of the company at a specific point in time and (2) summarizing the company's performance over a period of time. Achieving these two objectives means financial statements that provide internal customers of financial data with information on the company's ability to pay bills and meet obligations (liquidity) and generate additional equity (net income) for owners. Likewise, financial statements can provide information to certain external customers of data whether they are banks, equity partners, or governmental authorities.

Need for Statistical Data

Not all data needs are financial. Data customers may demand data that is not generated by a general ledger. Information like headcount, accounts receivable aging, bookings, and backlog are examples of vital information that the finance function produces. This data is typically referred to as *statistical* data. Some nonfinancial data may fall into this definition; however, most of this information is based on, or a derivation from, financial data. Components of fixed asset or reserve rollforwards are prime examples. The beginning and ending balances themselves are standard balance sheet items; components such as disposals, additions, translation adjustment, and the like may not be. How is this data gathered, stored, and interpreted? Statistical data must be considered part of the finance strategy just like other standard general ledger (P&L and balance sheet) data. Internal data customers may be the greatest consumers of statistical information, although certain external filings may demand statistical information as well.

Recognize the Mode of Data Delivery

Part of anticipating data customer needs involves understanding the mode of data delivery most likely to be demanded. The company will have, at some time or another, rigid, well-defined external reporting requirements as well as open-ended, less-defined internal reporting needs. Finance infrastructure addresses these varying needs in different ways. Handling predictable, recurring external reporting requirements may require a reliable consolidation and reporting tool that can generate predesigned P&L and balance sheet reports quickly and easily. The emphasis may be on speed in these circumstances. The demands of the finance organization may be to review results for outliers and articulate variances. If the organization is growing quickly, there may be an ongoing need for standard and nonstandard data analysis. Companies that employ economic value-added (EVA) models or dynamic valuations of the business may seek data to manipulate and fashion into nonstandard forms. Data requirements for these models epitomize the need for *data availability* as opposed to financial reporting. More complex infrastructure may be required to serve this purpose. Data warehouse and online analytical processing (OLAP) technology are examples of advanced tools that can meet more advanced, open-ended data needs. Because resource requirements will be so disparate between the need for rigid reporting requirements and open-ended data availability, the finance strategist must fully understand and anticipate these different data needs and incorporate the appropriate actions into the finance strategy.

LINKING DATA CUSTOMER NEEDS TO FINANCE STRATEGY

Recognizing the Impact of Tier 2

Knowing *who* needs *what* and *when* coupled with understanding the organization's ability to address these needs will enable the strategist to integrate data customer needs into the finance strategy. Although developing the finance function with customer needs in mind may seem a natural progression for many organizations, incorporating these needs into the core of the strategy will require constant focus and flexibility. Businesses evolve, as well as data customers and their needs. Every business is different, but the necessity of maintaining focus on core, static needs while sustaining a posture of flexibility for shifting or additional needs is somewhat universal. To this end, many key areas of integration must be addressed. Achieving success will mean focusing on the considerations in each of the tiers of the multilevel approach and incorporating Tier 2 into them.

Linking Milestones (Tier 1) to Data Customers

Businesses will encounter certain watershed events in their life cycles as they grow. Examples of these may be a target acquisition, multinational expansion, or a public offering of stock. Some milestones may be anticipated while others may not be. It is the challenge of the finance strategist to put the company in the best position to navigate successfully through these milestone events. These milestones may involve providing financial statements for a due diligence exercise or providing an enhanced look at company performance to management and key executives. In either case the onus is on the finance function to produce financial reports and perform analyses that serve the appropriate data customer.

The needs of certain data customers have been discussed already in detail. It is important to note that part of approaching these needs strategically is anticipat-

Exhibit 5.3 **Company Life-cycle Milestones and Anticipated Data Customers**

Event	Financial Statements Needed	Data Customer
Bank loan	Balance Sheet, P&L	Bankers, auditors
Business combination	Balance Sheet, P&L, Cash Flow Statement	Auditors, attorneys, acquiring business owners
Multinational expansion	Varying P&L and Balance Sheet data requests	Foreign tax/government authorities
Public offering of stock	Balance Sheet, P&L, Cash Flow Statement, Ancillary filings	Auditors, attorneys, Securities and Exchange Commission, underwriters
Private placement	Balance Sheet, P&L	Auditors, attorneys, underwriters

ing when they will be encountered during a company's life cycle. Some data customers will be encountered repeatedly in different milestone events while others will be encountered in particular circumstances only. Exhibit 5.3 depicts potential milestones and accompanying data customers.

The level of sophistication and detail required in generating financial information will be dependent on the company's life cycle events. The challenge of the finance strategist is to assess the current state of the finance function, particularly as it relates to accommodating these events and the data customers encountered. Are systems, processes, soft components, and the finance organization appropriate for the current stage of the business life cycle? Are future stages anticipated? Committing the organization to future life-cycle events may be ill advised if the finance function is not prepared to take on the data customers that will be encountered.

Company-wide strategies ultimately dictate which data customers are encountered and when. Not being prepared to meet the needs of data customers could prove costly, whether the organization is a closely held private company or a large public company. Lacking synchronization with expectations in this regard may mean:

- Missing earnings release dates
- Not making earnings estimates
- Not achieving critical liquidity or equity ratios
- Misrepresenting the company on paper in an acquisition
- Misinterpreting results and making faulty decisions

Any of the above circumstances may hurt the company at the negotiating table or in the court of public opinion. The only sure way to avoid circumstances like these is to anticipate life-cycle milestones where possible and devote careful attention to the data customers to be encountered and their informational needs. This evaluation will be particularly fruitful as it relates to strategizing infrastructure development.

Linking Infrastructure (Tier 3) to Data Customers

The development of relevant infrastructure at the Tier 3 level of the multilevel approach must be shaped by data customer needs. The three major aspects of infrastructure—finance organization, information systems, and data flow processes—must be customer-centric if the finance function is to be truly effective. Because information systems and processes are the foundation of finance infrastructure, the finance strategist must take pains to ensure that they are truly customer-centric. The following points are worth noting:

- *Finance organization.* Finance employees should be suited for the analysis, interpretation, and communication of finance information to internal and external data customers. Day-to-day operations may rely on perfunctory reporting schemes. Typically, the role of the finance organization is to address outliers or exceptions in company performance revealed by the data. The business organization may, however, be moving through a challenging time in its business life cycle. Hard economic times, a shifting market focus, the need for financing, and business combinations will demand extraordinary analysis and input from the finance organization. Sophisticated data customers in these cases may demand input on and explanation of the company's financial data. Because the packaging of financial information will be just as important as content, recognizing these circumstances and resulting needs enables the finance strategist to plan the finance organization appropriately.

- *Systems.* Information systems must suit the organization's ability to manage data. Information systems must be sophisticated enough to manage data in a manner that will serve external data customers. Having the ability to quickly and accurately produce data for auditors, bankers, or external authorities is imperative if the company is to navigate challenging life-cycle milestones. More important, however, is the development of systems to suit internal data customers. Complex systems with powerful functionality will be of little or no value if users cannot access data. The key is matching the skill set of internal users (data customers) with the system. Overly complex systems probably will not be used properly; in all likelihood their potential will never be realized, resulting in wasted dollars. The finance strategist and business owner must refrain from overbuying systems.

- *Processes.* Aligning the data flow process with the needs of internal and external data customers will be worth the effort as the business organization evolves. If the business has formal reporting requirements with the SEC or other regulatory authorities, timing and accuracy of the data will be crucial. Issues such as *time to close* will be a priority if these data customers are to be addressed properly. Absent these types of reporting requirements, the finance function will handle internal analysis needs. The company may opt for a less complex process with little detail or a detailed process that garners a wealth of data. Internal data customers may be more flexible on these matters than external data customers. The impact of process changes or upgrades on data customers is important to recognize. Will the overhaul of processes create downtime or degradation of the current process? The cost of such a *blackout* period may exceed the benefits of the overhaul that created it. Understanding customer needs must play a role in this component of the finance strategy.

Linking Soft Components (Upper-Tier Considerations) to Data Customers

Upper-tier considerations in the multilevel approach will yield certain unique data customers. Tier 4 and Tier 5 prompt the strategist to develop P&L and balance sheet–oriented models and policies. Although many of the same internal and external data customers may be encountered, their needs will vary based on the policies or data models the finance strategy seeks to develop. If management dictates a complex cash flow model, what will data customers expect in the way of data? Will the finance function be able to deliver the appropriate data in a timely manner? Will certain metrics set forth by the organization be reasonably addressed? Upper-tier policies and models must be easily understood by and accessible to data customers if they are to be worthwhile. If the internal data customers are less sophisticated, perhaps simpler versions of the models and policies should be strategized. For example, a complex Financial Accounting Standard (FAS) 95 cash flow model may be replaced by a simpler working-capital fluctuation model, which provides the same general cash flow results without requiring sophisticated analysis. Regarding accessibility, defining metrics but denying data customers access to the data that feeds them will not only result in frustration but also degrade the credibility of the metrics and the management issuing them. The finance function that understands data customers will make finance strategies more effective at inception and as they evolve with the company.

FINAL THOUGHTS

Strategizing the finance function is more than employing best practices and technology. It focuses on putting a structure in place that gives data customers what they want, when they want it. Constructing a finance function that does not serve users of the data wastes time and money. Staying in touch with current and prospective data customers and their needs is less about algorithms, formulas, and check lists and more about the culture of management. Working a customer-centric mindset into finance strategy will mean success or failure when it comes to finance function development.

6

DATA FLOW PROCESS

KEY TAKEAWAYS

■ Understanding the definition of data flow and the data flow process.
■ Understanding the need to convert data to knowledge.
■ Understanding the role and impact of the data flow process.
■ Understanding the key components and significance of data gathering, data processing, and data analysis.
■ Recognizing processes that are inadequate.
■ Understanding techniques for evaluating the data flow process.
■ Recognizing the manner in which discipline and documentation enable the integration of the data flow process into the business culture.
■ Understanding the benefits of common data standards.
■ Understanding how the data flow process will develop with the rest of the finance function.

ROLE OF PROCESSES

Processes Defined

The term *processes* means many things to many people. The term refers loosely to any chain of ordered actions or events that lead to a desired end. Processes have value in manufacturing, administration, or any of a myriad of nonbusiness contexts. The most predominant process in the finance function is the series of actions that contribute to the conversion of events and transactions in the company's business environment to knowledge. Tier 3 of the multilevel approach (see Chapter 4, "Multilevel Approach") outlines the considerations involved in developing this aspect of infrastructure. Data flow processes underlie and/or influence all aspects of Tier 3 and many facets of Tier 4 and 5 (upper tiers) of the multilevel model.

Data flow process represents the succession of actions that converts data from transactions and events external to the company into relevant knowledge to be used in decision making and financial statements. This cycle of data gathering, data processing, and data analysis must be broken down to a level of granularity that will enable the business owner/manager to create initiatives that incorporate the finance function into company-wide growth objectives. Processes in the small and emerging business may seem simple enough; however, as the company grows, the need to refine/review the data flow dynamic will become imperative. Being armed with the knowledge to understand in greater detail issues and concerns relating to data flow processes will serve the business owner/manager well throughout the strategizing process.

Data Flow Process and Creating Knowledge

Extracting accurate and timely financial data from the business environment and refining it for decision-making purposes is the foundation of the finance function. This process, however, often is taken for granted by the business community. The assumption is that generating accurate data for management is a natural offshoot of any finance endeavor. This misconception is perhaps most evident in academia, where most business leaders begin their formative training. Examinations and textbooks offer up challenges in the form of long elaborate problems to solve. Applying the concepts in question (be they accounting, finance, or otherwise) is not as daunting a task as sifting through the mosaic of information that is provided. Overlooking a minor, subtle piece of information can yield incorrect results. Strategically approaching these problems is key as students try to master the material in question. Where did all the information for the problem come from? How were account balances derived, and who declared the accounting treatments? Were the events yielding the transaction interpreted correctly?

The academic world assumes that the decision crossroads faced in examinations, textbooks, case studies, and business models are supported by reliable information. In the real world, applying the correct accounting concept to a circumstance is the easy part; the difficult part is *getting* the information. The formative years of businesses are marked by the challenge of gathering accurate financial data in a timely manner. In response to this challenge, organizations often fall into the trap of generating copious amounts of financial data that is neither accurate nor timely.

It is imperative that the small and emerging business be able to identify the difference between data and knowledge. Where data represents certain events and transactions in their most basic form, knowledge is the appropriate data refined and translated to suit certain circumstances at the right time. Creating knowledge is more than just gathering data; it is the state of awareness that bridges business needs with the capacity to generate information. The successful business owner/manager manages knowledge by staying close to the front lines of the business (operations) and linking everyday business needs with the organization's capacity to generate informational solutions.

Need for a Data Flow Process

Generating knowledge in the enterprise is more than a technological feat. It is a process that demands the capacity to access, store, filter, and discern the appropriateness of data. The blueprint for a particular company's data flow process is never final but always evolving. The components of this blueprint often touch on every aspect of concrete components of the finance function. The data flow process represents the protocols and procedures that envelop information systems. It draws on the skills of employees and their judgment in matching business needs to information availability. It also leverages the impact of information systems and bridges the gap between raw systems capability and company-specific needs. Processes must be customized and suited for a particular organization's needs.

The business owner or executive will spend a great deal of time making decisions. Hiring, firing, product purchases, product or service expansions, real estate divestitures—all these decisions require accurate and timely data. Where does it come from? How is it generated? Many executives blindly rely on their finance person or on out-of-box software to generate it for them. Surprisingly, they rarely challenge the integrity of the source of data, especially when time is constrained. Unfortunately, some executives are easily led to believe that data generated is always right. The reality is the data may or may not be appropriate for the circumstances intended. The key to determining the adequacy of data for the organization's purposes is understanding the effectiveness of the data flow process.

Making the transition from a struggling, emerging organization to a healthy, stable company will mean establishing a sound finance function—the core of which is the data flow dynamic. Developing a sound data flow process may not be as simple as implementing steps and actions for employees to follow. Issues of culture, knowledge of objectives, and view of the big picture must be addressed. Overcoming these challenges will be paramount in developing a sound data flow process. The case of Passalla Industries illustrates some of these issues.

Passalla Industries is a manufacturer and distributor of doors for a host of industrial and residential uses. The company has one central manufacturing site where it produces all standard and customized doors, which are distributed throughout the Southeast. The company is a traditional family-owned business with the patriarch and founder Victor Passalla immersed in both the strategic and day-to-day decision making.

Passalla Industries has experienced a steady surge in business orders of late. Revenues in the past two years have gone from approximately $10–12 million to $50–60 million. This has pushed the manufacturing processes to unprecedented limits. Many of Victor's manufacturing process decisions are driven by gut feel from his three decades in the business. The last two years, however, have put him in a position where he must reassess his approach to supplies, raw materials, and production capacity. Having spurned the input of accountants (whom he refers to as numbers guys) in the past, Victor is coming to the realization that to thrive, he will have to embrace financial data as it relates to his manufacturing process—something he feels he is not suited for at this time.

Historically Passalla's financial reporting has been limited to accommodating information requests from the CPA who prepares the tax return (a longtime family friend). The company is a Subchapter S corporation incorporated several years ago for liability and insurance purposes. Payroll, accounts payable, accounts receivable, and cash disbursements are done manually on a hodgepodge of applications—from 12-column paper (manual) to Quicken to Excel. Victor has been reluctant to invest in any information systems or computers for cash flow reasons and due to his fear of technology. Compounding this matter is his reluctance to open up his financial affairs to anyone other than family and his CPA.

Passalla Industries is in the process of acquiring a $2 million loan to expand its facilities to accommodate a greater volume of standard and nonstandard customer orders. Victor is growing frustrated with the information the bank requires regarding the financial picture of the business. He is equally irritated with the public accountants who are poring over the data he supplies and challenging its validity. Although many people are contributing to the effort of pulling the necessary financial data together, no *one* person is in charge of the numbers. This responsibility has fallen on Victor's shoulders, and he feels a little overwhelmed by the whole process and discouraged by the amount of his time it demands—time he would rather spend on operations. He is having a difficult time articulating the information requests to lower-level people, resulting in problems providing answers to the bank and the auditors. Victor's lack of finance/accounting background is becoming a disruption to current business processes as he struggles with clerks and order entry people to garner data for the bank.

Victor's son Jesse invested his knowledge of the Internet into Passalla Industries and created a comprehensive online ordering system that not only takes orders but expands the company's marketing exposure to a global level. The combination of this wide marketing net and Passalla's burgeoning national reputation has resulted in a surge of orders.

Jesse, educated as an engineer, is expected to succeed Victor as the company patriarch; however, Victor still retains all decision-making authority, especially as it relates to new technology in administrative functions. Victor reluctantly OK'd the website (after his son completed it) and has finally recognized its importance after positive feedback from his longtime customers. Use of the website has resulted in a great reduction in errors, as customers could input their orders directly and avoid the potential miscommunication that often happened though the phone ordering system on which the company relied.

The various door divisions are growing quickly, thanks to a generous bonus program that Victor implemented a few years ago. Quarterly bonuses can double the salaries of the division directors. The divisions are careful to track their financial data and submit it promptly for review at the end of each quarter. Victor often is suspicious of the results submitted to him for review; however, the success and rapid growth of the company have distracted him from acting on his unease. Each division keeps track of its own results as best it can. This situation has resulted in a number of various applications with varying definitions of revenue and expenses. Victor has made frequent unsuccessful efforts to unify the results and reconcile them company-wide. Preparing the financial statements for the bank loan is his most recent attempt at this exercise. His queries and concerns about the divisional results have been met with resistance and equal concern from the divisions themselves, which vehemently defend their results.

Passalla Industries is at a crossroads in its business life cycle. The key to ensuring that management is making sound business decisions in this time of rapid expansion will hinge on the development of a sound finance strategy, the core of which is a reliable data flow process. The following observations should play a role in developing the data flow process at Passalla:

- *Leverage the Internet for order processing.* The company has the ideal platform for eliminating a slow data entry process that is prone to error. Taking orders over the Internet will allow industrial and residential customers to communicate their needs around the clock without waiting for a customer service person to wait on them. This means minimized slowdowns or errors in recording and submitting orders for processing. Enabling an Internet order entry system for customers also will afford Passalla Industries the opportunity to gather market data from customers that it would not otherwise be able to accumulate. How will the company construct the infrastructure to interface with this valuable, cost-saving device? What are the implications of establishing a web-enabled order entry system for the rest of the organization? Could the resulting web platform serve as a mechanism for placing direct orders from vendors?
- *Keep Victor and others from gleaning incorrect information.* Serving as CEO/patriarch of the company, Victor Passalla has free rein over the company. However, he must exercise some restraint when it comes to handling financial data. Having a high level understanding of the finance function and how finance data is derived would benefit both Victor and the company. If this is not practicable, the next best thing is to select for all finance matters a "point person" who understands where data comes from and what the numbers mean. Installing a protocol for accessing data is difficult with high-level

executives and business owners; however, it is necessary in growing businesses whose financial data may be garnered and stored in inefficient or unorthodox ways.

- *Determine who's in charge of finance data.* Who is ultimately responsible for the validity and completeness of the finance data? Passalla Industries has no full-time person who "owns" the finance function, its individual components, or the information it produces. Of the people who attend to this function part time, none has a true finance or accounting background. This lack of organization may work for a short time for very small companies; however, companies that are mid- to large size and/or growing quickly eventually may find themselves without direction as filing requirements become more complex and the sheer volume of data generated by the business demands that there be someone with financial know-how. The lack of organization and hierarchy in the finance function breeds an everyone's-in-charge-no-one's-in-charge mind-set that robs the organization of financial focus. Sooner or later the organization will need to invest in proven human capital to manage the financial data the company must have to succeed.

- *Deal with multiple databases.* Business decisions must be made at the company and the division level. Information that drives decisions at all levels must reconcile and paint a consistent picture of the organization; otherwise, conflicting business initiatives may arise. How will the company evaluate results for the sake of bonuses and resource allocations? Will it rely on each division's individually derived data? How reliable (impartial) is this data? Passalla Industries' challenge will be not only to develop an easily accessible central storage site for data but also to convince the various divisions to give up their own pet databases. Doing this will not be an easy task, as division managers have grown comfortable with the numbers they gather. How will the company develop a central repository of data, and how will it ensure that the rest of the organization will use it?

- *Deal with different account structure/nomenclature.* The various divisions not only have their own stores of financial data, but they catalog and reference them differently. This creates a challenge for developing an overall, comprehensive financial picture of the company, which adds to the challenge of comparing results companywide. Eventually this Tower of Babel must be translated and unified to enable the quick consolidation of data across the company and allow for a fair, objective evaluation by management. Establishing a universal methodology for interpreting activity will add to the timeliness of company-wide data and enable quick, "high-level" decisions. Does the company choose an existing account structure from a division and mandate its use across all divisions when creating a standard chart of accounts? Will the company create a composite chart of select items from all charts of accounts? How much time will it take to create such a chart of accounts? How will Passalla Industries gain buy-in from the divisions?

- *Unify reporting functionality.* Passalla Industries' current regular reporting requirements are fairly light. Data for the tax return and cash disbursements/cash receipts data seem to be the only real recurring reporting requirements. The company is getting a taste of acute reporting needs, particularly with the due diligence required for the bank loan. The fact that Passalla Industries is struggling with this is a sign that it may not be prepared for future watershed events in its life cycle. Formal reporting will be imperative as the company grows in size and complexity. As orders continue to trend up, Passalla Industries must be able to plan and forecast future manufacturing needs. To do so, focusing on internal reporting becomes imperative. Gathering data for the tax return and for the debt compliance is becoming a dreaded task. It does not have to be this way, however. The company must design a central repository for data that can be translated into the various reporting forms. Whether it is for formal, external reporting purposes or for informal, internal reporting purposes, reporting from data that is gathered once will benefit Passalla Industries, especially since it does not employ a full-time finance staff to gather detail data for various filings. Creating an easily maintained one-stop shop for financial data that can accommodate reporting needs will strengthen the company's decision-making capacity in this time of accelerated growth.

Properly positioning Passalla Industries to face current and future business challenges will hinge on the development of a reliable data flow process. Doing this will include developing methodologies for identifying and gathering data from the business environment, processing it in an efficient and timely manner, and analyzing it before applying it in decisions that will drive the company forward. Passalla Industries will have to face the challenges of developing a cost-effective data flow dynamic that will serve its pending informational needs. It will have to focus on developing a comprehensive finance strategy before setting foot in the (potentially) dangerous world of technology and consulting expenditures. The most urgent needs for now center on the need for a data flow process. Because the design and functionality of this process will play a pivotal role in strategy development, understanding the basic components of the data flow process is critical.

DATA FLOW ECOSYSTEM

A key objective in the decision-making dynamic of any organization is linking decision making to the events and transactions the company encounters in the business environment. Financial statements (either formal or ad hoc) are the language by which the state of the company is communicated to others, whether they are inside or outside the organization. They are also the means by which decisions that move the company forward are made. The most critical consumers of finance data within the organization are found in the *decision support system*. This system typically comprises the managers and analysts who report directly to the executive level. Small and emerging businesses usually have a simple decision support system—the owners and those who directly support them. Relevant and timely information is what drives the decision support system. The key component in the system is the capacity to generate financial statements and reports. The small and emerging business will inevitably mature, resulting in evolving/changing data needs. Included in these evolving needs will be that of external, third parties that provide financing or become stakeholders. These data customers will rely on financial statement data to make judgments regarding their relationships with the company. Knowing this, it is critical for business owners to understand how efficient their finance function is at interpreting data and translating the company to financials.

Companies of all sizes often overlook the dynamics of converting data to knowledge. The data flow dynamic consists of operations (the front lines of the company) transferring information to management, which then makes decisions that drive operations. It is crucial that the organization's finance function gather sufficient information in a timely manner. Next, the data must be processed, or compiled in a way that is representative of the entire organization as well as its component parts. Finally, the data must be analyzed and either validated and forwarded to the decision support function or adjusted. These three key parts of the data flow dynamic are illustrated in Exhibit 6.1. Ideally, data gathering is performed by, or is a part of, operations, while processing and analysis are a function of the administrative part of the organization. Understanding the overall function of the data flow dynamic is dependent on examining these three distinct components.

Data Gathering

The data gathering step is the foundation of the data flow dynamic. The wisdom in the adage "Garbage In, Garbage Out" holds true in this context. Nothing neutralizes a well-planned, well-financed data flow dynamic (or finance strategy, for that matter) as effectively as bad information. The data gathering component of the data flow process must have three characteristics to be effective and relevant:

1. *Automation.* The objective of automation is to minimize the redundancy or impact of manual input. Just as too many cooks spoil the broth, too many clerks will spoil the process. Data input errors and nefarious data manipulation can be kept to a minimum if the gathering process is automated. This is the best argument for putting order entry or the customer

Exhibit 6.1   **Data Flow Process**

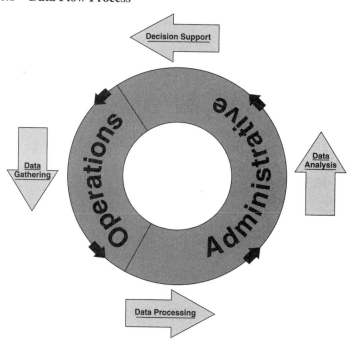

sales function on the Internet. Many organizations have welcomed technology in data input and have this aspect of their process *webified*. Companies that have not are missing out on an important platform for
inexpensive, powerful processing. The small and emerging business
owner is at an advantage when it comes to implementing a web-oriented
data entry process. Business disruptions usually can be managed more
easily in smaller business settings as opposed to large, complex businesses with remote operations. The cost savings and efficiencies gained
by automating this aspect of data gathering are just now becoming quan-
tifiable. A study by the International Technology Group in Los Altos,
California, compiled the data in Exhibit 6.2 for a variety of transaction
types conducted digitally over the Internet.[1]

Automating data gathering is not only a matter of good practice from
a cost perspective but also a matter of quality assurance. Having the sales
and revenue data input by customers electronically via carefully crafted
digital templates will add to the accuracy and timeliness of data. In particular, such an automated process will allow the company to skip manual
data input routines and move into the processing function quickly and

Exhibit 6.2   **Cost of Transactions Comparison**

Transaction	Conventional	Internet-based
Process airline tickets	$8	$0.77
Schedule package pickup	$6.22	$0.62
Process order (parts)	$12	$1
Process order (computer)	$65	$6.85
Process purchase order	$130	$28
Billing (utility)	$1.75	$0.30
Billing (retail)	$2.77	$0.88
Customer service query	$22	$2.32
Issue insurance policy	$580	$275
Sell car	$450	$155

Source: International Technology Group

efficiently. Relying on clerks to key data exposes the organization to human error. Passalla Industries is typical of an organization that can benefit from such a process enhancement. The website created by Jesse Passalla allows the company's retail-distributor customers to order electronically. This cuts down on the frequent miscommunication of order quantity and order types that has plagued the company in the past. Orders come directly from customers, with no room for misinterpretation by order takers. Another benefit is that direct retail customers have access to Passalla Industries' complete line of offerings. Allowing customers to browse the myriad of customization features from their home or office transforms Passalla into a true round-the-clock establishment. The customer-friendly template Jesse developed allows for the mixing and matching of standard door features and the ability to specify nonstandard customizations.

2. *Uniformity.*   Having a clearly defined, uniform data gathering methodology goes a long way toward developing a bulletproof data flow process. A uniform process will lessen the impact of employee attrition in the finance department and make troubleshooting easier if issues arise. Uniform processes are particularly critical for small and emerging business owners, given that they wear many different hats from month to month. The demands of other parts of the business may distract these owners/executives, making a uniform, easily replicable process all the more important.

Inexperienced managers/executives are particularly susceptible when it comes to dealing with nonstandard transactions. The tendency, especially in small companies, is to treat every transaction as a unique, stand-alone event. This may be a step toward a customer-oriented culture; however, when it comes to the data flow process, there can be *no exceptions*. Exception-based processes are, and always will be, a stumbling block for the finance function. Although exceptions cannot be avoided, understanding that exceptions should be tolerated on rare occasion will keep the data gathering process on track. Nonstandard transaction situations typically generate unauditable results and become time consuming and error prone. The data gathering methodology of processes must be clearly documented to a point where every transaction can be handled in a routine manner and not rely on specific knowledge of employees.

3. *Scalability.* Scalability allows businesses to expand data gathering methodologies in an economic and efficient manner. Can the data gathering process be enhanced to include other tools or functions without disrupting the process itself? If the business acquired another similar organization tomorrow, how difficult would it be to replicate the gathering process at the new operation site? Where small companies break down in their ability to gather accurate and timely data is when they expand via acquisition or otherwise. Even if their core headquarters site is gathering data efficiently, remote sites with different data landscapes often suffer as the gathering process is not clearly defined or does not fit the expanded environment. The finance strategist's goal is to create processes that are immune from disruptions or rework if the business environment or the organization changes.

Data Processing

Once data is gathered and input into the system, it must be processed and made available for analysis. Although the organization may be small and relatively simple, reporting needs may be complex. Internal reporting and analysis needs may cut across products, territories, or a combination of both. More than likely the business has external reporting needs of some kind, such as federal and state tax filings, financial statements for debt compliance, or SEC filings. The objective is to quickly and efficiently perform all processing in one centralized repository, in any format needed to serve reporting needs.

It is important to remember that data per se is not knowledge. The objective in developing an efficient and useful data flow process is to gather data and convert it to knowledge for data customers. The role of processing data will greatly impact the analysis and interpretation of data gathered in the company's business environment. The following three considerations will be prominent when conceptualizing a methodology for processing data:

1. *Create a central repository of data.* There should be one official storage place for company numbers. It should be easy to access and be updated in

a timely manner. It is not uncommon for data to be stored offline from mainstream systems, based on purpose or use. Tax data, product/service performance data, and/or external reporting data may be stored and managed in exclusive applications. The difficulty arises when this data is reconciled. Do final results differ? Why? Where? Fast-growing companies often find themselves having to deal with this dilemma. Which numbers will be used to determine resource needs, performance bonuses, or expansion/contraction? Issues like these beg the need for the centralization of data storage. The objective in the finance function is to focus efforts and resources on analysis and decision making. Time spent reconciling data across the organization is time *not* spent creating solutions for the business. Establishing a shared cache of data eliminates the need to constantly confirm data validity. The culture of information sharing should replace the culture of reporting, especially as it relates to internal reporting and analysis. Developing a central repository of data will be crucial for Passalla Industries. Victor's ongoing concern that the individual business units are manipulating results may be valid. However, he has neither the platform nor the tools to investigate his suspicion. Conceptualizing, creating, and rolling out a central repository of finance data may be the easy part. The hard part will be mandating that all division managers run their door divisions from the central repository. Victor will have to overcome the skepticism and distrust of these division managers of numbers that they did not generate.

2. *Leverage automation.*   Similar to data gathering, a fully automated processing engine adds speed and accuracy to the processing function. Moving from the gathering phase of the data flow process to the processing phase involves positioning the data gathered in such a way that analysis by the finance organization (employees) is maximized. Transferring this data into various logical forms while preserving its integrity is a formidable challenge in and of itself. Moving this data into logical forms and preserving detailed comparability to prior periods makes this challenge seem herculean. The potential for error in this exercise makes a manual processing function out of the question. Additionally, the likelihood of oversights and the exposure to unscrupulous manipulation render a manual processing function undesirable. An electronic processing function allows technology to do the heavy lifting related to mathematical and logical operations as well as to the disposition of (potentially large amounts of) data classified in a myriad of ways. Charging employees in the finance organization with mundane processing duties may leave them feeling underchallenged and expose the data flow dynamic to error. An electronic processing function minimizes errors (both intentional and otherwise) and enables the finance organization to focus more intently on analysis.

Exhibit 6.3   **Information Roll-ups Using Common Data**

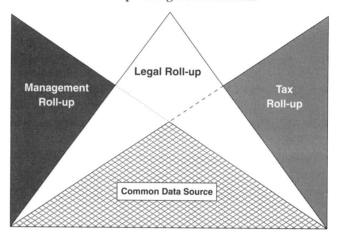

3. *Preserve versatility.*   The processing engine also should provide consolidation roll-ups that satisfy as many business needs as possible. Can the push of a button yield company data in the proper format for tax reporting, legal reporting, or internal analysis? Exhibit 6.3 illustrates this point.

The foundation of the capability to roll-up data to suit various functional areas of the business efficiently is the establishment of a basic level of data common to the disparate needs of the business. The example in Exhibit 6.3 outlines three different reporting needs of the organization served by one data source with a minimum amount of manual intervention. Even though these data looks are different, managers/executives have the comfort of knowing that all information is coming from the same data source.

Data Analysis

The analysis aspect of the data flow process must be the primary focus of the day-to-day activities of the finance function. Management will assemble a finance organization to address the everyday data needs of the organization as the company grows. Managing the data flow process means addressing two key objectives—creating an efficient data flow process and building a body of knowledgeable, professional staff to analyze and interpret the data. Employee turnover will present a continual challenge in the case of the latter objective. Creating a stimulating and fulfilling work environment, however, is one of the most effective tools in retaining employees. Keeping *gathering* and *processing* functions to a minimum and making *analysis* the focus of the finance staff will serve to motivate staff and encourage them to seek long-term careers in the organization. Designing the finance function in such a way that its employees must focus on analysis will hone their business skills and convert them to strategic-minded business partners.

The analysis function is focused on reviewing the data gathered and processed, refining it, and translating it to knowledge. Doing this means examining period-end data to determine the completeness and accuracy of the data. This examination may involve comparing current period data with historic data and determining its suitability. Adjustments often are needed for misstated or incomplete data. Analysis does not end there, however. Interpreting the company's financial results also means translating relevant data to a user-friendly format. Reports, either paper or electronic, are the tangible output of the finance function. Management and executives have their favorite reports to review each period to understand company performance. The analysis function should be focused on creating, fine-tuning, and delivering these reports to management as quickly and effectively as possible. Smoother data gathering and data processing will beget more effective analysis as time allowances and access to large amounts of data become more routine. This is good news for the organization as the finance function can focus its energy on more synergistic tasks, such as creating business models and what-if analysis. Emphasis on data analysis as finance function evolves will ensure finance will always add value to operations.

Addressing the data flow process means that the small and emerging business owner is not simply addressing a menu of tasks but establishing one aspect of culture for the organization. The lack of a progressive attitude could present the biggest challenge. The quest to gather timely and accurate information involves not only establishing effective components of the data flow process but also controlling the *mix* of time and effort spent by finance employees on its three components: data gathering, data processing, and data analysis. The statistics in Chapter 1, "Doing Business in Today's Environment," indicate that managing this mix is becoming a bigger challenge. Understanding the data flow process and its core components prompt the strategist to employ a process that is relevant for the organization. The next challenge is to fairly assess the current *as-is* data flow process and move forward with developing the more efficient *to-be* process.

EVALUATING CURRENT PROCESSES AND CONCEPTUALIZING FUTURE PROCESSES

Need for an Efficient Process

The small and emerging business owner must have a realistic grasp of the current data flow process before conceptualizing an improved one. Defining the as-is process provides the basis for action items in implementing the to-be data flow process and finance strategy. Certain considerations must be outlined to ensure the strategist assesses the as-is data flow process objectively. Chief among these considerations involves employing a sound evaluation methodology and identifying best practices to measure against.

Over time, most processes evolve; however, a distinction must be made between structured growth and haphazard change. Typically, small organizations with limited, homogeneous events and transactions rarely put a lot of thought into their data flow processes. This is often due to the straightforward nature of business activity and the limited volume of transactions. It is when organizations grow that processes become an issue. Varying environments and disparate customer needs create a more heterogeneous transaction landscape and create exceptions to the core process. Expanding overseas and dealing with invoices and billings in foreign currencies with unfamiliar government withholding practices is a typical environmental change that challenges conventional processes. Expanding revenue recognition and payment terms is an example of varied transaction types that also stretch the bounds of processes. *Workarounds* and *overrides* that result from these situations inevitably create slowdowns in data delivery or errors in the processed data.

Exhibit 6.4 is a schematic of a data flow process for a multinational company before it reassessed and overhauled its process. The far left, far right, and upper left margins of the exhibit represent local operations in overseas locations. The company had these local sites preparing submissions of total activity, then separate submissions for their industrial and retail business unit activity that represented different slices of the total activity. Separate disconnected consolidations were produced in each of the geographic regions as well as separate consolidations for the product business divisions (industrial and retail). This maze of submissions with varying requirements, nomenclature, and personnel created a burdensome and ineffective submission routine for the finance function. The most painful symptom of this inefficient process was the generation of unreconciled reports. Each region and division presented its own version of events to executive management. Due to the conflicting reports, management had difficulty making strategic decisions, paying bonuses, and reporting results to the shareholder community. Ironically, management was reluctant to overhaul this process, assuming these types of issues were a part of doing business. Managers noted that the finance team always got things done. They were paralyzed by their own if-it-ain't-broke-don't-fix-it attitude.

One symptom of an out-of-control data flow process is the just-get-it-done mentality that may underlie it. Often management is oblivious to broken processes for many reasons, not the least of which is the willingness of finance staff to just get it done. Although this may be a testament to staff commitment, it may be an indictment of the data flow process itself. This may be reason enough for management to dig deep and evaluate processes on an ongoing basis. The evaluation is a good opportunity to question staff and understand what is actually happening with the current data flow process. Are core procedures outdated? If so, do they need

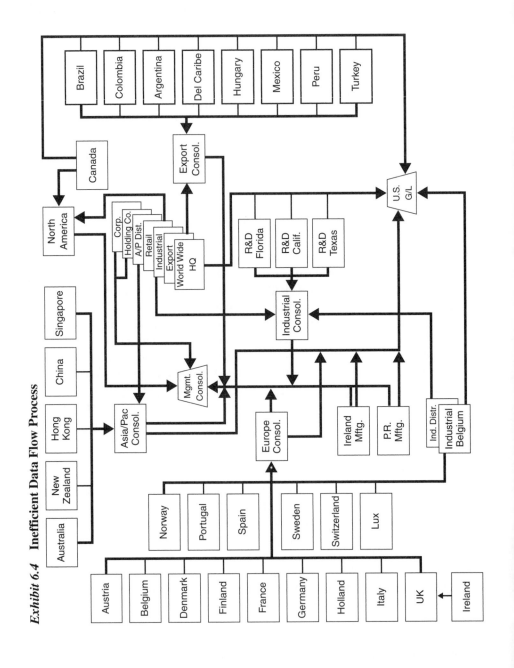

Exhibit 6.4 **Inefficient Data Flow Process**

minor refinements or a major overhaul? How much exception-based transacting do they handle? It may be found that improving poorly performing or inadequate data flow processes is less about design and more an issue of discipline within the finance organization.

Process Mapping

Interviewing staff and mapping processes will be key to understanding the current as-is process. Translating and recording what is done and when will provide an objective base from which to work when defining or redefining the data flow process. A template like the one in Exhibit 6.5 is helpful. During a typical close, each staff member should record what he or she is doing and how long it takes. All members of the finance team must put a chronological schematic of their actions on paper, providing a way to identify roadblocks and inefficiencies. Each day of the closing period, in this example, is broken down into eight hour increments. Any and all actions related to the period-end close are recorded chronologically. The actions are listed in the "Task Description" column while the time spent on the action is listed in the "Time to Complete" column. Tasks that must be achieved before another task can be performed are noted in the "Dependent on Task" column. Some tasks, in this case, are not dependent on others (i.e., tasks 1, 2, 5, and 7 through 10), while certain other tasks are dependent on others (i.e., tasks 3, 4, 6, and 11). It is worth noting that the final three tasks (tasks 12 through 14) are dependent on the completion of tasks 1 through 11. Evaluating the data flow process in this way enables one to identify bottlenecks that are sometimes not obvious to those directly involved in the process.

The goal is to achieve a perfect downward trending, stair-step configuration in the shortest amount of time. This would indicate a well-ordered process. In this example, task 2 appears to be a bottleneck. If this task is shortened, task 11, which is dependent on task 2, may be completed earlier in the process. The process owner may consider starting task 3 earlier on Day 1, immediately after task 1 is complete. This move will allow for tasks 4 and 6 to begin earlier. Besides mapping the current process, participants should be asked to list any peripheral barriers that do not appear on the chart. For instance, limited access to a specific line printer equipped to run reports or the limited availability of part-time employees to perform analyses are examples of factors that may limit the speed and quality of this process.

Benchmarking/Best Practices

The next step in evaluating the data flow process is to benchmark the process against those of similar-size companies in similar industries. Laying out the current, as-is process provides an understanding of both how it unfolds and how long it takes. Improving the process, however, requires establishing a standard to measure against the as-is. Is the current process ahead of the pack or behind?

Exhibit 6.5 **Process Mapping Template**

For: German Subsidiary

Task Number	Task Description	Dependent on Task	Time to Complete	Day 1	Day 2	Day 3	Day 5	Day 6
1	Run rental asset depreciation report	N/A	4					
2	Load creditors' invoices & close for month	N/A	16					
3	Review and adjust doubtful accounts	1	3					
4	Reconcile bank accounts	3	4					
5	Reconcile lease accounts	N/A	4					
6	Run accounts receivable report	3,4	3					
7	Prepare accruals	N/A	3					
8	Calculate commissions	N/A	8					
9	Review accounts and make adjustments	N/A	4					
10	Prepare I/C analysis	N/A	1					
11	Prepare service charges & allocations	2	2					
12	Prepare P&L and Balance Sheets	All of the Above	5					
13	Prepare Service P&L	All of the Above	3					
14	Complete submission to corporate HQ	All of the Above	10					

Source: Chris Muccio

Some process fixes may seem intuitive; however, real improvements may be too subtle or esoteric to detect, let alone employ. Organizations like the AnswerThink Consulting Group[2] and the Gartner Group[3] specialize in compiling statistics related to finance organizations as well as identifying best practices. Typical statistics are those related to dollars spent on the finance function and percentage of time spent on analysis versus transaction management. These organizations also keep statistics on average days to close the books of companies in similar industries. *Best practices* is a term that describes business solutions employed in a certain industry that lead to optimal performance. Examples of solutions in this context may be closing processes or information system configurations. Benchmarking and identifying best practices will provide a framework to set standards for an improved, to-be data flow process that will serve as the cornerstone of the finance strategy.

After benchmarking similar companies in the industry, the company with the process flow in Exhibit 6.4 overhauled its data flow process to resemble that in Exhibit 6.6. The focus was on a central repository of data from which all data customers could draw information. The win for this organization was to establish single submission sites from the different regions. This significantly reduced the time to close the books and enabled ample time to process and analyze data. The business units (industrial and retail) and the geographical regions were able to access accurate data that was available promptly after each month-end close, giving management confidence that all reporting would be based on the official data of the organization.

INTEGRATING DATA FLOW PROCESS WITH THE BUSINESS

The data flow process does not stand alone but serves as an integral part of the finance function. If any one aspect of the finance function has the most significance or requires the most attention, it is the data flow dynamic. Establishing the process itself is essential, but equally important is integrating the process into the business itself. Doing this means affirming its significance in the culture of the organization and ensuring it helps maximize all aspects of the business it supports. Discipline, documentation, and standard nomenclature are major aspects of the process that will ensure its success. Although these topics do not define the data flow process per se, they will shape the context in which it operates and help maximize its effectiveness.

Discipline

Discipline as it relates to data flow processes must be adhered to at all levels of the organization. Discipline in this context refers to the adherence by process participants to well defined, well communicated steps and procedures that illustrate a

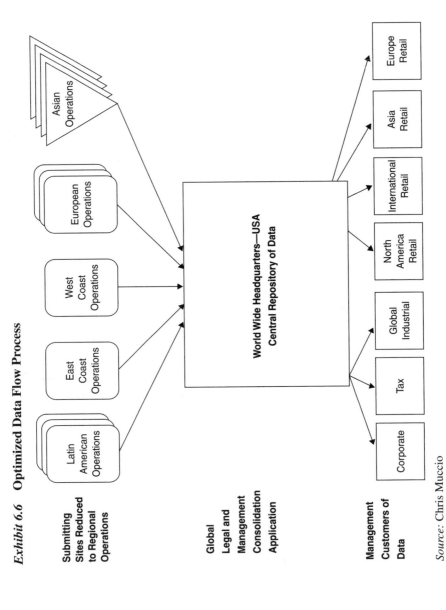

Exhibit 6.6 **Optimized Data Flow Process**

Submitting Sites Reduced to Regional Operations

Latin American Operations

East Coast Operations

West Coast Operations

European Operations

Asian Operations

Global Legal and Management Consolidation Application

World Wide Headquarters—USA Central Repository of Data

Management Customers of Data

Corporate

Tax

Global Industrial

North America Retail

International Retail

Asia Retail

Europe Retail

Source: Chris Muccio

Exhibit 6.7 **Schematic of the Data Flow Dynamic: Role of Discipline**

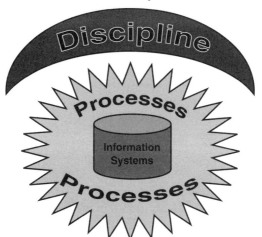

process. If processes govern systems technology (information systems), then discipline governs processes. Exhibit 6.7 illustrates this aspect of the data flow dynamic. Oddly enough, many strategists will create effective processes while discounting the role of discipline. Doing this equates to passing laws and neglecting to enforce them. Given the small or relatively simple nature of the data flow dynamic in many small and emerging businesses, strict adherence to codified steps and procedures may not be an issue. However, as the business evolves and processes become more complex, the culture of discipline will either galvanize a process or severely degrade it.

An example of discipline in the finance organization is the scripted manner in which a clerk inputs an invoice or transaction into the data system. Discipline also applies at the top of the organization. Bypassing key decision makers (managers) and posing extraordinary information requests to clerks is a breakdown in discipline often committed by higher-level executives and business owners. The case of Passalla Industries illustrates the disruption and inefficiencies bred by lack of discipline at the top. Victor Passalla's ad hoc information requests of low-level employees not only distracts the finance organization from its day-to-day tasks but results in incorrect data passed on for official purposes. Staffers who do not completely understand information requests may react with answers that are both inappropriate and misleading. Victor's lack of knowledge of the data flow process is dangerous in that he may not be querying the correct personnel or asking the right questions in the first place. Well-thought-out processes will accommodate both standard and nonstandard information requests regardless of the circumstances. Excessive exception-oriented information requests and data processing that represent persistent departures from the standard process, however, will create distractions and inefficiencies that degrade the speed and accuracy of data flow.

Poor discipline may be as innocuous as allowing extra time for a submission or tolerating workarounds in processes. Sticking to processes, employing time schedules, and mandating accountability represent key aspects of discipline in the data flow process:

- *Adhering to processes.* Establishing well-documented processes and holding members of the organization responsible to them are central to good discipline. If left unchecked, data flow participants may think nothing of deviating from scripted processes during the normal course of business. Although slight deviations may not prove fatal, over time the goal of speed and accuracy may become compromised if exceptions become frequent. Prolonged deviations from promulgated processes may, at the least, slow processes down and, at the worst, mutate them into ineffective procedures. Excessive camaraderie in the workplace and plain lack of oversight are the two main contributors to this phenomenon. Obviously, discouraging camaraderie in the workplace is not healthy for the organization. However, having check lists and documentation in place that ensure procedures are followed will go a long way toward keeping people on track. If the objective requirements of process participants is made plain, the temptation to deviate will be curtailed.

  Emphasis on speed and accuracy should be secondary to the emphasis on process utilization in the short run. This holds true especially in the early years of the business. Allowing a get-it-done-at-any-cost attitude to prevail in the finance organization may get results in the near term but could erode the effect of processes and procedures over time. The following example illustrates the impact of this management style:

  > Alfred R. works as a consolidations accountant in an organization that has put a renewed focus on reducing the time to close the books. The initiative is to occur in gradual increments. A generous reward structure has been put in place to facilitate the time-to-close behavior necessary to further this goal. The company has set strict ground rules on how to input data into its central repository. Data is either loaded electronically or input via a journal entry process—both methodologies flush with sound documentary characteristics. It is never acceptable to key data into the system. The time to close has been steadily reduced; however, exceptions that were normally encountered are now resolved by keying in correct amounts instead of reloading or journaling the data, in the interest of time. This quick-fix mentality has begun to create audit issues as no one is certain how the numbers in question are getting into the system and who is responsible for them. The local sites responsible for the submissions cannot be held accountable, as their submission documentation conflicts with system output. The

corporate headquarters finance group is beginning to deem the time-to-close initiative a failure, as resolution on deviations resulting from data input errors is requiring an inordinate amount of time to troubleshoot, which is nullifying any time savings the process presents. The real cost to the finance function of this failing initiative is the lack of buy-in to the process by users that has arisen from this difficult troubleshooting process. The local sites have lost confidence in the system because of the data conflicts, and they view the whole process as a burdensome, unreliable exercise. Although the time-to-close initiative for Alfred R.'s company was well conceived, the lack of follow-through has denied it the success it sought. The combination of the just-discussed issues has resulted in an unpleasant spike in closing time as sites have deemed the submission process a lesser priority and are uncooperative during troubleshooting exercises.

The lesson to be learned is that sticking to the prescribed process is essential. If a deviation is warranted—and certain situations will dictate this—it should be done on a true exception basis and not allowed to become routine. Review of processes should be part of normal operations. The small and emerging business owner/executive may find that through this type of continuous improvement, a workaround may supercede a process step altogether. Additionally, executive objectives and mandates must support processes and not conflict with them.

■ *Employing time schedules.* Putting out a calendar with date and time requirements will effectively communicate expectations to data flow participants, most important to data customers. While doing this may seem to be overkill in the small organization, as a matter of culture it will prove invaluable as the organization grows and new members of the finance organization are added. Publishing a calendar has two purposes. First, it gives all adjoining departments the ability to plan for the close, ensuring ample resources are available. Second, it communicates deadlines to participants and data customers in different time zones (if necessary). Doing this is especially important if the organization has operations overseas. If headquarters is on Eastern Standard Time with operations in the Far East, timing deadlines may have different meanings (e.g., does *noon* mean noon EST or noon PST?). Often, data flow process participants operate in a totally different day. Enforcing time requirements is difficult enough without the confusion of interpreting published times. Organizations must take into account different time zones and make clear what is due and when.

■ *Mandating accountability.* To achieve the objective of timely and efficient data flow, all process participants must have a clear understanding of expectations and duties. Accountability may be a sticky topic in many organizations. Making a commitment to accountability can be construed as cultivating a blame culture in the organization. When a breakdown occurs, it must be clear where the breakdown happened and how it will be corrected. After process roles have been communicated to the organization, the expectation of absolute follow-through should be made clear. The use of a score card or performance measurement report that tallies breakdowns in the process will help. Listing key metrics and recording achievements will give the organization the ability and (it is hoped) the motivation to ensure nonperformance issues do not occur or recur.

Documentation

Documentation must be as complete and up to date as possible at any given time. Processes should be carefully described and on file in a central location, ideally published on an intranet or accessible network directories. Documents that outline the step-by-step activities of all users (or class of users) should be created with screen-shot images (if possible). Doing this will facilitate troubleshooting (where breakdowns occur) and provide guidance for new users until they are trained. Having adequate documentation on hand also helps infrequent users. If the close occurs in the early part of the month, users may access the system briefly at that time, then not access it again until the next month. Knowledge retention may be a problem in circumstances where employee turnover is an issue. Knowledge retention issues are acute in organizations where new users are a constant or in the early stages of system/process development. Keeping the development team focused on developing systems and processes is critical in the latter case. Although the development team may be used to support the user community, guiding the general user community through learning curves for an extended period of time may put development initiatives at risk. It is imperative that companies keep up-to-date documentation on hand in all areas of the organization.

Common Data Standards

The term *common data standards* (CDS) refers to the need to establish a universal language within the company's finance organization. Establishing standard nomenclature and terminology for such items as units of measure, price lists, product types, entity structure, and chart of accounts will cut down on confusion in communicating results or processing information company-wide. While doing this may sound basic, if common data standards are not established, certain events in the company life cycle, such as acquisitive expansion, will present challenges for the organization.

Documenting a framework of standard terminology and units of measure will help minimize confusion as the organization grows, especially in the early years of the business. For example, if the organization measures orders in bundles, which may be measures of 12 components, and the business expands by absorbing another company, chances are the new organization may measure orders by individual components. Confusion may result when discussing backlog and bookings or, worse, valuing inventory and cost of sales. Taking an inventory of all relevant measures of data and unifying them in a single document of common data standards will minimize miscommunication and information processing errors throughout the business life cycle. Documenting official data standards is similar to compiling a policies and procedures manual. Even if this manual outlines *how* to conduct business, CDS will provide the *language* to do it. A policies and procedures manual and CDS will work hand-in-hand in serving as a platform for processes and reporting.

CDS will expand as the organization grows, and this should be expected. The following considerations must play a part in the development of CDS:

- *The CDS must be periodically reviewed.* This is necessary given that certain standards may become irrelevant, others may change, and new ones may arise. Keeping the review of CDS on management's radar as a standard maintenance procedure will ensure that the CDS does not become obsolete.
- *The CDS must fit the business.* The finance strategist must take stock of the products or services the business sells and understand how they are sold when developing/maintaining CDS. This is crucial, as these standards are referenced in reporting and define budget and forecasting needs.
- *The CDS must be compatible with information systems.* The CDS will serve as the foundation for the data flow process, defining the language and nomenclature in which data is defined. Careful consideration must be given to information systems or proposed systems when conceptualizing the CDS. Information systems will be sensitive to units defining data to be loaded and processed; therefore, definitions of compatible units and transaction measures is vital.

Exhibit 6.8 suggests a listing of Common Data Standards.

Some standards may evolve naturally in the organization or be implied as a function of operations. Price lists, cost price components, and terms of payment/delivery are examples of standards that evolve as a matter of doing business. Others do not develop naturally—hence they will take some effort to define. Examples of these are charts of accounts and transaction types. Whether dealing with data standards that already exist or those that need refinement (or development), documenting all standards and communicating them throughout the organization is necessary. The role of CDS may seem abstract to small, simple operations; however, investing the time and effort into documenting the nomenclature of operations will ensure seamless business combinations (acquisitions and divestitures)

Exhibit 6.8 **Sample Listing of Common Data Standards**

Common Data Standard	Description
Product (service) descriptions	This clearly identifies products and services the company offers. Variations and combinations of product/service mix are enumerated as well. In establishing a standard, company-wide profit and loss line items are more readily defined. This aids in defining *buckets* for revenue and expense recognition. This is an important standard for multiproduct and service organizations.
Languages	Defining official company languages is critical. The standard is cogent particularly when it comes time to produce documents for customers, suppliers, or employees in a global setting. This refers to both computer system language and conversational language.
Product and service prices	This standard allows for a scalable schedule of prices for standard products and services throughout the organization. It is particularly valuable in multiproduct and service organizations. This serves as a standard for sales force and data entry personnel.
Shipping	This standard defines the company's methodology by which product is to be shipped to customers. This standard aligns sales force, customers, and support organization to ensure no delays occur in the revenue cycle.
Units of measure	This defines the standard for product or service measurement. Establishing the official measures for certain products/services standardizes the communication of activity for P&L and balance sheet purposes. Standardization throughout the organization allows for greater uniformity for reporting, budgeting, and forecasting purposes.
Payment methods/terms	This standard addresses the terms extended to customers. In particular, it outlines the period within which invoices are to be paid and the amount of any accompanying discounts if they are paid early. This standard aligns sales force, customers, and support organization to ensure no delays occur in the revenue cycle.
Customer types	This standard defines classifications of customers to allow for proper data/transaction processing. This standard is useful for multiproduct and service organizations that deal with varying retail, wholesale, or international customers. Clearly defining customers in a transaction is crucial to facilitate information system logic for processing.
Supplier types	This standard defines classifications of suppliers to allow for proper data/transaction processing. This standard is useful in identifying payment and order terms quickly and accurately.
Chart of accounts	This defines the standard account nomenclature to be used in entering financial transactions into the company information systems.

and that unexpected spurts of growth and/or turnover in key positions do not hamper information processing and reporting.

Standard Chart of Accounts

The Standard Chart of Accounts (SCOA) will be the cornerstone of Common Data Standards. The CDS, as a practical matter, is not used by the entire organization. However, the SCOA underlies virtually all aspects of the finance function, particularly the data flow dynamic. Data customers review the results of operations compiled from source data originating in the SCOA format. The development and implementation of a SCOA is an all-or-nothing proposition. This concept can escape even the most seasoned finance executives and cause a host of global finance infrastructure breakdowns. It is worth reviewing the reasons why a comprehensive, relevant SCOA will serve the development of the finance function:

- *Need.* When discussing the need for a SCOA, it is necessary to understand what not having a SCOA will mean to the finance function, particularly the data flow process. Having a central repository of data will dictate a standard slate of account balances that define the official company trial balance. Data submissions with disparate charts of accounts will require manual input or conversion workarounds to get data into the central repository. Navigating these workarounds could slow the process and expose the organization to misstatement errors. Because acceptance by all system users is the foundation of an enterprise-wide process, buy-in from the global community is essential. Having local sites translate data from their account structure to that of the differing corporate structure every month may hamper buy-in. Additionally, it may create confusion and errors, at least, while at worst it may warrant rejection of the process and impair ownership of data by submitting sites. If the translation process is too burdensome, altering data at the headquarters site could impair the sense of ownership needed to foster accurate and timely data submissions.
- *Comprehensiveness.* The SCOA must be comprehensive enough to house all transactions the global or multiproduct/service organization encounters. While this sounds basic, certain countries may require particular accounts be kept for local statutory reporting. Keeping remote sites in compliance with their statutory reporting requirements is a priority and should factor into development plans for the SCOA. Surveying both the types of transactions the organization encounters and local statutory accounting requirements must be the focus of the strategist's research for this initiative. The development of a SCOA must be linked to the development of the policy and

procedures manual. The accounts that drive accounting methodologies (in the policy and procedures manual) will be defined in the SCOA.

- *Relevance.* The company's SCOA must be relevant to the business. Pet accounts inherited from acquisitions or left over from an earlier time in the company's development should be abandoned when it's certain they are not representative of the organization. This applies to accounting in foreign locations as well. The finance strategist, however, must be aware of certain accounts that either don't exist or must be maintained in different business and/or geographic settings. For example, the term *common stock* commonly used in the United States to classify equity, is not used in most Central European countries. The term "stock" in a European context often refers to what is called "inventory" in the United States and may be construed as such by foreign data customers. *Paid-in capital* may be a more suitable term for *common stock. Common stock* would be neither suitable nor relevant as an equity account for European users. If the company has significant balances in these line items, being clear on the definitions and when to use them is essential to avoid misstated financials. Another example of relevance in the SCOA is the use of FAS 109 (deferred taxes) accounts. Asking foreign controllers to populate these may be futile, as the complex framework making up this concept is specific to U.S. GAAP only.

Regardless of company size, the focus on how the account structure suits local and headquarters' reporting needs is critical to ensure all needs are met without creating a large, unmanageable listing of accounts. The SCOA may be as simple as 20 to 30 lines or as long as 2,500 to 3,000 lines. It must serve as the basis by which information systems are built and become the basic language of data input efforts. The finance strategist must take into account the operations in all corners of the organization when conceptualizing a SCOA. Every possible account, addressing every possible event or transaction, must be considered when conceptualizing an account structure. One size does not fit all when it comes to a SCOA, so flexibility in design is critical.

A SCOA that fits the business will do more than enable the data flow process. It will establish a powerful platform for the finance function to expand and integrate components of infrastructure. The finance strategy will, over time, dictate the upgrade or implementation of various hardware and software components to facilitate a certain business purpose. Employing infrastructure tools, however, will mean nothing if they are not defined with the same component definitions. For example, employing an ERP to gather data at the lowest levels of the organization and linking it to a powerful consolidation and reporting tool to facilitate reporting will be meaningless if the two are defined with different charts of accounts. A smooth data flow from the ERP to the consolidation/reporting tool may be hampered by data that is cataloged in different ways. Can mapping files be created to accommodate these differences? While this may be a solution, how are the mapping files defined? Are they accurate? How often are they maintained? Establishing a comprehensive SCOA and mandating its use throughout the organization will eliminate issues with infrastructure and process integration and the need to create workarounds. It also will pave the way for allowing the data flow process to develop along with infrastructure.

DEVELOPMENT WITH THE REST OF INFRASTRUCTURE

Chapter 4, "Multilevel Approach," explains how strategizing is an ongoing process based on a living model that outlines concrete and soft components of infrastructure. The considerations that characterize these components will change as the business evolves. Because the data flow process represents such a fundamental aspect of the finance function, its evolution must be kept in check. Is the data flow process serving the organization's needs? If it is not, has it *ever* served the purpose? If this is the case, what changed? Knowing when to alter or upgrade the data flow process and when to leave it intact will provide a sense of stability not only to the finance function but to the strategizing process. What drives changes? The small and emerging business must understand what aspects of the finance function will impact the data flow process—both soft and concrete components—as well as what it will take to make changes and what they will mean to the rest of the strategy.

Concrete and Soft Components Impacting Data Flow Processes

A discussion on the development of data flow processes must include the impact that development and maintenance will have on the rest of the finance function, and vice versa. An effective data flow process will achieve a state of equilibrium or balance with finance infrastructure (concrete components) and leverage its component parts. The reverse is also true—infrastructure will drive the quality of the data flow process. Two important aspects of infrastructure that impact the data flow process are the finance organization and information systems:

1. *Finance organization.*   The finance strategy must dictate the complexion of the finance organization. This includes the quality and characteristics of finance employees and the technology tools they employ. Depending on where the company is in its life cycle, the finance strategy will have to identify and serve the data needs of the organization by, among other things, determining the level of expertise of finance employees. Their level of expertise and skill set will dictate their ability to multitask and troubleshoot effectively. The general skill set, however, must evolve with the business *and* the finance function. In the early years

of development, the focus may be on simply translating the external environment into data quickly and effectively (data gathering). At this stage, the business may need classically trained accountants. The business, however, will evolve, and the finance function may be looked to for innovative and effective analysis, which may require more finance- or business-oriented employees who can focus on creating business solutions for the organization. What does this mean for the data flow process? The process must be suited for the employees who ultimately make it work. If finance employees are strictly accounting oriented, then they are suited for active participation and troubleshooting in the data gathering and processing phases of the data flow process. The analysis aspect of the data flow process may have to be automated or considered a work-in-process until this employee profile changes. If the finance organization is made up of nonaccounting employees, then the data flow process must be heavily automated on the gathering and processing side and interactive on the analysis side.

Technology tools also must be suited for the data flow process. How much automation is needed to troubleshoot and monitor the data flow process? Are desktop machines powerful enough to buoy the data flow process? Are laptops more appropriate for process participants? If so, are they powerful enough? Recognizing the need for technology and having the willingness to invest in it will ensure that the data flow process will not be hindered by the inability of participants to do their job.

2. *Information systems and the IS organization.*   The core of the data flow process will be the network and software technology (systems) that drive it. This is outlined in more detail in Chapter 7, "Investigating Information Systems." However, it is worth discussing a few key points as they relate to the data flow process.

The mind-set in developing a data flow process should center on the integration of process steps and technology that fit the organization and achieve the desired ends. The finance strategist must not rely on processes alone to achieve this end or depend on systems alone to perform this function. The term *information systems* may refer to a single, out-of-the-box package or a customized mosaic of applications and programs. Regardless of the structure, IS refers to hardware and software that make all applications in the finance function work. The best results will be achieved with carefully crafted processes that maximize the functionality of systems and technology. Weak or incomplete processes will render the most well-thought-out and advanced systems useless. Additionally, well-thought-out processes fall below their potential with inadequate or inappropriate systems technology. Neither processes nor technology should be conceptualized and developed exclusive of each other.

A key factor that colors the effectiveness of the data flow process and the finance function is the definition of roles for maintaining IS and technology. Whether the database administrator is part of the finance organization or not, someone who can resolve maintenance issues effectively must be available to maintain the system. The data flow process should be a sliding scale of process and technology. The more technology-heavy it is, the more exposed it will be to maintenance issues. How the finance strategy defines knowledge transfer regarding systems is key. Ideally, users should be as self-sufficient as possible in managing the process as well as trouble-shooting systems issues. The complexity of software applications and technology dictates reliance on database administrators for help when it is needed. The narrow window of time involved in a close may yield more issues than a single database administrator can handle. Having experienced *power users* spread evenly throughout the organization can lessen the impact of errors or breakdowns in systems technology. Conceptualizing a power user certification process is especially useful in organizations with active users in disparate time zones, such as the East Coast of the United States and the Far East.

What role will soft components of the finance function play in the data flow process? Although the role may be difficult to define for the small and emerging business, the data flow process dictates the company's ability to populate complex analysis models and evaluation metrics with data. What type of detail must be gathered for cash flow models or return on equity models to be effective? How timely must data be for these models to remain relevant? These issues define key aspects of the data flow process and must be addressed before the process is considered adequate.

What Is Needed to Change the Data Flow Process?

Many organizations employ a data flow process, whether effective or not. One of the goals of the finance strategy and the multilevel approach is to continually assess the effectiveness of the data flow process and, where possible, employ upgrades/improvements. Employing upgrades may seem routine and innocuous, but just what does it mean? Changing the process may mean upgrading or altering key templates that local sites use to submit data. It also may mean reconfiguring key technological interfaces that enable connectivity and functionality for remote users. Will changes like these require a level of coaching or education for process participants? How will the knowledge be transferred? What will happen if changes are made and no knowledge or guidance is provided? Changes may look good on paper, but in practice they may create more problems than solutions. This does not mean forsaking process upgrades, but the finance strategist must note that any changes in the process must be carefully thought through and evaluated to avoid potential business disruptions. Adhering to simple rules, such as not employing a process change during a quarter close, at year-end, or during a critical business milestone event, will ensure that changes are made without degrading the end product. Will process changes require input and assistance from nonfinance people? Identifying and securing resource needs before they are required will ensure that process changes are executed quickly and effectively.

Impact of Changes on the Finance Strategy

Often components of the finance function evolve and change concurrently. This may be good for the overall finance strategy, but it may create challenges in keeping all aspects of the finance strategy in sync. Counting on the data flow process to mature to a level of functionality may be the premise behind the development of certain soft components of the finance function. What would a delay or shortcoming in process development do to the soft components? Will it render them useless or partially impaired? Certain process upgrades may enable other aspects of the finance function to be upgraded. Does the finance strategy allow for necessary upgrades? How will an enhanced data flow process contribute to the development of the rest of the finance function? The finance strategist must maintain a high-level view of the finance strategy and understand how the data flow process will change current aspects of strategy and create new areas of development and consideration.

FINAL THOUGHTS

Strategizing the finance function involves identifying company data needs and positioning the company to serve them. Attention to concrete and soft components of infrastructure will predominate for small and emerging business owners as they attempt to establish elements of the finance function, in some cases for the first time. The data flow process lies at the heart of the finance function and will endure, whether it is suitable for organization needs or not. Mobilizing company resources to enhance an existing data flow process or establish a new one is the challenge of the finance strategist. Information systems will be the most critical and difficult to harness of all the finance components that impact the data flow process.

NOTES

1. Eric Krell, "Upfront," *Business Finance,* September 2000, p. 14.
2. AnswerThink Consulting Group, 1001 Brickell Bay Drive, Ste 3000, Miami, FL 33131.
3. The Gartner Group, 56 Top Gallant Rd., P.O. Box 10212, Stamford, CT 06904.

7

INVESTIGATING
INFORMATION SYSTEMS

KEY TAKEAWAYS

- Knowing what defines Information Systems (IS) in the context of the finance function.
- Knowing how IS considerations fit into the multilevel approach to strategizing.
- Realizing the value in maintaining a company-wide view in conceptualizing, implementing, and maintaining IS components.
- Understanding the need to analyze data customers and their needs when designing IS.
- Understanding how processes will impact IS.
- Knowing the value and need for up-front and ongoing planning when it comes to IS.
- Understanding the organization's capacity to implement and maintain IS.
- Understanding key concepts in choosing appropriate applications.
- Realizing the value in developing good documentation.
- Understanding key considerations in implementing IS components.
- Knowing how to conceptualize maintenance and support programs.

INFORMATION SYSTEMS CONSIDERATIONS
IN THE MULTILEVEL APPROACH

Defining Information Systems

The term *Information Systems* (IS) can imply many things and invoke dialogue from the technical and complex to the theoretical and esoteric. Throughout the strategizing effort, the small and emerging business owner must investigate both aspects of this broad topic. As outlined in Chapter 2, "Finance Function Defined," information systems refers to the backbone technology—servers, switches, operating systems, protocols, and software applications—that serves the finance function.

Issues related to the appropriateness, suitability, and scalability of IS must be dealt with before the technical aspects of platforms, interfaces, and peripherals are considered. In this discussion IS focuses on the former, particularly the need to understand the conceptualization, implementation, and maintenance of IS in the context of strategizing a relevant finance function that will endure.

Working Information Systems into the Multilevel Model

Chapter 4, "Multilevel Approach," discusses how considerations related to IS fit into Tier 3 of the multilevel approach to strategizing the finance function. The objective of Tier 3 is to help define the role of technology in the finance function and utilize the skill set of employees. Maximizing the subjective role of personnel (making decisions and drawing conclusions) while minimizing their role in non–value-added tasks (data gathering and processing) are the goals of well-thought-out IS. However, strategizing IS means more than automating low-level tasks. Designing reliable and scalable systems that are easily maintained will be paramount as the finance strategy unfolds.

Appropriate IS cannot be conceptualized without fully grasping certain Tier 2 considerations. Are internal data customers more focused on historical reporting or prospective reporting? If the emphasis is on prospective reporting, what level of complexity is involved—is it budgeting, forecasting, or advanced business modeling? How usable will the system be for these data customers? Can a novice create reports and extract specific financial and/or nonfinancial data, or will the services of a technical expert be needed? Small and emerging business owners may be focused exclusively on internal analysis needs for growing the business and/or specific external needs that are statutory in nature (e.g., tax filings, SEC filings). Infrastructure development must be suited for these current needs and be positioned to meet customer data/reporting needs as the business grows.

Knowing that the environment of data customers will change and the needs of current data customers will shift, the strategist must carefully identify the Tier 1 considerations that relate to the business life cycle. Knowing that the business will be transformed into a multiproduct, international enterprise with complex public and tax filings versus remaining a closely held family enterprise will dictate the planning for IS development. Anticipating data customers and their needs over the short, mid-, and long term will enable a logical progression of IS development. Does spending $200,000 on a reporting package today make sense if the company will outgrow it within the year? Would investing $300,000 be more appropriate now if it will serve the company's purpose over a greater time horizon? Reviewing Tier 1 and Tier 2 considerations will give the finance strategist a fair assessment of the future and enable positioning finance function development for potentially complex, lengthy IS implementations.

Reviewing Overall Business Needs

Surveying the company's current and future needs is key to understanding IS that will be most appropriate for the organization. It may be necessary to go beyond the current infrastructure and explore the culture of the company to seek out appropriate IS design. The following case exemplifies the need to match up IS with company needs:

Stephens Machinery manufactures microwave components for wireless and broadband applications. Its products include modulators, demodulators, couplers, power splitters, and other devices for high-tech applications. The company was founded by Ron Stephens, who had been a longtime employee of a company that survived on government contracts for manufacturing these electronic components. Ron recognized a market niche in producing these electronic components in odd or custom lots. He acquired the rights to produce the components from his former contractor-employer and has built his business into a $10 million-per-year operation. Although it is not a public company and does not have the pressure of complex, periodic filings, the business is in a constant state of change as products are added, dropped, or reconstituted to fit short-lived markets and customers. Because of the shifting nature of its business and the detail of data it must gather and classify, Stephens Machinery is constantly rebuilding its finance database and restating its historical data figures to keep up with its changing business. It currently employs a consolidation and reporting tool, which serves as its primary repository of data and suits its finance staff with its user-friendly reporting capabilities. Although the consolidation and reporting tool is an advantage, the periodic rebuilds are extremely painful. They are time consuming and demand lengthy periods of downtime as the data is reshuffled. Often misstatements result; however, the organization accepts this margin of error as a part of doing business. The company employs a light enterprise resource planning package that is good at gathering data but is not well suited to reporting. The data is loaded into the consolidation and reporting package monthly to facilitate the simple historical reporting and light budgeting that the company relies on for decision making. Stephens Machinery has a slim finance staff and an even slimmer IS team. Ron knows that analysis of the business will have to improve as it grows. These difficult decisions, however, center on which area to enhance, finance or IS. Ron and his management team know they will need to upgrade finance systems as they anticipate making acquisitions and expanding the slate of products produced. Although there is a general awareness that the finance and IS areas must be upgraded, the organization has grown comfortable with the current tools in place and opts to forgo the painful task of overhauling the as-is and instead settle for what is in place now.

Although Stephens Machinery's entire finance function is in need of a comprehensive strategy, its IS are worth examining. The company relies on its consolidation tool to do most of its data storage and reporting. While its current needs are being met, it is fair to assume that the company will experience some growth in the next few years. Keeping systems in line with data needs will be a challenge for owners and those strategizing the finance function. These issues must be addressed:

- *Flexibility.* Relying on a single consolidation and reporting tool has its advantages for Stephens Machinery's finance team—simplicity and ease of maintenance. However, its simplicity seems to betray the finance team when it comes to reconfiguring the data. This arduous exercise is accepted as standard fare when it comes to maintaining the system. The finance organization, however, must realize that these maintenance exercises are disruptive and non–value added. The irony is that as soon as the data is reconfigured, changes in the business render the application obsolete. The infrequent windows of time to rebuild the application often leave the organization with an inadequate repository of data for extended time periods. The organization needs to pursue an application that is flexible enough to accommodate changes in the business quickly and painlessly but high-powered enough to accommodate prospective analysis capabilities.
- *Enabling growth.* The current application is well suited for reporting on historical data; however, the organization will have a need to engage in stronger *prospective* reporting. The company currently is doing limited budgeting and forecasting, but it also must create what-if models for the business based on the myriad of custom or odd jobs it receives from its governmental contracts. Having the capacity to reclassify historical data and project performance based on these reconfigurations will be a powerful tool for Stephens Machinery. Investigating tools that enable this kind of data management, particularly On-line Analytical Processing (OLAP) technology, will be necessary for the firm to ensure the accuracy of restated historical data in the event of a reorganization. The first step for the company is to understand the shortcomings of the current, rigid data repository it employs and focus on the capability of more advanced tools.
- *Stability of platforms.* Upgrades to finance applications will be important for the company to move forward in its business life cycle. Upgrading means installing new applications and necessary peripherals on solid network foundations with adequate connectivity. Although management at Stephens Machinery may realize that the application it currently employs is inadequate, it may not have the systems platform to install something more powerful. Are servers adequate to house and run new applications? What about connectivity? Can users access the core application site cleanly and enjoy

its full functionality? The firm's reluctance to upgrade to something more advanced may be rooted in weak network platforms. What capacity for storage and speed will serve the organization now and in the future?

■ *Installing/maintaining.* Stephens Machinery must consider who will install and maintain the complex network components and software applications before moving forward with system and application upgrades defined by a finance strategy. The current finance and IS teams are not equipped to overhaul company-wide network configurations. Additionally, the current capacity to maintain and support the completed structure is also suspect. Will the organization rely on consultants and temps to install complex network upgrades and software applications? What will this cost? How will knowledge be transferred to in-house staff? Who will maintain network upgrades and applications? The organization will have to invest not only in increased headcount in the IS support area but also in education and training for current employees. Aborting installations or living with substandard support will limit the return on an IS investment and leave the community of data users frustrated. Lacking a full understanding of what is involved with system and application upgrades may create more problems than those encountered with the limited systems currently in place.

Ron Stephens will have a number of issues to address as he moves forward with a finance strategy. He may employ a finance strategist to handle them or take the entire endeavor on himself. Regardless of the approach, the company will be faced with matters related to processes, hardware, and software as well as decisions on who will design, install, and maintain it all. Bankrolling the project also must be dealt with. Systems requirements will be of particular interest to the strategist as they may require a significant commitment of financial resources, something the company will need to start budgeting for *now*. It is important to avoid distractions in this area and keep all IS decisions in the context of the company's needs and the finance strategy. The challenge will be to avoid getting bogged down in the many options that are available in the systems world. The objective in strategizing, particularly as it relates to IS, is to maintain a high level vision of the business and its needs.

MAINTAINING THE HIGH-LEVEL VISION FOR STRATEGIZING

Reasons to Maintain a High-Level View

Developing information system components, whether they are network, application, or hardware related, can be an arduous task. High price tags for equipment and expertise as well as long time horizons for subtle return on investments (ROIs) place a substantial burden on the strategist to ensure that IS are appropriate for companies now and in the future. Understanding data needs and conceptualizing the tools that will accommodate them requires focusing on the *total picture* when it comes to understanding the business. Keeping this high-level view of the business will allow for:

- *Minimizing rework.* Many organizations consider the IS world an insatiable abyss siphoning off the company's financial and human resources. Certain systems components and applications undoubtedly will require ongoing maintenance; however, *overhauling* obsolete or inadequate system elements is clearly a non–value-added task. The reason for such activity is often a pattern of shortsighted systems decisions. Lacking a holistic, company-wide view when it comes to planning produces such decisions. Failing to recognize that an application that serves company needs now will be inadequate in 12 months sets the company up for an expensive repurchase (of a new application), a costly reinstallation, and paralyzing downtime. Maintaining a bird's eye view of the business, though not fool-proof, will help the organization minimize systems rework. The challenge for Ron Stephens at Stephens Machinery is to project the company's foreseeable data needs as far into the future as possible when conceptualizing finance applications. He will want to avoid outgrowing anything that is put in place for at least the next two to three years.

- *Signaling when to upgrade.* A high-level, company-wide view of the business and its needs will allow the organization to adequately assess when systems components are ready to be replaced or upgraded. Moving too quickly or waiting too long to replace or upgrade certain systems components means degrading the return on the company's investment and the finance function's ability to serve its data customers. Stephens Machinery's finance systems fall into the latter category. Getting the most out of what is in place is one thing, but letting outdated systems dictate the capability to gather, process, and analyze data is another. While the high-level view means understanding the business from a functional standpoint, it also means seeing the time perspectives. Maintaining a high-level view of the organization will enable managers/owners to recognize the most appropriate time to act on potentially expensive system changes.

- *Clearly defining needs.* Management/owners must have an unbiased view of organization needs. When it comes to systems and data needs, often the squeakiest wheel is addressed. This may not be the most appropriate way to manage systems needs, however. Ensuring that the maximum benefit is derived from needed expenditures requires a judicious assessment of everyone's needs. Where possible, the finance strategist must seek commonality in purpose with systems implementations. Spending limited company resources on a high-priced luxury tool for one area of the business will not help the organization when another crucial area lacks the basic necessities. Looking past or penetrating the tunnel vision that characterizes certain parts of the organization will allow the finance strategist to address everyone's needs. The small and emerging business may not have to struggle with this challenge as much as larger companies. Companies like Stephens Machinery are centralized enough that most company decisions and data needs are focused on a central group of individuals.

■ *Ensuring systems fit the organization.* Overall appropriateness for the organization must be the goal of the finance strategist when conceptualizing systems needs. If the entire organization is only as good as its weakest link, the finance strategy must be prepared to identify where the weak links are. Shortcomings in the organization may be characterized by areas having weak leadership or overwhelming task requirements. Regardless, strong systems will benefit the entire organization, not just the "important parts." Knowing this will lead to a comprehensive understanding of the business and its component parts.

Dependencies in Maintaining a High-Level View

What will impact the finance strategy author's high-level view of the organization? The level of knowledge and experience in the management ranks will impact the high-level view of the finance strategist. Management that neither appreciates the need for a clear understanding of the company and company objectives nor facilitates this understanding among finance strategists will derail development of a strong long-term strategy. Rejecting a strong administrative function also will impede its development. This is often the case with shortsighted, now-oriented decision makers. Organizations that become focused on eliminating back-office functions as opposed to leveraging them will foster shortsightedness or, worse, shortcircuit an otherwise strong finance strategy altogether. A rapidly shifting business environment can impede a high-level view as well. The proliferation of changing business needs can distract the organization from its finance needs. This may lead to a myopic approach to managing tasks or the reluctance to invite the finance strategist to understand the overall business strategy. Stephens Machinery must implement a full-blown finance strategy, the most visible manifestation of which is the design and implementation of appropriate systems. To be successful, Ron Stephens will have to play a significant, high-profile role in the development of the entire strategy, particularly the systems configuration. Whether Ron himself develops it or hires someone to do it, he must be behind the entire project and its individual components. He will have to recognize that investments in time and money may not yield immediate or measurable benefits. His patience and commitment will be an important key to success.

Impact on Creating Strategy

The most important benefit of maintaining a high-level view of the organization when strategizing the finance function involves synchronizing all tiers of the multilevel approach. This is perhaps most important when conceptualizing IS. Understanding where the company is in its business life cycle (Tier 1 considerations) will reveal the data customers to be encountered. Understanding data customers and their needs (Tier 2 considerations) will enable customized infrastructure to be put in place. Making decisions on matters of infrastructure (Tier 3 considerations), particularly systems needs, will then seem less taxing. Additionally, linking upper-tier considerations, particularly analysis models and metrics, to the capacity of systems and applications to deliver timely and accurate data is dependent on maintaining a high-level, company-wide view of operations. This synchronization will allow the finance strategist to plan for appropriate systems and applications when they are needed, which will optimize spending and time dedicated to development and implementation.

Developing this understanding will take time for Ron Stephens. Depending on the urgency and need for data and enhanced decision making, Ron will have to reevaluate Stephens Machinery, identifying all pending business life-cycle milestones, defining data customers, and enumerating analysis models/metrics. As the company is small, this task is easier in the near future; however, it is clear that the business will change soon and begin to grow (presumably) at an accelerated rate. Ron Stephens must begin his multitier examination of Stephens Machinery before the accelerated growth begins.

Impact on Implementing Strategy

Having a high-level perspective of the organization will be critical as the finance strategy is implemented as well. This high-level view will be extremely important as processes are developed in concert with IS. Because processes are comprehensive by nature and extend throughout the organization, their design and implementation require a thorough knowledge of the business. IS are intricately woven into processes, as processes are designed to serve and/or leverage applications and the network platforms that support them. Keeping perspectives high will ensure that all aspects of the business are served by this infrastructure tandem.

The greatest benefit of a high-level view of the business is realized when unexpected roadblocks are encountered during strategizing or strategy implementation. It is certain that challenges will be encountered that will threaten the plan components and alter strategy design. Quick solutions may offer short-term relief but create more imposing long-term issues. Although it is tempting to opt for the quick solution, resisting an easy quick fix that may derail the entire effort and sticking to prescribed solutions or selecting a comprehensive solution that serves the overall effort will serve the finance strategist best. Avoiding a shortsighted approach to handling challenges will make those imposing game day decisions much easier to navigate.

Impact on Maintaining Strategy

The finance strategist also will have to consider enhancements and adjustments to the system as time passes. This will be particularly relevant as Tier 3 systems considerations are addressed. Will a modular approach be the preference, where bolt-ons and add-ons are the methodology for growth? Will the preferred method of maturation be the evolution to and through various applications altogether? Ultimately IS will involve a dizzying array of server, network, and application technology that will require a well-thought-out progression. Maintaining a high-level view of the organization from a functional and time standpoint will enable the finance strategy to lay core foundations of network technology that will enable applications to evolve over an extended period of time. Awareness of solutions that have long-term merit and the financial trade-offs that accompany them will pay dividends for the finance strategist and the organization.

INITIAL CONSIDERATIONS

Reviewing Information Systems

Moving forward with a finance strategy and putting it in motion will mean understanding all potential roadblocks and how to overcome them. Because so many aspects of the strategy are interrelated, changing direction in any area of the plan will have a ripple effect throughout. While some changes will be inevitable due to shifting business circumstances or adjustments to the strategy team, they must be minimized and carefully controlled. Nowhere is this more relevant than with the system aspect of the finance strategy. Laying out the blueprint for system design—defining the specifications of applications and defining the network platforms on which they are supported—must be carefully and thoroughly executed. Changing a specification or element of functionality may mean significant revisions to the application layout or the network design. The worst-case scenario would involve a change in user requirements or specifications that renders an application or network component useless—an expensive realization.

Building information systems can be expensive, both in time and money. This is especially true in the absence of good planning and design. Costs in initial outlays for hardware, software, and consulting can be eclipsed by rework and additional outlays for system components not originally considered. To avoid downtime, roll-out delays, and expensive rework it is worth reviewing a few initial considerations before moving forward with design and implementation.

The most important of these involves reviewing data customers and the processes interwoven with systems components. The finance strategist also must review the current systems structure and assess the ability to roll-out and maintain system components.

Tier 2: Reviewing Data Customers

The finance strategist must plan key financial applications to meet the needs of data customers. This means understanding the output on which they will depend as well as their capacity to use the system. Being customer-centric when conceptualizing and designing an information system is crucial not only in the initial stages of design but throughout implementation and maintenance. Chapter 5, "Analyzing Data Customers," presented a number of detailed classifications of data customer types and characteristics. It is worthwhile to review the following data customer characteristics and how they impact systems design:

- *Internal versus external data customers.* For whom is the system created? Internal and external data customers both have an interest in the financial data generated by the finance function. The question to ask is: Who has more to lose if the system is not up to the task of translating data to knowledge? In many cases the external user community will be the ultimate consumer of the financial data generated by the IS. Statutory filings with tax authorities, the SEC, and financial institutions are examples of documents compiled from data accumulated by systems and supporting applications. As a practical matter, internal data customers (management and owners) will be impacted on a day-to-day basis to a greater extent. Business decisions from fixed asset acquisitions to bonus computations to product line expansion/disposal will depend on the knowledge generated by IS. Internal data customers will not only rely on the systems for data to do their jobs but they will, to a certain extent, *own* the systems and the processes that enable them. Reliance will beget accountability as users see that good decisions can come only from good data, which is yielded from suitable systems.
- *Sophisticated versus unsophisticated data customers.* Gauging the sophistication of data customers will factor prominently in systems design. Internal data customers/users may be sophisticated, unsophisticated, or both. The implication is the potential for knowledge transfer of administrative and maintenance tasks to the user community. Giving the user community the knowledge and confidence to troubleshoot systems and applications will make for a more satisfied user community. The less users are dependent on administrators, the more quality time and usage they will receive from systems. Sophisticated users may better understand the gravity of making changes to the system in midstream, hence they may appreciate the planning process more than unsophisticated users. Conversely, sophisticated users may demand cutting-edge applications and performance regardless of the practicality of implementing such tools. Unsophisticated data customers/users

will no doubt accept the systems conceptualized and delivered from the outset. Unfortunately, they may not have a clear vision of their needs and therefore deprive the development stage of crucial input. They may initiate system change requests after the system is in place, when making changes/ enhancements may be impractical. External audiences may be sophisticated or unsophisticated regarding matters of reporting only. Although they may not be a part of system development, their need for complete and timely information should be understood.

■ *Financial versus nonfinancial data customers.* The finance strategist who designs systems must understand the need for nonfinancial data customers to use the system. Issues of accessibility and ease of use will be paramount. The development of processes that gather nonfinancial data will play a pivotal role in this regard. Because data gathering efforts and interfaces focus mostly on financial users, IS will be inherently suited for the finance team. However, this platform of data flow should extend to the nonfinancial world where practicable, whether it is human resources, product line managers, geographic division managers, marketing people, or production personnel.

Tier 3: Understanding Processes

Developing a finance strategy will not be a linear exercise. Nowhere is this more relevant than in the development of systems and processes. Chapter 6, "Data Flow Process," discusses in greater detail the dynamics of data flow processes and their role in the finance function. Specifications and capability limits of IS will directly affect the data flow process. Highly specialized, powerful IS may require a minimal process to buoy it. Weak or limited IS, however, may require comprehensive, invasive processes to enable their effectiveness. The finance strategist must have a firm grasp on this sliding scale and be clear on the limitations of certain systems configurations versus others. This dynamic will define, among other things, spending thresholds for the finance strategist. Can expensive extras and accessories be left off the development plan and instead be addressed by the process? Understanding the interrelationship between IS complexity and process design in a particular finance function will be critical to strategy development, especially as it relates to other dependencies and aspects of the strategy.

The interrelationship between processes and IS may be dictated by factors that go beyond systems sophistication. The environment in which the company does business will define to some extent the data flow process requirements and the limitation of systems. Global organizations are particularly in need of well-thought-out processes. Rather than basing the systems planning process arbitrarily on systems technology or the data flow process, the business environment may demand that a comprehensive data flow process be developed that factors in geographic distances, local reporting requirements, and personnel limitations. Issues related to language, knowledge of statutory filings, and local culture may demand that less sophisticated users drive the data flow process locally. This will mean the development of a strong process that may or may not limit the choices for systems development. Matters of varying country infrastructure will impact systems development as well. Connectivity may be less reliable in less-developed nations than in more advanced ones. With this in mind, strategists must consider whether investing in powerful finance applications would make sense. If remote locations cannot utilize certain functionality because of inherent infrastructure limitations, investing large sums of money in powerful tools may not be the solution.

Staffing Needs

One of the most important assessments the finance strategist will have to make is who will follow through with system installations and maintenance. Ideally the organization will want to keep this function in-house; however, certain issues may demand the input of specialized knowledge sources. Will the organization seek outside consultants to guide it through the thorny process of systems design and implementation? If so, how will it secure adequate knowledge transfer of system nuances to internal personnel? Should the organization simply hire knowledgeable professionals from the outset and have them design, implement, and maintain the system components? There is no best answer to these questions; however, the small and emerging business owner may not have the luxury of either purchasing expensive systems components or hiring the professionals to manage them. What alternatives are there?

The concept of renting systems capability from outsiders must be investigated and understood. This approach to systems implementation and design is embodied in the application service provider (ASP) model. The explosion of Internet technology has enabled this business model to flourish. The model is based on software companies hosting finance applications on their own local servers. These hosts attend to implementations, upgrades, operations issues, maintenance, and application disposals. Customers subscribe to these hosting services and simply maintain Internet connectivity for their employees to access the applications and enjoy their functionality. The core concept is that *renting* is better than *owning*. This model works for small and emerging businesses that are short on time and money when it comes to implementing their business model. Advantages to the ASP model include:

- No need to burden the company with expensive installation routines
- No need to maintain a resident IS expert to maintain applications and peripherals
- Upgrades to applications are relatively seamless and timely
- Maintenance often is included in the agreement
- Backups and disaster recovery are assured

The down side to ASPs is that the company has little control over the applications themselves. If customization is needed to ensure that systems meet data customer needs, host companies may be (for a myriad of business reasons) reluctant to alter their slate of offerings and comply. Other disadvantages include:

- Internet access and connectivity must be adequate to ensure full usability of the applications
- Long-term contractual commitment may be required
- The company is not in control of its own data
- Customizations are not an option
- The agreement may involve applications that are underused or not needed
- If the ASP goes out of business, the company may be left with significant service downtime

The finance strategist must examine the ASP model thoroughly to determine if it is appropriate for the company. Although there are trade-offs, the model has benefits, especially for the small company that needs to have a quick up period. Getting past these initial strategy considerations (particularly the role of processes and the understanding of data customers) as they relate to systems development leads to developing a comprehensive project plan.

PLANNING

Why Plan?

The disposition of IS, whether they involve network, hardware, or software components, requires significant preparation and planning. Upgrading or installing system components, whether it is within the context of a finance strategy or not, will have many key dependencies and considerations. Whenever a complex systems project is taken on, competent, proven professionals must be sought out to help in the planning and implementation. This is imperative when such projects involve intricate knowledge of technical specifications and specialized concepts and theories related to networks, systems, and the like. Although small and emerging business owners may have built their businesses with a strong do-it-yourself attitude, the systems aspect of business development works best when qualified professionals are involved.

Strategizing the finance function involves conceptualizing and planning the role of IS, a step the strategist must fully engage in, long before equipment purchases, consulting contracts, and time-consuming implementations begin. Conceptualizing the layout and design of systems will require choosing a particular philosophy of design and maintenance and understanding the impact of the general approach and philosophy chosen. Depending on where the organization is in developing a finance function, this process can be seen as either a subset of strategizing or a part of the finance strategy itself. Regardless of the motivation and form, this planning process must consider the general philosophy of decentralization versus centralization, the suitability of the organization to implement and maintain applications, and the capacity to develop relevant documentation.

Centralized versus Decentralized Designs

Early in the planning/strategizing process the finance strategist must determine to what degree applications and processes will be centralized. Determining whether the IS and finance function will be centralized or decentralized often is rooted in the management style of owners or culture of the business. Dictating uniformity in processes, as well as application and system components, embodies centralization. Centralization also may prescribe the location of all core hardware and software applications in one designated site company-wide. The true characteristic of centralization is the use of uniform, prescribed processes throughout the organization. Decentralization in its purest form is the opposite of centralization, especially as it relates to location and specifications of core applications and network tools. It is also characterized by the propagation of nonstandard processes made up of tasks that are conceptualized and implemented by the various components of the organization.

In reality, no finance function is totally centralized or decentralized. Processes and systems, in practice, fall somewhere on the continuum that bridges these two polar concepts. The finance function usually is *more* centralized or decentralized; hence the terms refer to the general philosophical approach to finance. Centralization in some cases is a more rigid approach to managing the finance function. Centralization travels with words such as *accountability, discipline,* and *structure.* Nevertheless, decentralized approaches can include all these things as well. Key factors in applying centralized and decentralized approaches to the finance function are often related to the geographical and cultural scope of the business. Small or domestic organizations often are more suited to centralized infrastructure. Commonality in time zones, issues faced, and competence level of process participants makes centralization more palatable to the organization. Multinational organizations face challenges related to statutory reporting rules and availability of qualified finance staff. Limited infrastructure may be a challenge in some countries. Challenges like these may require varying approaches to data flow and systems issues. As a result, the finance function for multinational companies ends up with a core, centralized component and peripherals that are decentralized.

Advantages of one philosophy over the other are circumstantial. Centralization implies uniformity, which makes troubleshooting easy and minimizes the impact of turnover. Decentralization, however, implies flexibility and the capability to overcome challenges in unique ways. Centralization often leads to rigidity and the inability to accommodate unique circumstances or presents solutions that create more challenges than they solve. If planned poorly or applied inappropriately, centralization can result in unnecessary hierarchy and bureaucratic hurdles. Decentralization may enable the development of processes or systems that are counter to the overall objectives of the finance function. Allowing the loose development of finance function components may enable blatant inefficiencies to infiltrate the finance dynamic and degrade the function as a whole. Centralization and decentralization can and often do exist simultaneously. Regardless of the approach, accountability and results-oriented management still can be preserved.

Discussing the concept of centralization and decentralization is particularly germane when defining the organization's IS configuration. Systems and processes will serve as the backbone for the functionality of the finance function. Beyond understanding the difference in philosophies, the issue of centralization and decentralization will manifest itself in these key areas:

- *Maintenance and management.* Centralized systems and applications are often the norm with small and emerging businesses. In the case of multinational or geographically spread out organizations with users in remote locations, centralization presents challenges as well as advantages. Maintaining system components in one secured location will allow for the concentration of expertise in the application location site and make changes and updates simple and quick. Decentralized systems design requires a degree of application administration to occur locally, something for which small local sites may not be suited. Changes and updates often can be incorporated incorrectly or untimely. In the case of a worldwide user community, the application may be accessed 24 hours a day, seven days a week, which may make downtimes for maintenance or other reasons detrimental to the user community, a drawback to centralization. Server space and hardware costs will play a role in utilizing a centralized versus decentralized system. Having one application in a central site is cheaper to care for than multiple, remote applications. License issues and hardware expenditures also will factor into the design solutions.

- *User community/data customers.* Knowing how many users and where they will be located is key when determining whether the finance function will be centralized or decentralized. A large number of remote users may dictate maintaining regional applications or data sites. Such a quasi-centralized configuration requires that regional administrators or knowledge champions exist to enable troubleshooting and general application maintenance. This configuration will enable process users who are in various time zones or geographic locations to avail themselves of maintenance programs that are timely and relevant, as opposed to purely centralized processes and system components. The goal is to alleviate issues related to periodic maintenance downtimes that would impact the user community. Although this configuration requires strategically placed professionals, adept at systems administration, it will ensure that system issues (if encountered) do not paralyze the entire user community but rather the local or regional site in question. Small user communities or those in very close proximity would benefit from centralized configurations as the administrative function would be less apt to fall in the hands of the users themselves. Applications can be centrally located and maintained.

The ability to roll out the system and transfer knowledge to new and remote users will be an issue if the organization is in a growth mode. It may not be an issue if the company is static or in a purely emerging state; however, if the company is expanding via acquisitions or otherwise, taking on new users and data customers will be a constant. Should the finance function demand the adaptation of a uniform centralized process or allow the freedom for employing nonstandard, homegrown solutions? How will new users view a prescribed data flow process? How long will it take for them to master a new process? What level of expertise will be required at the local site? If centralized system components and processes are employed, a quickly expanding user community will require good documentation and logical processes that are easily transferred. Will old, existing processes have to run parallel with newly adopted processes? Undoubtedly redundancy will be required during the transition period to a centralized system. The finance strategist must have a plan in place that allows for fast and effective transfer of system components, especially higher-level finance/accounting applications. Initial setup and conversion to the prescribed process will take time and depend on the competence and cooperation of the user community and data customers inherited or new to the organization. Decentralization allows for less coordination but embodies more risk. Process and system development is left to the discretion of the new user community. Matters of motivation and commitment may be more relevant here than that of documentation and knowledge transfer.

- *Scalability.* The finance strategist must address the need to expand both the scope and the functionality of systems in the finance function. The finance strategy must address the capacity to incorporate new applications or adapt to infrastructure changes. Addressing the issue of scalability is different in centralized environments compared to decentralized ones. Will a highly centralized, inflexible finance application deny new users the functionality they need for local statutory reporting? Would simple data requirements suffice if full-blown process participation is not feasible? Although well-documented, highly structured systems and process requirements may seem easy to transfer, they may not be relevant. Conversely, relying on new users or expanded reporting sites to develop their own solutions for data and reporting requirements could leave too much to chance and expose the finance function to breakdowns in reporting. The challenge of scalability goes beyond measuring how long solutions will be relevant and instead must address the ease of system expansion.

- *Support/maintenance.* Once the system is in place, how will ongoing support be handled? Are dedicated IS professionals available for support if systems issues are encountered? The landscape of the support model is dictated by the degree of centralization of the system itself. A centralized system lends itself to a focused IS support team in one location. Decentralized systems require a level of expertise distributed throughout the organization. Creating a network of knowledge spread evenly throughout the organization is essential to maintaining the applications and maximizing their usage. This may be the method of choice for a 24/7 application with many users in geographically remote locations at varying levels of expertise. Establishing and maintaining a remote support web may be a difficult initiative to execute. Establishing power users or application champions at local and regional locations may foster the transfer of knowledge and develop adequate support expertise. Maintaining a certification process and reward structure for achieving a level of readiness from a system standpoint may inoculate the organization from latent weaknesses in the data flow dynamic.

Finance function design depends on the management philosophy as it relates to centralization and decentralization of tasks. The finance strategist must understand the particular philosophy to which the company subscribes, especially as it relates to systems design. Understanding the basic approach to the finance function will enable more accurate systems design planning and cue the finance strategist to consider the organization's ability to follow through with implementation strategies.

Ability of the Organization to Implement and Maintain

System design and development, as a general rule, follows the one-third, one-third, one-third rule; planning, system construction, and testing must be dealt with in equal measure. Because systems design and development is not mutually exclusive of the finance strategy, the strategist must keep these three phases of design and development in mind as the finance function is built. The finance strategist must consider the capacity of the organization to initiate and finalize the systems design, implementation, and maintenance aspect of the finance strategy. Planning this aspect of the strategy will demand knowledge of the resources available and a level of expertise that can be lent to systems development issues.

Many organizations fall prey to the part-time bug—that is, the resources that will be dedicated to systems development on a part-time basis. Implementing IS infrastructure is a challenging task and should garner full-time, qualified resources. Dedicated human resources will have the time and focus for troubleshooting that part-timers will lack. Specifically, a full-time project manager will strengthen the odds of finishing a project on time and within the means estimated. The finance strategist may decide either to preside over systems development or to delegate to another. Regardless, this task must be undertaken by qualified professionals who are subjected to as few distractions as possible.

The systems roll-out plan should focus on utilizing as many in-house professionals as possible. The temptation to outsource may be high. Outside specialists and consultants may be necessary, particularly when it comes to installing systems initially. In the early phases of planning and development, the opportunity to transfer knowledge and cultivate a wide base of understanding for the systems configuration must be clearly grasped. The finance strategist must keep in mind that the strategic aspect of systems development should remain within the company's control and that use of outsiders should be carefully managed to ensure proper knowledge transfer. Technical expertise should be procured to keep projects on time and within budget. Keeping the knowledge transfer and learning curves in-house will facilitate future development of the overall systems structure and user community in the end.

Choosing Applications

The finance strategist will spend considerable time and effort determining what systems components will fit the organization's needs. What software applications will be relied on to perform the critical tasks that make the data flow process effective? What network components will be put in place to house these applications and make them work? Will the finance strategist choose simple off-the-shelf applications or internally generated ones? Perhaps the plan will involve building a database from scratch using the various languages and architectures that facilitate data storage. Maybe the final solution will end up somewhere in between, utilizing a proprietary out-of-box database augmented by a made-to-order system of code and languages.

Buying systems components can be a confusing and daunting process. Making well-informed decisions is a challenge, given the numerous choices, options, and combinations of hardware, software, and consulting support. Although this discussion will not provide all the answers to selecting the right applications for all finance strategies, it provides some areas to consider before signing contracts with vendors. Every situation is different; the one constant is the need to research and carefully evaluate needs and the tools that will address them.

The first step in moving forward with application purchases is understanding organization needs. This is often a circular equation, as needs will dictate the tools to address them, which in turn may shape the needs of data customers. Rather than jumping in and putting expensive solutions into play before finding an equilibrium between systems tools and data customer needs, employing a model like the multilevel approach to strategizing will allow the strategist to plug in solutions and judge the impact on data customer needs. Having a firm grasp of customer needs and the resources available to address them will be key to this aspect of strategizing.

The finance strategist will have to be prepared to endure presentations from software vendors who are not only good at what they do (selling) but are under tremendous pressure to sell product. Expenditures for finance software can range from tens of thousands to millions of dollars. This is perhaps the most important reason why the strategist must have a solid grip on the company's needs. Strategists must base buying decisions on software offerings that are available *now.* Buying software applications based on prospective upgrades is dangerous and often leads to unfulfilled expectations. Getting key users and technical people involved in the buying process also helps. The application *is* what it *is,* and its capacity to generate appropriate solutions should be obvious to the vendor representing or selling the application. Having key users (who have a stake in the application's functionality) and IS experts (who have a stake in maintaining the application) ask questions directly to the vendor during demonstrations and sales meetings will ensure that all performance requirements are clearly articulated to the vendor. Including them in the process also secures their cooperation as the finance function continues to develop. Good sales reps appreciate pointed questions, which will help them to match the right tool to the customer.

When a major purchase is at hand (usually for the small and emerging business this is a purchase above $500,000), the finance strategist may want to designate a team to evaluate the options for a particular solution. The team may be composed of a group of key users, an IS professional, and the finance strategist or business owner. Companies may choose to hire a consultant to evaluate applications for their business needs. The company may or may not have the money for this option; however, hiring professionals who understand the technical specifications of tools on the market and how they accommodate needs for other businesses in similar industries may be worth the money. They also will be adroit agents for the company in meetings with vendors, insisting on seeing all functionality and features of software clearly demonstrated. If it is a substantial purchase, vendors may let a company try the product out in a limited setting in-house before buying the application outright. This will allow for the user community to put the software through its paces and ensure it possesses the functionality being sought.

Deciding whether to go with an off-the-shelf solution or an internally generated one will also be a challenge. Prepackaged applications are advantageous because they can be put in place quickly. The concern is, though, that they may create scalability issues. Can the application be expanded? Can additional applications be attached to it as needs change? Is there a capacity limit for data storage or design? Although prepackaged applications are advantageous when it comes to ease of implementation and support, the strategist will have to factor in the need to expand when considering an off-the-shelf product as a long-term solution. Free-designed applications provide flexibility and scalability; however, documentation must be meticulous as it relates to design and support. Using languages such as Oracle and SQL provide a broad canvas to create databases and storage applications. Consideration must be made, however, of the ability to create reports and generate dynamic analysis. Does a user need to be an expert in the application architecture to create reports? If a barrier to usage exists, users may become frustrated. The time horizon for a final, usable product also may be unreasonable. Many small and emerging businesses do not have the luxury to play hit-or-miss with application designs. Uptimes or completion dates need to be predictable and occur within a reasonable time period.

The organization may decide to outsource the applications and the functions they perform altogether. The most popular form of outsourcing is employing an ASP. ASPs provide benefits in the form of quick uptime, good support, and reliable backup/disaster recovery procedures. Before signing a contract with an ASP, however, the organization must be sold on the longevity of the company and feel comfortable with the financial commitment. While the organization can avoid the hefty capital outlays that characterize application purchases in the short to mid term, the finance strategist must be aware of the breakeven point where an up-front investment in application software equals the ASP contractual payments. The company also must be aware of the requirements to customize interfaces with the ASP and ensure connectivity is adequate. These IS-intensive topics must be addressed before the contract is signed to secure the full benefits these tools will offer.

Documentation

The development of systems and processes, if done correctly, will produce enough documentation to aid users in support and further development. Comprehensive documentation will inoculate the organization from turnover and provide guidance to users who do not have ready access to support personnel. New employees or users with shifting roles will especially benefit from comprehensive documentation.

The first step in preserving documentation is to mandate its existence. The finance strategist must make the accumulation and creation of relevant documentation a standard component of development and implementation. Those responsible for developing systems components must be tasked with providing comprehensive, easy-to-read, graphical documentation that describes applications and processes. Additionally, such documentation must be available to those who will need it. Useful documentation should be easily accessible *and* user friendly.

Documentation must exist, but what exactly does good documentation include? Descriptions of hardware and software components? Outlines of processes? The objective is to establish enough written documentation on all aspects of the finance function to provide enough guidance for a person new to the environment to succeed. Armed with this approach, documentation should cover:

- *People. Who* does *what?* This may be as simple as a roster of individuals and their role in the data flow process or as complex as a detailed list of job descriptions. This documentation should include notations from support staff and from those with intimate knowledge of systems configurations.

- *Processes.* Detailed outlines of the data flow process will be crucial to provide guidance for new users and a context for systems components. Maintenance and development will be dependent on understanding not only what applications and systems components exist but how they are employed by the data flow process.
- *Applications/hardware.* Documentation of software and hardware components will be referenced by many individuals, from laypeople to technical types. Detailed descriptions of configurations, settings, and alignments must be available in the case of breakdowns or maintenance. It must be assumed that those implementing and installing system components will not necessarily be the people maintaining them in the future. Key points of interest relate to clarity, completeness, and relevance. Extra effort should be put into writing in easy-to-read terms, without leaving out crucial technical matters. Graphics and illustrations in documentation can make it more easily understood. Keeping documentation in tune with upgrades and configuration changes is also important. Often the best documentation exists with initial implementations but degrades as applications, network components, and hardware upgrades are undertaken. Making documentation a priority when systems changes are engineered will be key to maintaining good written knowledge of the systems.

To be effective, the documentation must be in an accessible location for all relevant parties, whether they are users, data customers, or maintenance professionals. Intranet or network directories are often the best locations for frequently referenced material. Making documentation usable will be key to ensuring that system configurations and updates will be timely and appropriate. Availability, relevance, and completeness are factors that the finance strategist must focus on to ensure that documentation shadows system needs.

IMPLEMENTING SYSTEMS

If done correctly, implementation should be a well-scripted, predictable process. Although changes to existing parameters and the emergence of new ones are always a challenge, strategists and implementers must position themselves to avoid unforeseen events or considerations. Achieving success will go beyond the plan and implementation. Strategists/implementers will find themselves becoming cheerleaders, PR people, firefighters, and soothsayers before the task of implementing a comprehensive schematic of systems architecture is complete. The following 10 items, although not exhaustive, will provide a realistic checklist of considerations to be given attention to increase the odds of success in conceptualizing and implementing IS in a finance strategy:

1. *Secure executive backing.* When it comes to implementing new systems, many issues factor into the need for support from the highest levels of the organization. Enlisting buy-in from users is one key dependency that can make or break the roll-out of applications. Everyone is busy; however, certain projects must be clearly marked critical for all to see. Owners/managers must not only communicate to the organization that systems development and implementations are a priority, but they must create incentives for success and accountability for failure. The dedication of resources to systems development must be assured. Unexpected contingencies will arise with implementations, especially those that happen over an extended time period. Support at the executive level must be as strong when challenges arise as when things are going well. Prime movers of the organization must be committed to the project for its duration and ensure that all others in the organization are committed as well. This may not be as difficult for small and emerging businesses as it is for larger organizations. Regardless of company size and complexity, the executive level must be behind, if not a part of, the strategizing effort, especially as it relates to systems design and implementation.

2. *Work around key dates.* Implementations are difficult enough; however, mix them with critical deliverables and the finance function could put the company at odds with the business environment. Waiting to install new applications or key network components at year-end or during a quarter close could impair the company's ability to meet statutory reporting requirements. Working around these dates will ensure that the normal course of compliance will not be disrupted and will take the pressure off key users who may be intimately involved in the implementation process. Another issue involves avoiding critical reporting times when using a new application or system component for the first time. Running old processes and systems in parallel during critical times and waiting until off-quarter months to use new system components for the first time are good safeguards against hiccups in critical data periods.

3. *Establish a communication web.* Certain companies have geographically removed users. Regularly communicating results and status of the implementation will succeed in managing their expectations and give them a sense of inclusion in the process. A channel of communication established throughout the implementation should be parlayed into a communication channel that facilitates support and furthers systems development. Establishing communication with key users during the im-

plementation will make communication with these same users easier when they have maintenance issues. Implementers who were seen as forthcoming during the implementation stage will be seen as helpful and supportive during support and maintenance. Managing the relationship with system users this way will add to a positive, team-oriented finance culture.

4. *Deal with design changes.* Even though design specifications must be addressed in the planning phase, the finance strategist must be aware that issues will be discovered throughout the implementation. Many times the tendency is to maintain implementation momentum and gloss over a miss. The implementation team is best served if adjustments are made for specifications and requirements originally overlooked in the planning phase as they are encountered during the implementation. The cost of inconvenience in the interim and project slowdowns will pale compared to the cost of an information system that does not work properly or fit the needs of users.

5. *Monitor progress honestly and objectively.* Anyone who has been involved in lengthy, complex implementations can attest to the fact that sometimes these projects take on a life of their own. Part of losing control may lie in the inability or unwillingness to measure progress. The finance strategist will find time spent conceptualizing good measures of progress to be valuable to project follow-through. Establishing intuitive measures of completion is not only sensible but basic to good project management. The challenge may be translating results to these metrics objectively. Pressure from management, shareholders, and data customers may induce project leaders to hedge reporting actual progress. Knowing that the status of resources and other (potentially) dependent projects are hanging in the balance, the finance strategist and/or systems implementer must resist the temptation to be overly optimistic about project progress. Interim disappointments related to missed targets on component completions are easier to swallow than colossal overall project overruns. The organization will have to understand and appreciate that realistic and honest tracking of progress must be maintained to ensure that resource allocations are adequate and dependent projects can be monitored.

6. *Establish a framework to maintain while systems are being implemented.* Taking advantage of the valuable learning curves traversed and intimate knowledge gained throughout the implementation phase of IS development must be a priority of the finance strategist. The key is to ensure that company personnel have significant roles in the implementation process. Before ceding control to outsiders or consultants, the finance strategist must consider the cost of losing all the experience and knowledge that walks out the door when the implementation is complete. Many

organizations want to run lean and therefore minimize permanent head-count. Outsourcing certain nonrecurring projects often augments such objectives. Systems implementations often demand consulting and outside help. This is the unpleasant but very real aspect of dealing with cutting-edge technology. Keeping an in-house team that can sort through issues as they come up is worth the investment, especially if they are brought in on the ground floor of systems development and implementation. Converting the implementation team, in whole or in part, to a maintenance and support staff is a wise investment in the future. Troubleshooting and systems development will be addressed by individuals versed in systems configurations and data customer needs.

7. *Involve users.*   The need for buy-in and ownership of data customers as it relates to IS is paramount to development and implementation. It is the data customers who will reap the greatest benefits from powerful IS or bear the greatest burdens from weak ones. Involving users in the development, implementation, and testing of systems and systems components is the safest way to ensure they are getting what they want. This involvement will foster, at the very least, reasonable expectations regarding the systems being put in place. Finance strategists in larger organizations may find themselves unilaterally pushing systems down to the rest of the organization. Systems may be met with disappointment or outright rejection, as they may not fit the needs of the user community. Involving users in the rollout process will cultivate a pulling dynamic with regard to the systems as users will anticipate and appreciate the systems put in place. Pulling as opposed to pushing systems will create a healthier finance culture and facilitate further development of future systems.

8. *Manage expectations.*   System users and data customers should be involved in the planning and design phase; however, they also should be involved in the implementation phase to the extent possible. Target dates are missed for many reasons, often for reasons not related to the implementation. Users who have been promised certain tools to do their jobs may become critical of the entire initiative if the tools are not available at the promised times. These same users will be more understanding and even help with projects encountering extraordinary impediments if they are a part of the rollout. Their involvement also will expose them to the functionality the applications have to offer before they are in place. This may prompt timely changes and adjustments.

9. *Know when it is time to retreat.*   The finance strategist must recognize that something that works in theory may not work in practice. This goes for applications and system components as well as for the potentially arduous implementation process. When is it obvious that applications and/or systems components are not adequate? When is it obvious that an

implementation will never actually be finished or is simply too expensive to complete? Wrestling with these two questions is a challenge to most management teams. Maintaining objectivity and honesty throughout the implementation process may save the company from white elephants and broken tools that will be a drain on the organization in the future.

10. *Define when the project is done.* Resources in the form of consultants and specialized support staff are expensive. When the drain on overall company resources required to follow through with implementations is tallied, the need to finish projects satisfactorily and in a timely fashion is clear. The quicker these projects are done, the sooner other projects can be undertaken. Often peripheral or lagging issues take the greatest amount of time to iron out. The finance strategists and implementers must be poised to address these late implementation matters swiftly and decisively. More important, the project must be defined well enough so that project completion is unambiguous. Nagging or difficult-to-address issues cannot be allowed to bleed into unwarranted implementation efforts, which translate into unnecessary consulting costs and wasted internal staff man-hours.

Implementing systems components defined by the finance strategy will require discipline and careful monitoring. This operation is crucial as systems will be the key to meeting data customer needs and will help the finance organization operate at its optimal level. Beyond implementing, the finance strategist must position the finance function to maintain and support the applications and systems components that sit at its core.

UP AND RUNNING: MAINTENANCE

Once the system is up and running, the issue of maintenance must be addressed. Systems design must conceptualize, to some extent, the maintenance model. Excluding an ASP model, network and application components will need to be maintained, serviced, and upgraded on site when necessary. Issues of timeliness are particularly important when systems downtimes occur. The ideal model for maintenance involves retaining all individuals who have participated in conceptualizing and developing the system components. Doing this ensures that the knowledge of nuances and workarounds specific to the company's customized system and application configuration is translated to a knowledgeable support staff. The following considerations should factor prominently into the finance strategy as it relates to maintaining the company's IS:

■ *Assessing outsourcing versus in-house.* This refers to maintaining a support team within the organization versus employing an outside firm to address maintenance needs. Both solutions can work but must be customized to the company's needs. The finance strategist must be aware of resources to dedicate to either solution. Engaging an outside firm may seem the obvious solution from a cost and logistical perspective early on; however, trade-offs related to staffing quality, knowledge level, and knowledge retention should be reviewed. Additionally, the strategist must be aware of the breakeven point on investing in an in-house team versus periodic costs to a third party. The most logical solution may be a blend of the two, with certain key support personnel remaining in-house while dedicated staff are contracted to perform day-to-day support.

- *Understanding downtime tolerance.* Maintenance and support always has a time element. The more dependent users and data customers are on applications and the data they produce, the more reliability will be demanded from network, hardware, and application components. When the network goes down, will the company come to a standstill? Can finance and nonfinance people still be productive if systems components break down? A state-of-the-art, comprehensive system configuration may make the finance function the most productive; however, it is vulnerable to outages and breakdowns. If breakdowns in systems components put company initiatives at risk, the finance strategist must devise an effective *and timely* support plan to minimize the fallout.

- *Identifying hot times.* Certain time periods will be more crucial to data customers and system users than others. Closing periods, whether they are monthly, quarterly, or yearly, are examples of time periods where systems outages are the most damaging. Additionally, the time that immediately precedes filing deadlines will be critical for users who are dealing with statutory time frames. These requirements may be tax or SEC related and demand many different system users contribute to the final product. The finance strategist must build in routine and nonroutine upgrades and maintenance routines around such time periods.

- *Defining disaster recovery plans.* Owner/managers as well as the finance strategist must provide for systems failing or degrading to a point that they are unusable. Although many avoid this topic altogether, the organization must realize that planning for worst-case scenarios does not imply weaknesses in design but rather allows for a plan of action to combat an extraordinary circumstance. A disaster recovery plan may provide for offsite data storage or alternate *hot sites* for data customers to continue with company business if the physical plant is lost or destroyed. Excepting natural disasters, the most likely catastrophic event will relate to lost or corrupted data or a downage in key network components. A good finance strategy will provide for such events and prescribe a data restoration or maintenance plan that is timely and effective.

One of the goals of the finance strategist is to devise a long-term system maintenance plan that will endure system and personnel changes over the life of the business. Many issues will figure prominently in this plan, particularly the level of centralization/decentralization of the finance function and the skill level of data users/customers. The conceptualization and planning phase of system development is the ideal time to create a schematic of a reliable maintenance plan. The implementation process will represent the best opportunity to lay the groundwork for an effective maintenance plan as the in-depth knowledge of system configurations is laid bare. Harnessing this knowledge and converting it into a solid support plan will serve the finance strategy best. Regardless of how the design and implementation unfold, the ongoing maintenance plan will play an important role in the long-term success of information systems and their component parts.

FINAL THOUGHTS

Conceptualizing, implementing, and maintaining IS can be a complicated undertaking. Implementing application solutions will be the gateway to a host of new initiatives and challenges. Issues of logistics, implementation resources, and roll-out timetables prevalent in the conceptualization and implementation stages will give way to issues of education, maintenance, and further systems development as the finance function matures. Maintaining a realistic outlook on this aspect of the finance function will keep IS development an ongoing strategic goal for the overall business. Creating a culture of continuous improvement will position the organization to think prospectively and develop solutions and alternatives that anticipate the needs of users. The challenge is to resist the temptation of adopting easy, quick solutions that may preclude a progression of future development. The ideal posture the finance strategist must take regarding IS is to make continuous review and update of applications and systems components a permanent part of the finance strategy, regardless of where the business is in its life cycle.

8

FINANCIAL REPORTING

KEY TAKEAWAYS

- Understanding where financial reporting considerations fall in the multilevel approach.
- Knowing the role of financial reporting in the finance function.
- Recognizing the most commonly used financial statements.
- Understanding the difference between standard and nonstandard reporting.
- Understanding the difference between internal and external reporting.
- Recognizing the impact accounting methodologies have on financial reporting.
- Understanding key issues in developing relevant accounting methodologies and policies and procedures.
- Understanding the importance of developing internal analysis and measurement tools.
- Knowing how to prioritize reporting needs.
- Knowing how to distinguish between historical and prospective reporting.
- Recognizing key issues in maintaining the reporting function.

UNDERSTANDING THE NEED TO REPORT FINANCIAL DATA

What Does Reporting Mean?

Strategizing the finance function involves conceptualizing and designing infrastructure that will suit the organization's data needs now and in the future. Although this is no easy task, the strategizing effort eventually must focus on higher-level, soft components to ensure development of a relevant finance function. This means addressing upper-tier considerations (Tier 4 and Tier 5) of the multilevel approach to strategizing. Developing the reporting aspect of the finance function is the key summary objective of upper-tier considerations for the small and emerging business owner. *Reporting* in this context refers to (1) the capacity to translate data into formal or informal presentation formats and (2) identifying and developing analysis paradigms, growth models, and metrics to aid in decision support. Conceptualizing these two major aspects of reporting is critical to the design of the finance function, particularly infrastructure. Eventually, the small and emerging business owner will need to develop certain balance sheet and P&L strategies that support the reporting effort. The capacity to develop these aspects of the finance function will dictate success in internal and external reporting efforts. Laying the foundation early and developing the capability to generate meaningful reports will make for a strong finance function that will lead the business forward and allow for adjustments and change when necessary.

The urgent demands of the day-to-day operations in the early, precarious stages of business development may occupy the attention of the small and emerging business owner. Notwithstanding, there will always be a need for reporting, whether it is formal financial statements or esoteric analysis models. What's involved with producing financial statements? How suited is the business and its finance function to producing them? What are the key dependencies? How will the finance function keep up with internal and external reporting needs? The first step is to understand the need for reporting.

Purpose of Financial Reporting

One of the biggest challenges the small and emerging business owner will encounter involves understanding how the company is performing. The most accurate depiction the company will convey comes through the financial data it generates. It is the challenge of management/owners to report this data effectively, which includes translating it into intelligible financial statement form.

Reporting, as it relates to the finance function, represents the actions or exercises that transmit data harnessed by the data flow process to data customers. These actions include creating reports, presentations, or other platforms of data delivery. Reporting in the enterprise focuses on identifying and assessing data in the business environment as it relates to the organization's objectives to key decision makers. Key decision makers in this case would be the small and emerging business owners/managers. Financial reporting helps owners make decisions regarding their investment in the organization or aids creditors in assessing whether to lend funds to the business. Reporting also provides owners and other stakeholders information on the use of or need for the most important resource in the business—*cash*. Financial data, whether it comes as formal financial statements or customized evaluation metrics, provides knowledge on the utilization of resources. Whether it deals with people, equipment, dollars, or intangibles, financial reporting provides the ability to measure resources used to run the business and provide direction for future needs.

The small and emerging business owner will find that financial reporting shapes the company's relationship with the business environment. It may seem that financial reporting is merely the depiction of the business environment and how the company exists in it. In fact, this "one-way" relationship is a misnomer, in that

reporting dictates decisions that relate to resources within the company and the allocation of resources outside. This is especially true with financial data disclosed
in the public sector. Financial reporting also provides an indication of performance
relative to a business's peer group. Is the business doing better than others? Worse?
If performance is above or below industry peers, do owners/managers know why
and in what ways? Financial reporting plays a role in the decision-making dynamic
by providing a view of relative performance and the use of and need for resources.

The examination of formal reporting tools will lead the small and emerging
business owner to consider financial statement tools that will suit current and
prospective decision needs. Generally, the need will exist for two types of financial statements: those that illustrate company performance over a *period of time*
and those that measure the state of the company at a *point in time.*

Most Frequently Used Financial Statements

Measuring performance over a period of time will give owners and other stakeholders the ability to see how well the company's use of resources yields products
and services. Profit and loss statements are used to show how expenditures yield
income over a period of time—monthly, quarterly, or yearly. Overall, this statement
will provide information on the availability of cash, particularly the amount and
timing. The P&L is inherently based on historic information, which is not necessarily indicative of future performance but offers valuable insight into trends and
patterns in the external environment and inside the company.

Key to the usefulness of P&L statements is in the detail or components of income. Understanding these components provides practical insight into the historical performance of the company and its likelihood for future success. For
example, two companies with similar bottom lines may be distinguished by the
fact that one company achieved this number through solid margins and practical
expense levels, while the other achieved the number via an extraordinary event
(e.g., asset disposal, insurance proceeds). It is not practical to base a business
model on unpredictable windfalls. Good financial reporting provides an indication
not only of the amount and timing of cash flow but of the risk of attaining certain
cash flow expectations.

A balance sheet provides an assessment of the company's financial state at a
given point in time. In particular, it provides information on the details of company
resources, company obligations, and the interests of owners. The balance sheet
provides an evaluation of company resources available in the future as well as
commitments the company has made to outsiders. This type of financial statement
provides an understanding of the value of the stake each owner has in the enterprise by illustrating the value of equipment, inventory, and intangibles as well as
commitments and contingencies to outsiders.

The balance sheet serves to augment the information presented in the P&L and
provide information on the availability, timing, and risk of future cash flow. The

balance sheet presentation of inventory, accounts receivable, and accounts payable provides an indication of future cash flow and the anticipation of revenue. Analyzing the balance sheet over time is particularly useful as the ebb and flow of balances can be understood and translated into useful business decisions. Unique to the balance sheet is the assessment of capital structure and its impact on liquidity. Key stakeholders such as creditors and equity owners have an interest in the relative level of liabilities (both long and short term) to assets. Can the company meet its debt obligations from period to period? Will the company be able to pay out its dividend? The balance sheet is an honest depiction of the organization for both internal and external stakeholders.

The statement of cash flows combines P&L and balance sheet components to provide information on how the company utilized its most important resource over a specified period of time—cash. A formal cash flow statement will distinguish cash flow from operations, investing activities, and financing activities. If a company is publicly traded, it must prepare a formal cash flow statement in accordance with GAAP. Although the complexities of preparing a cash flow statement will not be addressed here, it is worth noting that small and emerging business owners must understand the uses or sources of cash, especially in the early stages of business development. They must motivate and base incentives for current and future employees on P&L items (e.g., revenue, margins) as well as the amount of cash generated or collected. Becoming familiar with this financial statement will aid small and emerging business owners with the decision-making process and ensure that managers/owners are in sync with business needs.

Certain aspects of financial statements may be mixed to help analyze the business. Creating ratios with balance sheet and P&L components will help the small and emerging business owner make decisions about customers and products. For example, Days Sales Outstanding ratios—made up of accounts receivable (balance sheet) and revenue (P&L)—help evaluate the quality of customers or the organization's efforts in servicing receivables. Inventory Turns ratios, made up of cost of goods sold (P&L) and inventory (balance sheet), help provide an understanding of the supply chain and how well inventory is being managed.

Understanding how these standard financial statements work and their value to decision makers is key, as most analysis and reporting is based on information derived from them. The strategist must have a clear understanding of the need for these basic financial statements and the level of detail that will be necessary to make them useful.

Standard versus Nonstandard Reporting

In many contexts, the term *reporting* refers exclusively to preparing formal financial statements. Preparing them for external and internal purposes depends, for the most part, on the ability of the finance function to produce financial information in a prescribed format. Some companies, however, will have requirements to relay peripheral financial information to data customers outside the organization. These nonstandard reporting requirements may have the same weight as formal, standard reporting requirements and/or a heavy consequence for noncompliance. Attention to nonstandard reporting requirements will be a particular priority for publicly traded companies. What are these reporting requirements? How should they be addressed? How do they impact the finance function and strategy?

Nonstandard reporting requirements may come about as a result of legal obligation, regulatory requirement, industry practice, or voluntary management disclosure. This type of reporting is unique in many ways to publicly traded companies, although privately held companies also may engage in nonstandard reporting. Examples of nonstandard reporting include:

- Press releases (quarterly earnings or otherwise)
- Reporting to the U.S. Census Bureau
- Responses to or reporting for tax audits (state and federal)
- Filing the Form 8K, Current Report Pursuant to Section 13 or 15(d) of the Securities Exchange Act of 1934
- Management Discussion and Analysis (MD&A) in corporate annual reports and Form 10K, Annual Report Pursuant to Section 13 or 15(d) of the Securities Exchange Act of 1934
- Filing prospectuses and offering investment circulars

What makes this reporting different from standard reporting requirements? The circumstances that give rise to it and/or the motivation for a desired end distinguish this type of reporting from that of standard reporting—producing balance sheet, P&L, and cash flow statements. The following factors distinguish nonstandard reporting from standard reporting requirements:

- *Irregular timing.* Requests for data/reports by governmental agencies will have timing constraints that go beyond the standard timing for data requirements in the organization. Where standard reporting comes in annual, semi-annual, quarterly, or calendar-month increments, tax notices may have response time increments anywhere from 10 to 90 days from the date of the notice. For public companies, a Form 8K filing is required (per the SEC) to disclose a significant event within a reasonable time period after the event occurs. The finance function must be prepared to manage planned reporting requirements and be able to respond quickly and intelligibly in nonstandard time frames.
- *Urgency.* Although some nonstandard reporting is done in anticipation of a significant, desired business life cycle event, most is done in response to an authoritative request for information. Inaction may have consequences for the business. This type of reactive reporting must be accurate and timely.

Initial responses to notices for tax audits, whether at the federal, state, or local level, may not require financial information per se, but simply an acknowledgment of receipt of the notice. The brevity of that response may induce a positive, qualitative evaluation by authorities regarding the organization and lessen the blow of an examination or lien. The finance function must be suited to respond to various requests.

■ *Compulsory responses.* Most nonstandard reporting is *not* optional. Regulatory authorities, governmental bodies, or the general public may issue demands for information to which the business must comply. The right to do business, access to public funds, or market capitalization may be at stake if an organization is reticent regarding a nonstandard data request.

Addressing nonstandard reporting requirements will require the ability to respond in a timely manner with accurate and relevant data. This sounds simple, but because this reporting is either nonrecurring or unorthodox in nature, it is not unusual for these requests to get lost or misinterpreted, or simply be ignored. For example, notices of tax audits usually come in writing, with a time-sensitive response required. Actions are dictated by the passage of time and the response or lack thereof of the target company. What is in place to ensure that written notices are delivered to the proper personnel and interpreted properly? Small and emerging businesses are susceptible to these communication breakdowns as divisions of duties and definition of roles sometimes are vague or unclear.

The finance function must be able to handle nonstandard reporting requirements. Establishing a full-time owner of finance and accounting may be the most important step in handling these types of issues. Creating an environment/culture of awareness in matters of finance also is crucial in handling nonstandard reporting requirements, especially in a small organization where few people handle many different responsibilities. The strategist, as it relates to the multilevel approach, must review the business life cycle (Tier 1) and understand the potential for nonstandard reporting requirements before they are encountered. Realizing which stages of growth or life-cycle events expose the business to these requirements will allow for provisions to be made and an awareness to be established.

Internal versus External Reporting

Just as the company will change and evolve, so too will its reporting needs. The small and emerging business owner must be aware of these shifting reporting needs and have the capacity to accommodate them. One of the most important distinctions that must be made when it comes to addressing reporting needs is that of internal versus external reporting needs. The finance function must be equally suited for both. How will the stages of the business dictate the nature of reporting? What demands will these two types of reporting put on the finance function?

Reporting that focuses on internal analysis needs and drives day-to-day decision making is called internal or management reporting. The majority of these reporting needs will be internal, revolving around analysis for in-house decision making, in the early stages of the company's life cycle. The overall objective of internal reporting is to provide the information necessary to ensure that resources are maximized and strategic decision making is reliable. The complexion of management reporting will change as the company evolves. Measuring, understanding, and applying new metrics to help make strategic decisions for the company in a dynamic environment lie at the core of management reporting needs. Reviewing operating expenses or revenue run rates in the early years may evolve into analyzing receivables days-sales-outstanding and inventory turns or cash flow versus revenue trends. The design as well as the detail of financial data reported will improve or shift with the company's changing needs. Internal reporting needs may focus on standard reports and financial statements (balance sheet, P&L, and cash flow statement) or on more customized analysis and evaluation tools. The finance function must be synchronized with the needs of internal data customers to be certain that internal reporting needs are being met.

The organization, if it is not already, may be charged with statutory reporting requirements as it matures. These filings are an example of *external* reporting requirements. These reporting requirements often are detailed in their content and timing of release. Public filings and disclosures with governmental authorities are good examples of external reporting requirements. They may be an integral part of the company's growth cycle. Financial statements generated for these purposes must follow a certain format with certain time frames for filing. Many small and emerging businesses fall in the trap of relying on financial statements prepared for external purposes to suit internal reporting needs. Although these financial statements may seem to provide enough information to run the business in the short term, the need for granularity and specificity in reporting will eclipse the value these rigid statements provide to decision making. Over time these financial statements will have limited value-added impact for the organization. Filing these timely and accurately will keep the company in compliance with legal or contractual obligations and nothing more. It is worthwhile to focus on developing the processes that create these statements, with the object being to minimize manual input and time. These financial statements, especially in the early stages of company development, may be the only regularly produced reporting instruments. Burgeoning companies are best served to shape their internal reporting needs from these financial statements and use the processes for developing them to hone their internal reporting routines.

Unlike internal financial statements, the production of external financial statements must become a process-driven exercise. Internal financial statements will be shaped by the demand of internal data customers, refined and reevaluated regularly, and should be a continual focus of the finance function. The finance function must ensure that external financial statements are prepared accurately and in a timely manner; the goal is to spend as few resources on generating them as possible. Automating the preparation of Form 10Q, Form 10K, audited financial statements, tax returns, and government census reports should be the aim from the outset, as the company gains little value-added benefit from generating them.

Key Dependencies

Many entrepreneurs and executives find that maintaining the financial reporting aspect of the business is a burdensome distraction to operations. The ability to translate the business into relevant financial reporting tools, whether they are for internal or external purposes, goes hand-in-hand with doing business. Whether it is fulfilling the data needs of owner/managers or complying with an external/statutory reporting requirement, the finance function must be prepared to generate accurate and timely financial information. Key areas or dependencies that will dictate the quality of reporting are:

- *Sophistication of management.* Not only will management/owners be charged with interpreting the data that results from the reporting process, but they also will make decisions regarding the processes and resources that yield the reporting. Management must have an understanding of the business that goes beyond operations. Operational decisions cannot be made if good information cannot be harnessed and passed on to management. The finance function must be carefully strategized, funded, and maintained to ensure that the information ecosystem stays intact at all times.
- *Appropriate accounting methodologies.* Do accounting methodologies translate the company accurately to financial statement form? Is the revenue number reliable? How about cost of sales and operating expenses? Reports and financial statements will be of no value to the organization if the information presented is unreliable. The finance strategist must ensure that the accounting methodologies are employed correctly before allowing the organization to rely on reports, metrics, or automatically generated data models.
- *Changing business.* Businesses are always changing, and reports that were relevant in the past may not be appropriate in the future. The finance strategist must understand this and be poised to identify aspects of reporting that will always be needed (e.g., balance sheet, P&L, cash flow statement) and those that will change with the business (e.g., ratios, turnover, operating leverage, financial leverage).

To achieve success, small and emerging business owners must master financial reporting early on. Whether it is internal, external, formal, informal, standard, or nonstandard reporting, the business has a vested interest in ensuring the finance function is suited to meet *all* reporting needs. Although different companies may interpret the upper tiers of the multilevel approach to strategizing differently, the small and emerging business owner is best served by focusing on the capacity to create financial reports. Considerations related to optimizing balance sheet and P&L presentation are one and the same with reporting at the early stage of the business life cycle. The finance strategist must next understand and incorporate accounting methodologies into the finance function.

EMPLOYING ACCOUNTING METHODOLOGIES TO SERVE CURRENT AND FUTURE NEEDS

Role of Accounting Methodologies

Financial reporting is a critical aspect of the finance function as it is the way in which the company is communicated to stakeholders, whether internal (management and owners) or external (creditors, governmental agencies, and absentee shareholders). Ultimately it is the owner of the business who is responsible for the accuracy of data disseminated in financial statements, a point worth noting especially when external data customers are significant. How the finance function deals with the challenge of data issues and financial statement preparation, particularly misinterpretations, bias, and ambiguities related to data, is ultimately the owner's responsibility. Avoiding these potential shortfalls in the reporting process will depend, to a large extent, on the implementation of uniform, relevant, and practical accounting methodologies that fit the business.

The common set of standards and procedures set forth by the accounting profession are embodied in GAAP. These principles and practices represent, in some cases, very specific rules on accounting for specific transactions in particular industries or general guidance on how to approach circumstances and events. Because the goal of GAAP is not to prescribe the correct treatment for every possible transaction that could be encountered in every business circumstance, a certain level of judgment must be exercised when applying GAAP. A transaction may fit more than one GAAP treatment, depending on the business circumstance. This level of subjectivity makes applying GAAP more of an art than a science. Nevertheless, establishing the accounting standards that fit the business and applying them consistently will underscore the financial reporting effort. Finance strategists must discern such matters as what accounting treatments to use and when. They also will have to identify the manner in which certain rules will be applied. Is it appropriate to be aggressive or conservative with revenue recognition? Should expenses be capitalized or charged to the P&L? Although one would think taking a conservative stance on applying accounting principles would be the rule, executives and managers have an obligation to act in the best interest of owners (shareholders). If the company is publicly traded and market capitalization (shares outstanding × share price) is the chief metric, management may have an obligation to be aggressive with certain accounting rules to fulfill their duty as data stewards for the owners. This is a very subjective and controversial area. It is enough, though, to understand that many gray areas exist in applying GAAP to the company and that financial reporting will be heavily dependent on how it is interpreted by the organization and applied to the company's circumstances.

Role of Policies and Procedures

Establishing clear, consistent accounting methodologies is the first step to ensuring that financial reporting is adequate. The finance strategist will be charged with creating a mechanism that employs all accounting and reporting methodologies consistently over time and across the organization. Publishing a set of company-wide finance policies and procedures will lend uniformity to the entire finance function and ensure that all members of the organization have a uniform resource for processes, accounting treatments, systems maintenance, and the like. Creating a policies and procedures manual may be as simple as accumulating certain documentation related to the finance function or as complex as codifying best practices developed from careful studies and research.

Not having key finance policies and procedures documented and available in one location could be expensive to the organization. The lack of uniformity may result in costly learning curves, inefficiencies, turnover, and high training costs. A more subtle cost of not having clearly communicated policies and procedures will be incorrect or inadequate financial reports produced by the finance function.

Policies and procedures can apply to any aspect of the organization; however, in the context of the finance function, they define what accounting methodologies are to be used and how they will be applied. They also outline how processes are to be followed, particularly *who* does *what* and *when*. This area is particularly critical as it relates to time-sensitive closing processes. They should clearly communicate management's expectations for specific job tasks and include a clear definition of the policy, its purpose, scope, and the steps (if necessary) that accompany it. The policy and procedures manual must be easily accessible to all relevant members of the finance team. It may reside on an intranet website or common network directories or be stored in a shared area of the office. Finance strategists must go beyond creating policies and procedures and challenge the organization to ensure that they are being used properly. To do so they must rely on the culture of the enterprise and strength of management.

Benchmarking and Seeking Consensus

The business owner/manager will have two perspectives in approaching the application of GAAP to the organization: external and internal reporting. The objective in applying GAAP to the business for external reporting purposes is to find the most defensible position (whether it is aggressive or otherwise) for the company's reporting objectives. For internal reporting purposes, needs will center on translating the business accurately to financial statements to facilitate analysis and decision making. In most cases the level of sophistication of data customers (both internal and external) will dictate the quality level of accounting and disclosures. Where does the finance strategist go to seek guidance on applying GAAP to the business?

The most reliable methodology for applying GAAP "correctly" to the company's circumstances is to see what the business's peer group in the industry is doing. Crucial areas of reporting are revenue recognition and the treatment of expenditures. The best place to go for guidance is to seek out public disclosures of companies in similar industries. The SEC's Form 10K provides the most comprehensive disclosure of accounting results and policies. This is an annual filing of results and policies required by public companies as dictated by the SEC. A key area of Form 10K as it relates to accounting policy is Footnote 1 to the financials, "Summary of Significant Accounting Policies." This footnote allows the company to explain the way it employs certain accounting methodologies peculiar to its circumstances. For example, seeking guidance on how to book research and development and software costs may be as easy as going to Footnote 1 of the financial statements in Form 10K for Microsoft and IBM. The biggest challenge for the finance strategist is identifying public companies in the business's industry. The Internet is a good resource, particularly the SEC website (*www.sec.gov*). Bloomberg Professional™ service is also a useful tool for this purpose, although it is a subscription service. Bloomberg Professional™ service may be the quickest path to Form 10Ks issued by companies in similar industries. Other resources for benchmarking may be a local CPA or industry gathering. Oddly enough, one of the most effective ways to benchmark may be a simple phone call to a controller or CFO of a company in a similar industry. Professionals often welcome the opportunity to network and share thoughts on these matters.

Why is it important to seek a consensus on accounting methods? As indicated earlier, GAAP are far from detailed rules set in stone. They are as their name implies—a widely held consensus of acceptable methodologies. Data customers will, however, seek consistency and consensus with the rest of the reporting world. If the company is private and/or closely held, applying GAAP may not be an urgent matter. However, doing so becomes an issue when and if the business seeks financing, pursues public funds, or wishes to be acquired. Employing GAAP inappropriately in financial statements may result in adjustments to them during the due diligence process. Examiners (auditors) who are well versed in industry accounting will use this consensus approach to evaluate the fairness with which the company's financial statements conform to GAAP. Almost overnight company results can be significantly diluted if they are not prepared initially in accordance with GAAP. Waiting for an important event in the company life cycle to find out that GAAP has been employed inappropriately may be expensive and lead to a besmirched management reputation and/or the expense related to a due diligence process that does not yield financing. If the purpose for being examined is stymied because of financial statement adjustments, the whole company suffers and the business life cycle could be drastically altered.

Developing Accounting Methodologies

Translating the business to financials will require management/owners to determine the level of aggressiveness of certain accounting positions. Purists in the accounting world maintain that the company's performance is what it is and there is no room for editorializing results. Practically speaking, the objective of external reporting is to make the company look good on paper without materially misrepresenting results. The objective for internal reporting purposes is to translate the company's performance and financial state accurately. There are two potential pitfalls to avoid:

1. Making the company look good in the near term at the expense of the future
2. Sacrificing presentation on one financial statement to enhance that of another

To navigate these issues properly, the finance strategist must employ a companywide approach to preparing financial statements and setting accounting policy.

To avoid making the company look good in the near term at the expense of the future, the finance strategist must understand revenue streams and disbursements. If accelerating revenue from a certain transaction serves a reporting purpose now, what are the effects on reporting in the future? An example of this dilemma is recognizing the steady revenue from operating leases over an extended period versus accelerating the lease payments and employing sales-type lease accounting. Although many other factors affect the use of sales-type lease accounting, in this circumstance the steady revenue stream would be eliminated in return for a lump-sum revenue number today. This may be good if the company is positioning itself for an acquisition, but it may backfire if the company is public and feeling pressure to make periodic earnings estimates indefinitely. Essentially the company would be mortgaging future revenue for a quick hit now.

Avoiding a sacrifice on the presentation of one financial statement to enhance that of another also requires an understanding of revenue streams and disbursements. A good example involves the deferral of expenses. If the company is trying to maximize earnings, it is tempting to capitalize expenses (i.e., put them on the balance sheet rather than on the P&L). Doing so also may distort the long-term view of financial statements. This approach will have an impact on other financial statements, unlike employing sales-type lease accounting, however. Inconsistencies may result when analyzing the P&L in relation to the statement of cash flows. A telling statistic is comparing cash flow from operations to earnings over time. A rate of growth in cash flow over time that lags behind the rate of earnings growth is a red flag to financial data customers. Although certain company initiatives are expected to have this effect (a planned investment in infrastructure over time, for example), systematically window-dressing earnings by moving P&L items to the balance sheet eventually will create a situation that is difficult to explain to stakeholders. Companies that overcapitalize expenses fall into this analytical quagmire, as do companies that take advantage of nonrecurring write-offs. Companies that regularly announce restructuring or special below-the-line charges are a prime example of offenders in this area.

Both cases illustrate that financial statements as a whole must be taken into account when considering accounting policy. The finance strategist will be compelled to maximize company results on paper and position the company for the future or at the least avoid putting the company in a disadvantaged situation. Regardless of reporting needs, the finance strategist must ensure that the finance function translates the company accurately to financials to give data customers the opportunity to make well-informed decisions.

A unique circumstance that is worth discussing as it relates to applying proper accounting methodologies to the business is the issue of addressing foreign GAAP. Multinational companies face a unique challenge in dealing with both statutory reporting requirements of a particular country in which they do business and U.S. GAAP requirements. Public or private, if the company is doing business in other countries, it will have to submit to local reporting rules. Local GAAP in a particular country may be made up of International Accounting Standards (IAS), its own particular accounting rules, or a combination of the two. These rules vary from country to country, and ignorance of the rules is no excuse for not complying. How well has the finance function mastered the foreign rules that govern operations? How well is the company converting foreign GAAP financials to U.S. GAAP?

How will the different levels of the organization address the knowledge level of local and U.S. GAAP? It is not uncommon for a multinational company to hire local professionals to manage a local subsidiary. When cultural and language considerations are factored in, this is often the best way to position the local subsidiary for success. Although local professionals may be familiar with local GAAP, how familiar are they with U.S. GAAP? This becomes an issue only when the world headquarters consolidates the worldwide data. U.S. personnel more often than not assume that the data they receive is in U.S. GAAP form, while local professionals submitting the data assume the U.S. team will convert it where necessary. Unless told otherwise, the headquarters team has no reason to believe any differences exist in the first place. This creates concern when management is looking at data submissions from many different countries. Two issues must be addressed here:

1. What, if any, differences between U.S. GAAP and foreign GAAP exist on the financials?
2. How challenging is the process of converting foreign GAAP to U.S. GAAP?

The finance strategist must understand where the differences in accounting methodologies lie. Are there differences in revenue recognition, expense accruals, or the recording of intangibles? Whether the GAAP conversions are done manually or automatically, the time and effort put into making conversions every period can create slowdowns in the data flow process and leave it prone to error.

This issue has become a hot topic with the SEC of late as more and more big-market players are competing globally. The SEC's goal is to arrive at a consensus on global GAAP. The chances of this happening within a reasonable amount of time are slim due to the myriad of cultural and governmental barriers. However, it is worth noting that the SEC and external data customers are aware of the impact of foreign GAAP on the financial statements, which behooves all multinational organizations to address the issue in some way. If the business is currently or intends to be multinational, the finance strategist must:

- Understand the differences in revenue recognition methodologies
- Know when hyperinflationary accounting must be addressed
- Know when thin capitalization rules must be addressed
- Understand the treatment of intangibles for both local and foreign GAAP purposes

CREATING MODELS FOR INTERNAL ANALYSIS AND MEASUREMENT

Value of Internal Analysis Models

Preparing financial statements and creating models and analysis tools are both subsets of financial reporting. Models and analysis tools are internally focused although they may be based on external needs and reporting requirements. The most critical time to establish analysis models and measurement tools is during the early stages of business. Even though a company may not be sophisticated enough to create and manage a collection of such tools, having a small number of simple measures will offer a framework/measuring stick for growth. Knowing what aspects of business work and do not work is critical. Waiting until all company resources are exhausted before realizing that an aspect of the business model did not work is detrimental to business success. Analysis models, even simple ones, will provide a way for the small and emerging business owner to gauge progress and avoid failure.

Developing and Maintaining Internal Analysis Tools

Generating analysis tools and metrics will enable managers/owners to gauge company progress and provide the platform for making adjustments to the overall business strategy. How will management develop effective tools that are reliable and relevant? Weak and irrelevant tools are just as ineffective as strong tools that cannot be populated with accurate data or interpreted properly. These two areas of concern will drive development of analysis tools/metrics.

The small and emerging business owner must understand the areas of business that must succeed in order for the entire organization to flourish. The early stages of business development will be dependent on profitability and cash flow. Issues related to capital structure, turnover, and operating leverage may be important; however, the ability to generate revenue and free up cash will secure the foreseeable future of any organization and position it to succeed.

Another factor shaping analysis tools lies in the finance function's ability to deliver data in the appropriate form. Does it gather the necessary data? Can it gather the data in a timely manner? These matters represent an upper-tier consideration that, in the multilevel model, will affect lower-tier considerations. Pegging tools and metrics that depend on data/information that the data flow process cannot gather or process will result in weak management tools. Additionally, how will these analysis tools change as the business changes? If the organization pursues a different strategy or changes its market focus, will these analysis metrics still be relevant? For example, managing margins (sales less cost of goods sold) in a low-volume business may be different than doing the same in a high-volume business. Although high margins may be necessary in a low-volume business, a high-volume business may be representative of a low-margin business. Both business models are valid, but the business profile must fit the circumstances.

Understanding the underlying assumptions of analysis tools will also drive their development. The assumptions, dependencies, or limitations must be understood before the ratio, model, or line item is relied on to make decisions. For example, when using balance sheet accounts for performing ratio analysis, using average balances is more meaningful than using ending or beginning balances. Ensuring that the data used in the tool or model is accurate and timely is another key area of concern. A metric or ratio should not exist on its own, it should be compared to the company over time or to other companies in a similar industry. Ratios and metrics should never be taken out of context or used to rationalize a decision; rather, they should stand as part of a series of measures that augment the owner/managers' subjective understanding of the business.

The level of sophistication of the data customers who will interpret and analyze these tools also plays a role in developing them. The capacity of management/owners to understand these tools and translate their meaning into workable initiatives or strategies will play a role in their development. For example, financial ratios that focus on working capital components of the balance sheet will be lost on decision makers who do not understand the relationship between current assets and current liabilities. Analysis of working capital is particularly important when it comes to cash flow analysis. Because many inexperienced entrepreneurs do not understand the dynamics of certain crucial areas of the balance sheet, namely inventory and accounts receivable, developing metrics and analysis models that focus on these areas will be of little value to them. The combination of poor analysis tools and management inexperience may result in decision making that is misguided in the most critical area of the business: cash. These soft components of the finance function must be easily interpreted and clear to all data customers regarding what they imply about the business.

Types of Internal Analysis Tools

Analysis tools derived from company-generated financial data may come in the form of simple, line item reporting metrics or relationships between classified data elements. Examples of the former are revenue, margin, earnings before interest and taxes (EBIT), and net income. These measuring tools are straightforward and consist of certain line item accounts on financial statements. Analysis tools that represent relationships between classified data elements come in the form of balance sheet and P&L ratios. Ratios can convey very powerful information regarding a company's well-being and performance. They also can be relatively complex to construct and decipher. Due to the limitations of certain ratios and analysis tools, the small and emerging business owner should take time to review upper-tier considerations of the multilevel approach to strategizing and determine a slate of analysis tools to use to evaluate the business.

Simple financial reporting metrics are based on financial statements prepared by the company. The power in these analysis tools is their simplicity and objectivity. They are limited, however, in their reliance on the data that defines them and the methodologies used to derive the balances. Upper-tier considerations of the multilevel approach will impact the effectiveness and reliability of these analysis metrics. Understanding management's analysis needs will help the finance strategist develop infrastructure that adequately feeds these measures. Most small and emerging businesses rely on P&L-oriented metrics to measure success. The following analysis tools provide valuable input on the performance of the company:

- Revenue
- Margins
- EBIT

- Net income
- Operating expense
- Total equity (positive versus negative)

Financial ratios come in a myriad of forms and serve varying analysis needs. They can analyze anything from simple liquidity, to profitability, to capital structure. The small and emerging business owner will benefit best from simple ratios that focus on areas that are the most critical in the early years of the business. Using *critical* as the chief criteria narrows the focus down to cash/liquidity ratios and profitability ratios. Ratios helpful in this regard include:

- Cash and marketable securities divided by current liabilities
- Cash and marketable securities divided by sales
- Cash and marketable securities divided by total assets
- Cash plus marketable securities and current receivables divided by current liabilities (quick or acid test ratio)
- Current assets divided by current liabilities (current ratio)
- Net income divided by revenues
- Net income divided by shareholder's equity
- Net income divided by total assets

ISSUES IN CREATING FINANCIAL STATEMENTS

Measuring the Level of Urgency and Motivation

Financial reporting, whether it is for internal or external purposes, must be prioritized. Finance resources must be dedicated to urgent reporting matters before less important reporting issues are addressed. The challenge for the finance strategist is to determine which matters of reporting deserve attention over others. Financial reporting matters will be segregated into two broad categories: (1) have-to reporting and (2) like-to reporting. Small and emerging companies, midsize companies, and large companies accumulate financial data and perform some reporting on a have-to basis. This have-to umbrella includes federal income tax reporting, state and local tax compliance, and bank loan covenant compliance. Companies that are publicly traded will, in addition to the filings just mentioned, file Form 10Q, 10K, and 8K and other statutory filings with the SEC. The major data customer for have-to reporting is external to the organization, usually a governmental authority. If the company has operations in other countries, it will have foreign tax filings and local statutory filings as well. The motivation for this type of financial reporting is based on negative reinforcement, most notably fines and penalties.

The second category of financial reporting is like-to reporting. This reporting can be used for external or internal data customers. Examples of like-to reporting for external audiences would be the presentation of financial results for potential business combinations and public offerings. Examples for internal audiences would include reporting for bonus measurements or product divestitures. Like-to reporting is motivated by a potential positive end, which could be a payoff from selling the business, an accelerated market cap with an initial public offering, or a performance bonus. Like-to reporting does not come about as a statutory result of operations. The organization will not be sanctioned for not complying with these reporting requirements.

The finance strategist must be careful to sort through reporting needs and understand which reporting initiatives are critical to the organization. Finance infrastructure and related soft components are designed to suit the urgent reporting requirements while lesser reporting needs will either be minimized altogether or passed on to data customers or the finance organization to coordinate. The following example illustrates how motivation impacts the prioritization of reporting compliance tasks:

> Edward B. works in the external reporting group of a public company. The deluge of SEC and internal reporting requirements this company has demands the sorting and prioritization of reporting requirements. One of the reporting requirements he deals with is that of the U.S. Census Bureau. Because Edward B.'s company has a manufacturing component, these form requests by the Census Bureau are not only numerous but awkwardly complex. The rainbow of colors and assortment of sizes and shapes of these forms grace his desk every month, it seems. Edward B., like his predecessors, has noticed that there was no real consequence to returning the completed forms late. Additionally, he has found that no one at the Census Bureau ties the completed forms to anything. The only follow-up that is done is an occasional phone call when the forms are not filed on time. These realizations have led to the submission of the same numerical data each quarter or year (whatever the form demands), an exercise as easy as transcribing the same data to new forms each period. In spite of the imposing words stamped on the forms instructing to file or risk penalties and fines, Edward B. discounts the significance of these filings and uses old or dummy information to complete them. Edward B. has networked with his peers in other companies and found that his approach to handling the census forms is no different from that used in most organizations. Because this methodology can be followed with impunity, the results, which fit the level of reinforcement from this data customer, may be less than accurate.

Generally, efforts to assemble financial statements or a particular filing are driven by the intensity of the measure of reinforcement (good or bad) that motivates the organization. Fear of the IRS and dealing with bureaucracy to sort out penalties, interest, and interest on penalties is motivation enough to research all necessary IRS filings and follow through with them. An impending windfall from the purchase of the business by an eager buyer is an example of motivation to prepare comprehensive financial statements in a timely manner. Parlaying the motivation to report financial data to have-to and like-to terms is a simple way of linking actions and results.

Historical versus Prospective Reporting

Key to gaining perspective on reporting needs involves equating have-to and like-to reporting to historical and prospective reporting. Have-to reporting includes state and federal tax returns as well as SEC filings. These reports are usually based on actual events and transactions that have already happened, hence they are historical in nature. *Like-to* reporting, budgets, forecasts, and financial models are typically forward looking or prospective in nature. As opposed to historical reports, these reports are to some extent based on assumptions. Historical-based reporting, it may seem, has no value to the company other than to keep the organization in compliance with reporting authorities. However, historical data has apparent value to the organization in that it reveals the results of past decisions and hints at the economics of the business environment and how it affected the organization. Historical results, therefore, must be compiled and interpreted properly for any organization to flourish. Depending on the sophistication of the finance function, the organization must be poised to leverage historical data into good decisions.

Accurate prospective reporting by nature adds value to the company's strategic direction. Budgets and forecasts provide performance benchmarks and give the organization a way to communicate results to external data customers, if necessary. Business and financial models based on historical performance are typically heavier on the prospective side. These models provide the backbone for acquisitions, divestitures, and mergers—significant events in the business life cycle. Following this logic, it stands to reason that companies would do everything in their power to ensure maximum effort is put into prospective (like-to) reporting while minimizing the effort and time put into historical (have-to) reporting. Understanding these relationships will require revisiting the role of motivation and how it drives the finance function.

Historic Needs

Success in the early years of the business is heavily dependent on the ability of management/owners to optimize resources. Resources, whether money or people, are typically scarce in the early years of business development. While historical data may be nonexistent or sparse in a young company, as time passes a track record of performance will be established. The ability to view the past and assess the use of resources will hinge on accurate financial reporting.

Gauging historical performance against both peers and the company itself will augment decision making as the company moves from an emerging/developmental stage to a more stable, mature stage. Do results reflect decisions made by management or a fortuitous environmental event? Is the reverse true for bad results? As the management team and the company mature, analysis and decision making will become a matter of generating good data on past performance and knowing why (or why not) certain results were achieved.

Accessing historical data is the foundation of developing reporting and analysis capabilities. Part of the maturation process involves creating financial statements or reports that analyze the relevant aspects of the business, whether it is time, geographies, or a combination of the two. The evolution of these tools is an indication of how the decision-making framework is developing. For example, analysis needs that focus on performance results for a current period will give way to bilevel variance reports comparing current and prior-period performance. Bilevel variance reports may evolve into trilevel variance reports comparing current, to prior, to budget data.

The need for information to make decisions will drive finance function development as a particular suite of suitable reporting tools anchored by historical data becomes the mainstay of decision support. The need to discern and strategize will grow as the business becomes more complex. Accommodating this increased need for analysis will demand tools that not only interpret past performance but predict future performance as well.

Future Needs

Just as management will have a need to review the company's past performance, the need to be prospective (via budgets and forecasts) with company results will become imperative as the business grows. The company eventually will confront the need to grow and expand, which will lead to the difficult task of having to assess future performance with a fair level of accuracy. Estimating future resource needs and creating expectations for stakeholders are examples of needs that require reliable prospective reporting.

Excluding extraordinary circumstances, the ability of the company to flourish in a changing environment will depend to a large extent on the finance function's capacity to generate and interpret accurate prospective financial reports on a regular basis. Budgets and forecasts are an example of prospective financial statements that will serve recurring, prospective reporting needs. How will the company perform next month, quarter, or year? Does it take time for the company to ramp-up resources to penetrate/grow relevant markets? If the supply chain is complex, which is often the case with manufacturing organizations, there will be heavy reliance on budgeted revenue numbers to position production or distribution channels to meet expectations. Budgeted P&Ls may be prepared for one-, five-, or 10-year time periods. Forecasts must blend actual results with budgeted numbers to derive short-term targets, typically a year in advance.

Analysis and decision making will hinge on financial reporting tools that interpret data generated by the data flow process. Comparing actual results to budget results in a given period will give an indication of the company's performance. The organization may discover a need to budget balance sheet items for cash flow purposes or otherwise, in addition to P&L items. Although this is more complex and not as widely practiced as budgeting P&L items, mastering this aspect of budgeting may prove to be vital in developing the finance function.

Other Issues in Preparing Financial Statements

Much like choosing accounting methodologies that fit the business, preparing formal financial statements or less formal reports will require focusing on certain key dependencies. Chief of these dependencies is the need for good information. For financial reporting to have value to the organization, the finance function must be able to generate accurate and timely information. Understanding data customers and their needs is also crucial to establishing a sound reporting function. These Tier 2 considerations of the multilevel approach to strategizing dictate the finance function's ability to dispense data in addition to its capacity to gather, process, and analyze data. Having a grasp of the business and industry in which it operates is key to developing an effective reporting function. The finance strategist must work closely with operations and management personnel to ensure that the finance function and strategy is suited for reporting information adequately. Finally, the need to consult with experts to interpret GAAP cannot be discounted. This is particularly critical for organizations that have statutorily defined reporting requirements. Understanding how to treat transactions particular to the business and/or industry will aid in ensuring that data is captured, processed, and classified properly by the finance function, especially where reporting is highly automated.

MAINTAINING GOOD REPORTING

Establishing a solid reporting function will require significant effort from the strategist as the needs of data customers are matched by the capacity of the finance function to serve them. It is important to note that as the business changes, so too will the needs of data customers, whether they are internal or external. The finance function must be able to accommodate these changes. Maintaining the capacity to report financial data will be an ongoing challenge. Certain considerations must be factored into the finance strategy to ensure that the finance function is flexible enough to enhance the reporting function and stay synchronized with the needs of the business. These considerations can be segregated into two groups: external circumstances that will force change and internal circumstances that impact the ability to change.

Navigating external circumstances that will impact financial reporting maintenance will hinge on understanding the business's life cycle. Doing this means grasping Tier 1 considerations of the multilevel approach to strategizing the finance function. Certain events are more dependent on, or have a greater impact on, the reporting function than others. The following external events present challenging requirements for the finance function's ability to report financial data:

- *Acquisitions.* How well does the finance function of target companies mesh with that of the business? Data customers and the capacity to serve them may be very different in outside companies, something that may present challenges to the finance strategist. Considerations related to the centralization of processes and their maintenance will play a prominent role in acquisitive circumstances.
- *Going public.* Reporting requirements set forth by the SEC are specific in time and content. Private, closely held companies may be intimidated when they encounter these statutory reporting requirements for the first time. Preparing for these reporting requirements before they are required may be worth the effort. Can financial and nonfinancial data be harnessed quickly and accurately? Can the company's financial statements be held up to scrutiny from a GAAP perspective? The finance strategist must take these considerations into account as the finance function is designed.
- *New tax laws/accounting rules.* New laws and rules are particularly relevant issues if the company operates in a highly specialized industry. Does GAAP prescribe specific accounting treatments to revenue or expense recognition? Is there a standard to be promulgated in the near future that will impact the organization? Will the change in accounting standard alter the presentation format or financial statements? Will it change the way data is gathered and classified by the finance function? The finance strategist must be aware of areas of accounting or tax laws that may change and be certain the finance function is prepared to deal with them adequately.

Internal circumstances also must be managed to ensure that financial reporting can adapt to changes in the business. Although the greatest focus will be on infrastructure (concrete components of the finance function), soft components must be addressed also. The following areas of concern must be considered:

- *Time to close.* Meeting the reporting needs of data customers will mean gathering data in a timely manner. Doing so will impact the ability of the finance organization to analyze data (which affects data integrity) and deliver required filings on time. Managing the time it takes to close the books and consolidate the numbers company-wide involves awareness of data customer needs and the capacity of the finance function to perform this function. The finance strategist must be aware of the reporting requirements faced by the company when designing the data flow process and the information systems that drive it. How will life cycle events change the time-to-close initiative? Will they demand an as-is closing schedule of 10 days be reduced to five days? The finance strategist must anticipate such a circumstance to prevent data quality from suffering by accommodating a time-to-close need.

■ *Infrastructure.* The capacity to handle reporting/data needs *now* and the flexibility to handle *future* needs should underlie infrastructure development. Accommodating reporting needs will depend on the ability to gather, process, and store data in a logical manner. The finance strategist must be aware of components of infrastructure that are suited for reporting and be certain that tools that are effective in the current stage of the business life cycle are relevant in the future. For example, installing a strong ERP will lay a sound foundation for data gathering for the life of the company. The benefits may end here, however. ERPs are notorious for their lack of user friendliness in regard to reporting. The finance strategist must be aware of and plan for the organization's needs for robust reporting. It would be worthwhile, in this case, to plan for the implementation of a reporting tool on top of the ERP, before the needs of the organization demand it.

■ *Getting it right the first time.* The finance function is in a constant state of evolution, as is the company it serves. Because of this, certain aspects of the finance function will have to be upgraded as the company changes or the business environment shifts. Management/owners must, however, avoid settling for an annotated or inadequate finance function. A finance function that is chronically underdeveloped or behind the business will make the finance strategy less effective and degrade the company's ability to report. Staying on top of the finance function from the start will spare the finance and accounting organization from being perpetually behind the business organization and ensure that, at any given time, meeting new reporting needs will require only minor adjustments rather than major overhauls.

■ *Analysis paradigms/models.* When it comes to conceptualizing a company's finance function for the first time, upper-tier considerations may seem to follow infrastructure considerations. These considerations, however, must play a role in finance function development, especially as it relates to the capacity to report information to data customers. Analysis models and data metrics must change if the analysis is to stay relevant. The finance function must have the flexibility to accommodate data needs for this type of internal reporting.

■ *Reorganization.* Companies in the early stages of life-cycle development typically change their business model. Modifying products, services, or markets may mean gathering financial data in different ways. How does this translate to the reporting function? Will the need to focus on margins increase? Will operating expenses become more or less a priority? Critical reporting needs will have to be addressed at all times regardless of the business model. The finance strategist may have to ensure that the finance function remains flexible, particularly in the reporting area.

FINAL THOUGHTS

Financial reporting is the capstone of the finance function. The data flow process, analysis paradigms, and core fiscal results are manifested through the various modes of reporting employed by the organization. Strong reporting can enhance an otherwise weak finance function while inadequate reporting can degrade a strong finance function. The finance strategist must be mindful of the upper-tier considerations of the multilevel model that comprise financial reporting when conceptualizing and implementing the finance strategy. Awareness of changing needs and requirements of data customers, whether they are internal or external, should drive finance function development. The finance strategy must be in harmony with reporting needs and be flexible enough to add more reporting requirements or enhance existing ones.

9

WRITING THE STRATEGY DOCUMENT

KEY TAKEAWAYS

- Understanding the need to create a finance strategy document.
- Recognizing key benefits of a strategy document.
- Understanding the value of maintaining a high-level view of the business and finance strategy when creating the document.
- Recognizing the role that the multilevel approach to strategizing the finance function plays in creating the strategy document.
- Understanding key areas of preparation/discovery before creating the document.
- Understanding the value in logical initiative flow.
- Knowing how to apply an appropriate format to the document.
- Understanding the components and interrelationships between document format sections.
- Knowing the role of the strategy document in strategy implementation.
- Understanding the role of the strategy document in codifying measurement parameters and metrics.
- Recognizing the role of the strategy document in future strategy development.

PURPOSE OF DEFINING/DOCUMENTING THE FINANCE STRATEGY

Conceptualizing, designing, and implementing a finance strategy will demand generous amounts of time and effort, both in the initial stages of development and in the enhancement/maintenance stage. Whether the finance strategy is allowed to evolve over a period of time as it is implemented or designed and enacted quickly, the finance strategist will find an accumulation of notes and supporting documents to be the sum total of the tangible proof of a strategy. Eventually the organization will need a comprehensive, accessible record of the finance strategy. Creating a central document or series of documents that embody all aspects of the strategy will be necessary if it is to be put into action by the organization. Maintaining a record of the finance strategy will cultivate the philosophies and culture that must prevail in the organization for the finance strategy to be effective.

Putting final thoughts to paper will be the last step in the conceptualization stage of the finance strategy. Documenting data customer needs, systems configurations, and processes may be the primary purpose of this document. However, the strategy document also will serve to cultivate the subinitiatives that achieve strategy objectives as well as to monitor the progression of personnel charged with follow-through. By stating the objectives and scope of the overall strategy, the strategy document will serve as the common platform by which the finance function will be designed and evolved. A comprehensive strategy document will also:

- *Serve as a reference for current and prospective employees.* Depending on the size of the company, the implementation of strategy initiatives will involve a number of people in the organization. Some may be involved in different aspects of the business and/or be geographically removed from the chief strategist(s). The achievement of certain strategy objectives may be marked by a passage of time that spans months or even years. It is critical that all relevant members of the organization be aware of overall strategy objectives and the needs that give rise to them. A comprehensive document will achieve this. Not only will it make clear the critical aspects of the strategy, it also will mark the point in time in which they were conceptualized and put in motion. This document will make clear the initiatives that are passed on to peripheral members of the strategy team and clarify the purpose for initiatives inherited by latecomers. The strategy document will define for everyone *what* is being done and *why.*
- *Guard against the "lost generation."* Anyone involved in strategizing recognizes the value in consistency of thought and the longevity of team members. Developing a strategy is more than dictating the nature and timing of tasks and actions; it involves creating a synergistic consortium of philosophies and approaches to problem solving. Strategies are born from evolving thought processes that stem from a core of perspectives and opinions that blossom into paradigms that address problems and provide solutions. It is not unusual for organizations to lose sight of the purpose or reason for the evolution of certain tasks and initiatives, particularly when key contributors to strategies leave the organization. This lost generation of visionaries can leave the organization rudderless, as initiatives that consume the organization's resources lose their meaning. An unambiguous strategy document will guard against the turnover of strategists, allowing for all members of the organization to understand the components of the strategy as well as its rationale.
- *Define all initiatives.* In many ways the finance strategy is a chronological schematic of business objectives, bridged together with a series of minor ini-

tiatives. Knowing this, it will spawn a series of tasks and subinitiatives that move the organization toward achieving the objectives defined. Because resources will be at stake in the form of time and money, all initiatives must be relevant and purposeful. Most important, they must be able to be held up to scrutiny and rationalized. A strong strategy document will serve as the source for various subinitiatives that will define the finance function. Not only will the document define the vision and objectives of the entire strategy, it also will articulate the steps needed to fulfill the vision. Essentially the document will serve as an enterprise-wide strategic planning tool that lends a sense of urgency to the resulting initiatives.

■ *Serve as a "sell sheet" to executives.* Depending on the philosophy and knowledge level of management/owners, the finance strategy may come under fire or be subject to constant scrutiny. Small and emerging businesses will be particularly prone to questioning or even opposing initiatives that engender the strategy, as the prime movers may want the organization to maintain focus on growth and operational issues. The strategy document will serve as the sell sheet to executives or key personnel on a perpetual basis. Invariably, as time passes and the original intentions for the strategy and initiatives fade, a comprehensive strategy document will preempt naysayers or those lukewarm to strategy development and follow-through. The essence of the document will be to summarize executive management's vision of the company (particularly the finance function) through the finance strategy.

Although it seems like a simple task, putting effort into a comprehensive document is the most overlooked aspect of the strategizing process. Allowing key contributors to commit the strategy to memory exposes the organization to extreme loss if these employees leave the company. Most important, however, creating a comprehensive document allows the finance strategist to articulate, in document form, strategy objectives and how they will be achieved. The concepts will take form on paper. If the strategy does not make sense on paper, it will not do well when put in practice.

The need to think through and plan the critical aspects of the finance strategy document can be illustrated by the case of Downey Interiors. (The preliminary strategy document for Downey Interiors is presented in the appendix.)

Downey Interiors is a full-service interior design firm that specializes in commercial and nonresidential space planning and furnishings. The owner and founder, Deborah Downey, has grown her business from a handful of seasonal clients to a full slate of commercial customers including developers, builders, and large commercial real estate owners. Deborah's business began soon after she finished college while working for her father's well-established architecture firm. Her father was well regarded by the real estate and development community. Deborah noticed a need for quality spatial and interior design. In particular, she discovered that many luxury builders with whom her father did business were left to their own devices when it came to furnishing and decorating models used to sell their apartments and condominiums. Deborah began to provide input on these matters for a few of these clients and soon developed a knack for design and decorating. Ten years later she built the company into a multimillion-dollar business that provides spatial design, drafting, full-service interior design, and decorating to virtually all the major developers and builders throughout the Southeast.

Deborah, however, is at a crossroads in her business. Success has led to the need for more sophisticated administrative management, particularly in the finance area. Although her name is well regarded in the design community, she has developed a reputation for missing installation deadlines. This is creating discomfort among her longtime clients (who are even longer-time friends of her father) who rely on completed models to be the showcase of meticulously planned openings. Her mushrooming client list has put a strain on her logistical framework, which mobilizes key suppliers and manufacturers throughout the United States, Europe, and Latin America. The logistics consist of a web of convoluted, manual processes that are becoming more ineffective as her client list grows. The business itself is extremely sensitive to swings in the economy. Her design team (20 staff designers and 15 drafters) and logistics staff (10 expeditors, 20 warehouse people, and 10 truck drivers) lack the tools and technology to cut down on miscommunications with suppliers and vendors. This results in glaring inefficiencies such as duplicated efforts and process redundancies, which are translating into ill will among vendors and concern with clients. The business is cash oriented from a revenue standpoint, although Deborah extends credit to some customers. Although ample cash is coming in the door, Deborah is constantly experiencing liquidity problems and having difficulty meeting payment terms of vendors and suppliers. The company is not incorporated but is a proprietorship run through Schedule C of her tax return. The business is used to finance her lifestyle; she regularly withdraws cash to finance her own residential needs and passion for travel as well as the needs of her immediate and extended family. She is extremely generous and has certain family members on the payroll of Downey Interiors who are not directly related to the business. Deborah recognizes that the business is experiencing some difficulties as clients, employees, and suppliers are becoming increasingly frustrated with the shortcomings of the business. Clients are getting annoyed with the lack of timeliness of her services, while employees are becoming aggravated with the low pay. Deborah is befuddled by the fact that in spite of the steady increase in business and cash-in, she is unable to harness enough cash to sustain quality raises and retention bonuses for her staff. Turnover is becoming a recurring pattern and mounting challenge as she continues to lose her experienced, licensed designers. She has decided to hire a proven consultant,

Dan Walters from MCD Consulting, who can help her understand the shortcomings of her back office and create some quality solutions to position the company for continued growth. Dan has spent approximately four weeks studying the company, especially Deborah Downey's plans for the future. A summary of Dan's preliminary finance strategy for Downey Interiors can be found in the appendix.

PREPARING TO WRITE THE DOCUMENT

Maintaining the High-Level View

Creating the strategy document will involve codifying concrete items, such as process flows, systems components/specifications, and levels of professional expertise. It will also involve recording thoughts, philosophies, and vision objectives. The initial document should be created at the early stages of strategy development, before initiatives are put in motion and resources are secured. Knowing this, the strategist, in order to excel, must maintain a high-level view of the business and its environment to adequately translate the strategy to paper. In many cases, the strategist may find that the exercise of writing out the strategy will yield unforeseen enhancements or issues that may not have been considered in the early stages of strategizing.

The finance strategist may find that before getting into the nuts and bolts of the strategy, it is worth the time and effort to review the business as a whole—both where it is now and where the owners want it to be in the future. Doing this will freeze the state of the business at the time of strategy conceptualization and create a historical context for the strategy as it unfolds. This context will convey the reasoning behind the objectives and initiatives that make up the strategy as the business changes over time. The benefits of maintaining a high-level view are outlined in Chapter 7, "Investigating Information Systems." Although these benefits were put in the context of conceptualizing, creating, and maintaining information systems components, the same general benefits apply in creating the strategy document. The value in maintaining the high-level view is to resist shortsighted or quick-fix solutions that may derail the long-term health of the finance function. Avoiding a shortsighted view of the finance strategy and the finance function will make future development and evolution much more natural.

Staying within the Multilevel Approach

The heart of the strategizing effort is the multilevel approach, which serves as a working pallette for the strategist to develop ground-up components of strategy and plug in different components to the main body of the existing plan to assess their effectiveness or appropriateness. The author of the strategy document must not lose sight of this top-to-bottom framework when translating the strategy to paper. The audience or reader must be able to put all ideas expressed in a logical context. The multilevel model will allow for the strategy author to incorporate issues related to the business life cycle, data customers, infrastructure, and business models/metrics in their entirety.

The format of the document itself may or may not follow the format of the multilevel approach; however, the essence of its considerations and their interrelationships must be translated to paper. Such documents, especially those written by finance-oriented people, often tend to be narrow in certain areas or overly technical. Maintaining a high-level view and staying within the framework of the multilevel approach will help insulate the document from such a result until all supporting initiatives can be clearly thought through.

Understanding/Defining Resources

The written strategy must enumerate the objectives and initiatives in which the organization will engage to fulfill the finance vision. Initiatives and tasks are of no value if the organization does not have the resources to follow through. It is necessary, therefore, for the finance strategist to understand the current availability of resources and the organization's capacity to commit future resources to the overall effort as the strategy is defined on paper. This commitment of resources will impact the scope and timing of initiatives addressed. Resources to be considered will come in the form of manpower and dollars.

Fundamental to any plan or series of initiatives is the need for the lead and support cast to be clearly identified. They also must be suited for the tasks at hand. The overall strategy must be attributed to committed personnel, starting with the executive or ownership level of the organization. Tapping high-level personnel who have a vital interest in the success of the strategy will ensure the dedication of current and future human resources to initiatives when they are needed. The finance strategist must inventory the personnel and in-house knowledge level and gauge the willingness of management/owners to procure the know-how needed to avoid bringing the strategic initiatives to a standstill. Inevitably gaps will exist in knowledge that will have to be dealt with by hiring additional full-time people or using consultants. The finance strategist must be aware of this before the strategy is recorded and circulated throughout the organization.

Assessing fiscal resources will involve understanding dollars available and timing of their availability. The funds available will depend on many things, some of which are beyond the control of the finance strategist. Regardless, the strategist is best served in determining the total price tag of the finance strategy in the early stages of strategy documentation. Doing so will involve understanding all needs (personnel, consulting, hardware, and software) and potential business circumstances that could change the strategy. Defining the strategy on paper will play a key role in determining these needs.

No less important is understanding the *timing* of fiscal needs. Maintaining a high-level view of the strategy at this stage will help show *when* dollars are needed.

Total dollars available may be dependent on financing arrangements or built around the seasonality of the business to take advantage of cash flow. Understanding the timing of cash in will allow for the arrangement of initiatives in such a way that progress on the overall strategy is not impeded. For example, expenditures for expensive hardware and software may have to be postponed to allow for a round of financing. Committing to consultants before cash is available to buy hardware may saddle the organization with premature consulting fees. Maintaining a high-level view will allow for the finance strategist to address all preliminary initiatives in advance and ensure that throughout the implementation, financing issues do not become an impediment to the overall objectives.

Is All Research Complete?

The finance strategist may find that the time is not quite right to compose and circulate the definitive strategy document. Although writing out the strategy may illuminate certain issues initially overlooked and add clarity where ambiguity once prevailed, the strategist must resist relying on this exercise solely to formulate the strategy itself. The basic philosophies and vision of the finance strategy must be developed by management/owners and firmly grasped by the team implementing it when a document is created and circulated throughout the organization, knowing that certain initiatives may change, arise, or become irrelevant.

The multilevel model may serve as an appropriate check list for the finance strategy. Strategy should be put to paper when the finance strategist has an understanding of:

- The business and where it is in its life cycle
- The identity and needs of data customers
- Infrastructure needs
- The need for or current use of certain business modeling and metrics

Although none of these points needs to be thought out in detail, all should be acknowledged and defined in enough detail to be written down. The finance strategist and readers must keep in mind that the business environment and the business itself will be in a constant state of evolution; hence the above topics can vary over time. It is important to understand that creating a strategy document that is too vague or underdeveloped may damage the strategizing effort in the form of lost credibility (of the strategists) and a general discounting of the effort by managers/owners.

Awareness of Initiative Flow

Perhaps the most critical aspect of strategizing is identifying the tasks and subinitiatives that will mark follow-through. Success, however, will be dependent to a large extent on defining the *flow* of initiatives, that is, the way in which they unfold. Will they be addressed in a manner that maximizes resources and dependencies?

Carefully reviewing the layout of initiatives at the inception of the finance strategy will minimize potential standstills related to conflicts in resource availability or other dependencies. Once the strategy is put in motion, the strategist's principal role will be to manage changing initiatives as they are encountered. Thoughtful attention to initiative layout early will ensure that these reassessments are minimal. Important issues to address include:

- *Maximizing resources.* At the early stage of strategy development, the finance strategist must be certain that the ranks are staffed adequately with the right professionals at the right time, consistent with the flow of initiatives. For example, the implementation of a global consolidation tool will depend on the development of the process that encompasses it. The knowledge needed to develop the process may not be the same as that needed to implement the tool. Staffing efforts will take place over an extended period of time. Certain initiatives will be earmarked for completion first—a decision based on dependencies. Successfully tackling these strategy initiatives over time will require the strategist to be certain that staffing is well ordered, with personnel utilizing the knowledge gained in early strategy tasks to drive future initiatives. This ordered approach to addressing initiatives may mean designating current in-house staff to begin developing processes—an exercise that will prepare them to steer systems development. It is easy to enlist consultants to begin developing systems or other aspects of strategy in the early stages. However, a knowledge base built on outsiders or nonpermanent employees is knowledge lost when initiatives have been completed. The advantages of growing knowledge internally around internal resources cannot be discounted and should factor into the evaluation of resources throughout the implementation of the strategy.

  Because specialized experts and outside help may be costly, the strategist must arrange initiatives and pace the effort so as not to burden the organization with tasks that cannot be properly funded. Understanding budget constraints and planning around them will be imperative during this conceptualizing/documentation stage. Certain needs may seem more critical than others at the outset; however, the timing of availability of funds may dictate holding off on certain initiatives from the start until the organization is better positioned to address and follow through with them. This fiscal awareness must be tempered by the fact that casting aside crucial initiatives in the short run for budget reasons may shortcircuit the strategizing effort in the long term. The strategist, therefore, must be aware of the truly critical initiatives on which the rest of the strategy is dependent.

- *Identifying dependencies.* Logically arranging initiatives in the strategy will involve a prioritization that will allow certain initiatives to form a foundation of sorts, on which other initiatives can be based. Although many tasks will stand on their own, certain ones will depend on the achievement of others. Developing a policies and procedures manual, for instance, may not depend on other initiatives; implementing a reporting software may depend on the implementation of an ERP, which in turn depends on the development of processes and an IS platform. Dedicating resources to developing a policies and procedures manual may not be time critical. Resources for developing and implementing the ERP, reporting package, user processes, and IS platform, however, must be planned carefully.

Dependencies related to external and nonfinancial events also must be considered. Closing dates, manager/owner schedules, and significant life cycle events will dictate the capacity for certain initiatives to be addressed. The strategy document must be created with these dependencies in mind in order for it to gain acceptance from the entire organization and maintain credibility with management/owners. Arranging tasks graphically may be of help to the strategist. Because the strategy document will be the first depiction of the strategy for the organization to review, creating a clear picture of the arrangement of initiatives and their dependencies will promote success. Exhibit 9.1 is a simple depiction of a flow of initiatives for the finance strategy for Downey Interiors through March. (See the appendix.) This schematic of initiative flow will enable Deborah Downey's initial chief finance strategist, Dan Walters, to identify which, if any initiatives, are dependent on others. It will become clear which projects to engage first and which ones will have to wait. The most obvious initiative dependencies involve staffing. The hiring of a controller must happen before the development of a data flow process can begin. Application development for Hyperion Enterprise will not begin until the developer has been put in place.

- *Identifying achievable initiatives.* Many in the business community subscribe to the philosophy of *aim high,* knowing that even if they come up short of the target they will achieve better results than having aimed lower. Although this school of thought has merit, for purposes of developing a finance strategy, the strategist is wise to make the strategy implementation as predictable as possible, knowing that the unforeseen will have to be dealt with either way. Making the execution of the strategy as predictable as possible will mean taking on initiatives that are achievable. Not to be confused with underachieving, arranging initiatives logically will mean understanding resource limitations, timing needs, and dependencies when earmarking and arranging the chronology of tasks. Creating the strategy document may be the first opportunity for the finance strategist to view the entire time line of proposed initiatives and tasks. It also will allow for an assessment of how realistic and achievable the entire strategy and individual initiatives are.

Exhibit 9.1   **Initiative Flow for Downey Interiors through March**

Downey Interiors / Finance Strategy Initiative Flow	January	February	March
Develop first draft of strategy document			
Search for and hire controller			
Search for and hire IS consultant			
Search for and hire Hyperion Enterprise developer			
Search for and hire AccPac developer			
Develop Strategy Executive Summary			
Develop Schedule of supporting initiatives/tasks			
Develop communication Strategy			
Develop Chart of Accounts			
Create Data flow process document			
Create Hardware development Plan			
Create Network development Plan			
Create Data flow system design			
Create a preliminary Hyperion Enterprise application			

COMPOSING THE STRATEGY DOCUMENT

Determining a Format

The format for the document itself can be altered to fit the writing style and sophistication of the management team charged with implementing the strategy. The one *must* to writing the document will be focusing on its usability. The fact that the document will be circulated throughout the organization and relied on in the future is reason enough to develop an informative record of objectives and tasks. The finance strategist must recognize that this document will not only inform but also serve as a platform and motivation for action. Therefore, the components of the document must translate easily into manageable tasks and initiatives. A suggested format to serve this purpose is:

■ Summary of business
■ Define problems/objectives
■ As-is finance function
■ To-be finance function
■ Proposed actions
■ Key dependencies/issues to monitor

The particular arrangement and details of each area may vary, but this general format should be observed, especially for organizations embarking on a finance strategy for the first time.

Summary of the Business

The finance strategy must fit the business in both the needs it addresses and the ability of the company to follow through with relevant tasks and initiatives. The strategy in its manifest form must sell the reader on both the solutions proposed and the needs they address. Establishing the validity of needs to the reader requires a clear definition of the business and its current status in the environment in which it operates. The document also should indicate overall needs as they relate to the finance function. This section should segue into the problems/objectives section.

Referencing the multilevel approach will be imperative in the "Summary of Business" section of the strategy document. Chapter 4's "Tier 1 Considerations: Life Cycle" outlined the need to evaluate the company's past, present, and future and in so doing illustrate the need to develop a strong finance function. This part of the document will serve as the foundation for the presentation of needs and their solutions. Understanding Tier 1 considerations will serve to sell the organization on the need for long-term solutions that may be costly or demand comprehensive commitment from the leadership. Downey Interior's preliminary strategy document touches briefly on certain Tier 1 issues, particularly the quest for financing and the desire to expand the business model into the retail furniture arena.

The necessity to define the business and its needs is easy to discount when creating a document that is deemed to be exclusively finance-oriented. The finance strategist must keep in mind the fact that, as time passes, the business and its needs will change. Certain aspects of the strategy, therefore, may be questioned or challenged, whether the initiatives are being upgraded, changed, disposed of, or remain unchanged. The strategy document must clearly show that the business's situation dictates the need for the tasks and initiatives put in motion, whether the business has changed or not. New executives/managers who may become a part of the overall effort after its inception will depend on historical documentation for the duties they are charged with addressing. The business description will allow for this and enable an easier transition as tasks and initiatives are enhanced/upgraded to fit the growing business's needs and circumstances.

Define Problems/Objectives

This section of the strategy document outlines the primary needs of the organization as they relate to the finance function and the proposed solutions. The scope of the strategy is outlined as well as the challenges that are to be addressed. The overall strategy objectives also must be clearly articulated. Considerations that factor prominently in defining these three main topics include:

1. *Scope.* The scope section provides a statement of the impact of the finance strategy. It should not be long and detailed but rather short and pithy, enabling the reader to grasp the essence of the need for the strategy in a concise, easy-to-understand paragraph. Many small and emerging businesses may be burdened with a haphazard, inefficient finance function or be without one altogether. The scope statement may address the need to overhaul the finance function or develop one from the ground up. The appendix presents a scope statement for Downey Interiors that

focuses on the major concern of the company—the need to manage and report the cash position quickly and accurately. It also mentions the need to accommodate internal data customers and to serve future, external data customers.

2. *Challenges.*   The finance strategist must elaborate on the challenges and issues faced by the organization as they relate to the finance function. Doing so will mean taking the scope statement and defining in greater detail the issues to be addressed. In particular, this area of the strategy document identifies certain routine aspects of data flow that are not adequate and reporting requirements that must be addressed. The challenge for the strategy author at this point is to articulate these challenges in a finance context and also to show how they impact the business. Perhaps the best tool to make the most of this aspect of the document is Tier 2 of the multilevel model. Chapter 4's "Tier 2 Considerations: Data Customers" can serve as the basis for defining these challenges—or, more specifically, needs not being met. The organization's internal and external data customers must be the focus of this section. Downey's strategy document mentions data customer needs in the scope statement, then addresses them again in the "Key Challenges" section. The document clearly articulates the need for professionals to analyze and report on customers as well as the future need to prepare financials for financing arrangements.

3. *Solutions.*   The strategy document must define, in high-level terms, the overall objectives of the finance strategy. This section provides the opportunity for the strategist to do this. This discussion must be confined to the major intended accomplishments and objectives. The challenge in restricting attention to major accomplishments being sought revolves around distinguishing between major strategy objectives and minor initiatives that support the whole endeavor. The solutions proposed at this stage must be logically linked to enhancements to the business or business model.

Attention must be focused on Tiers 3, 4, and 5 of the multilevel approach when defining solutions. Topics of infrastructure, business modeling, and performance metrics factor prominently in this aspect of the document. Although the details of implementation may not be addressed here, the objectives must be clearly articulated. These objectives may come in tangible and less tangible forms. Examples of the former may be the installation of an ERP or consolidation tool. Less tangible objectives may involve establishing a solid base of knowledge and skill in the finance area to help create and enhance business models. Other less tangible objectives may focus on matters of data flow process enhancement, whether it relates to reducing the time to close the books or to enhancing the volume and reliability of financial information. Objectives must be specific and provide clarity and focus to the reader without being too pointed and mired in details. Downey was without a finance function altogether. The strategy author has enumerated the need for many Tier 3 upgrades, particularly development of a data flow process, development of systems infrastructure (network and financial applications), and the establishment of a core finance organization (hiring a full-time controller). The implied evolution of the finance organization hinges on the retention of the two software (AccPac and Hyperion Enterprise) development professionals. Upper-tier considerations are addressed, especially the need for developing analysis models that examine the business's major customer divisions—condominiums/apartments and business/commercial (and retail furniture division starting in Year 3).

As-Is Finance Function

A major component of the finance strategy document is the outline of the current state of the finance function. By defining the landscape of the current finance function, the specific areas to be focused on for improvement will be clarified. This depiction of the *as-is* finance function will serve as a natural extension of the listing of challenges noted earlier in the document. The as-is discussion should be comprehensive and relevant to the strategy objectives while avoiding irrelevant details. The strategy author must include all aspects of the as-is finance function, even if it includes weaknesses that will not be addressed in the immediate future. Doing this will leave the strategy open for further development as the business evolves.

A discussion of the as-is finance function serves to document the starting point of the strategy. More often than not, finance strategies will evolve over time, with some initiatives and tasks implemented sooner than others. The passing of time will mark the gradual fruition of benefits by the finance organization and the business as a whole. Reflecting on where the finance function began and how far it has come at any stage of the evolution of the strategy will serve the overall effort. The well-documented beginnings of a nonexistent or poorly defined finance function will serve to motivate the organization to continue with the finance strategy and to inspire those who may be faced with a particularly challenging slate of tasks. Reviewing the as-is finance function for Downey Interiors in the appendix reveals the lack of any organized finance function. The brief narrative indicates that the organization lacks a data flow process, information systems, finance organization, and reliable analytical tools.

To-Be Finance Function

This discussion is optional and necessary only if the objectives/solutions section is particularly comprehensive. The author may wish to include specific objectives, link certain solutions, or provide a time perspective to the solutions. For example,

the objectives of a certain finance strategy may be the installation of a global consolidation, ERP, and OLAP tool. Although these may be illustrated in parallel in
the document, the finance function evolution may employ these three in varying
combinations throughout the business life cycle. The global consolidation tool, because of its ease of implementation, may be prescribed first, followed by the ERP,
which may be implemented over a longer time period. The OLAP tool, which may
depend on the ERP being in place, may be intended to supercede the global consolidation tool. All three solutions in this case will serve a purpose at different
times during the finance function life cycle, although the planning and conceptualization for all three may have to begin immediately. The appendix briefly outlines certain key areas of Downey Interior's to-be finance function, particularly the
need for employing a controller to gain control of the administration of cash. The
need to develop and coordinate key financial applications that will eventually
serve as the foundation for a reliable data flow process is also defined.

Proposed Actions

This stage of the strategy document defines with more specificity how the organization will go about executing the strategy. This section provides more detail on
the objectives/solutions part of the document. The finance strategist uses this section to define relevant initiatives, resource requirements, and timing of deliverables. The following topics should be outlined:

■ *Key resources.* This section will have two components: (1) human resources
available and needed and (2) financial resources required. The nucleus of
the strategy team may already be in place; however, roles as they relate to
the strategy may not be clearly defined. This area of the document allows
for current finance and nonfinance personnel to be formally tapped and their
roles identified. This listing also enumerates roles and responsibilities the
organization may not be equipped to handle. The organization will use this
document to help in its search for outside help whether it be consultants or
new hires. The strategy document in the appendix approaches the topic of
personnel resources by listing the roles necessary for following through with
the strategy as designed thus far, whether Downey Interiors has the personnel to fill the roles or not. The "Personnel Requirements" section of the document defines these personnel requirements.

  Making financial needs clear at this stage allows management/owners
to become acquainted with the fiscal realities of follow-through. Fiscal
needs must be highlighted in the document as well: Hardware, software, or
other consulting requirements can be clearly defined along with the appropriate cost. Downey Interiors is facing an investment in hardware and
software of approximately $332,000. Additionally, it must commit approx-
imately $490,000 toward qualified professionals to execute and maintain the

finance strategy ($100,000 will be dedicated to a year's worth of consulting for initial strategy design and follow-through). Knowing that these numbers may change in either direction, the finance strategist (Dan Walters) should create an overall budget for Deborah Downey and Downey Interiors.

- *Hardware/software requirements.* Detailed descriptions of hardware and software components demanded by the finance strategy are documented in this section. The strategist's objective is to define the need to upgrade existing hardware and software to accommodate further systems enhancements or to communicate major structural components that must be purchased. Defining major software and hardware purchases in this document will be advantageous in that needs can be put in a logical context. A major part of the finance strategist's job is to secure the bankrolling and budgetary provisions as they relate to crucial strategy components. Communicating them clearly in the context of the entire finance strategy may make the need more palatable to company owner/managers. Downey Interiors will need to create a systems structure from the ground up. Not only will desktop computers, printers, and a server be needed, but also an additional software package (Hyperion Enterprise). One of the key software packages (AccPac) will be retained and developed further.

- *Preliminary strategy time line.* The strategy author should take this opportunity to create a time line summary of the foreseeable initiatives that make up the strategy. The time line may be either top level and summary in nature or detailed. The nature of the time line summary depends on the clarity of the tasks and initiatives and the development of the finance strategy itself. To the extent possible, the finance strategist must make certain that dates for deliverables and task completion are consistent. The critical factor is the arrangement of dependent initiatives and tasks. Many tasks must be achieved first before others can follow. Identifying these foundational initiatives is critical at this stage of documenting the strategy. The strategy author also must be aware of external or nonfinance events that could impact key dates. The dynamics of the initiatives proposed in the first three months of Downey Interior's finance strategy are outlined in Exhibit 9.1. Events in the business life cycle, such as financing arrangements, major filings, or comprehensive audits and evaluations, must be considered in the time line as they will demand resources that may be dedicated to the finance strategy. This area of the document may have to be revisited on a regular basis as events and issues are encountered that impact proposed completion and deliverable dates. The "Strategy Time Line" section of the appendix is a comprehensive listing of tasks and initiatives as they exist in the first draft of the strategy document. The line items listed do not represent all tasks to be achieved; however, they do represent the major initiatives and their general timing requirements.

■ *Major components and deliverables.* This section links, in more detail, *who* is responsible for *what.* The strategy author must go beyond general roles and begin to link major deliverables to individuals and/or groups. In this section of the document the strategy author can assign responsibility and establish accountability where necessary. Identifying key contributors or peripheral nonfinance personnel who will be depended on to help with follow-through could be critical to the success of certain tasks and initiatives. Generally the finance organization is the major contributor to overall finance strategy development and follow-through; however, success may hinge on certain professionals who fall outside the finance/accounting area. These part-time participants could represent weak points in initiatives, especially if the finance strategist has no capacity to dictate their actions. Listing who these people are and what their roles will be, no matter how minor, will ensure a record of support and will invoke either resistance early on in strategy development (which allows time for adjustment) or agreement of support. Agreement at this stage will make reluctance to follow through in the future that much more difficult. It also will signal to the organization that the finance strategy is and will become a permanent part of business objectives and culture. The "Major Components and Deliverables" section of the appendix groups initiatives into the 10 major areas of achievement important to the finance strategy of Downey Interiors. Some of these deliverables will require further planning with tasks and subinitiatives to be defined, although they may go beyond the scope of this particular document.

Potential Risk Factors/Issues to Monitor

The business environment is always rife with change. The author of the finance strategy document must be acutely aware of the changing business environment and circumstances that could lead to amendments or changes to the finance strategy. Changes that threaten or alter the finance strategy and supporting initiatives may come in the form of a shifting economy, changing customer base, disparate market trends, or cost/availability of technology and people. An unexpected (unfavorable) shift in the economy or changing customer base may necessitate abandoning certain initiatives that support the overall finance strategy. A favorable shift in the economy may allow for a rededication to certain initiatives or an enhanced focus on certain areas of the strategy. Monitoring internal risk factors is crucial, especially in regard to turnover in key areas of the organization.

Particular issues to be monitored may range from maintaining a knowledge base for software and hardware implementations to monitoring the stability of government infrastructure in foreign countries in which the company does business. The finance strategist must carefully evaluate all aspects of the strategy and be certain that these risks and issues are truly relevant. What would it mean to the finance strategy if the worst-case scenario were encountered? This section is critical for those who may be skeptical of the relevance of the finance strategy and its ability to be implemented. Skeptics may lie in wait for a bump in the road that may derail the overall effort or call it into question. Defining these bumps in the document will put all members of the organization on notice that certain events or issues may be encountered that could change the landscape of the overall effort. This section is not a list of excuses for the finance strategy to fall short; however, in this section the finance strategist can establish realistic expectations for all involved. Risk factors of note for Downey Interiors include the need to commit the organization to long-term information system construction and maintenance. The need to develop solid GAAP accounting methodologies for the company is also mentioned. These particular items communicate two considerations that could dampen the effectiveness of the finance strategy or impede its development altogether.

PUTTING THE DOCUMENT TO USE

The organization must ensure that after the document is written, the finance strategy is implemented. Doing this means mobilizing available resources and procuring those that are not readily available. The objective now shifts from conceptualizing and designing to action and follow-through. The finance strategist must contend with barriers to completion and internal and external events that may hinder accomplishing key tasks and initiatives. Three issues will require attention:

1. *Administering the strategy.*   Often the organization defines a limited role for the finance strategist. If the organization has hired a consultant or a contract employee to conceptualize and design the strategy, it may not be in a position to retain that person as the overall administrator of the strategy. This may be the case for small and emerging businesses due to budgetary constraints, or it may be that the consultant/ contractor does not wish to take on the role of administrator. Business owners/ managers must understand the role of the finance strategist from the outset of the strategizing effort to ensure that a proper succession of dedicated personnel has been arranged to put and keep the strategy in motion. The intention may be for a member of the management team to take on the role of administrator. If this is the case, the business should demand that the proposed administrator be involved, to some extent, in the conceptualization of the strategy. The organization also may demand that a comprehensive strategy document be crafted and communicated to the management team. The organization may want to keep the consultant/contractor for a limited time to ensure that an adequate

transfer of knowledge has been made to the administrator. The role of the strategist at this point is one of support, ceding the executive duties related to the strategy over to the new administrator.

2. *Developing/managing subinitiatives.* The strategy administrator's major role is to manage the subinitiatives and tasks that make up the strategy. More than likely, small and emerging businesses have to manage limited resources for these purposes. The challenge, therefore, is to utilize available resources wisely in achieving the desired end. Downey Interiors must create a data flow process where it never existed before. Doing this will not be a simple task but rather an iterative, evolving one that may demand considerable resources. The strategy administrator must be aware of who is most suited for these tasks and prepare them for the challenge. Significant up-front time may be required to explain the objective of the proposed process and the key dependencies/factors. This task also may demand steady monitoring to ensure that the process development stays within both the design parameters and the necessary time constraints.

   The strategy administrator also must dedicate time to the development of subinitiatives. Doing so may involve ensuring that certain subinitiatives or proposed tasks are relevant and constructive and do not create more issues than they solve. To this end, the strategy administrator may purge proposed tasks from workflow rather than initiating them. This high-level awareness of the strategy is vital given that many aspects of the strategy will be assigned to various parts of the organization, some of which are nonfinance areas.

3. *Making changes.* Change will be constant throughout strategy follow-through. Finance administrators may or may not be the strategists, but they must be knowledgeable enough to understand the dynamics of the strategy and its supporting initiatives and possess the administrative skills to coach personnel through shifting tasks and initiatives. The external and internal business environment is in a constant state of flux, which may generate significant changes to the strategy. For example, the system design for Downey Interiors may be impacted by a new requirement of vendors that all orders be done online (over the Internet). Downey must be prepared to refocus its efforts on developing the capability to place orders online or risk being cut off by key vendors. Additionally, an unreasonable time element may make matters more complicated. The finance strategy administrator, therefore, may be called upon to be the de facto strategist. Managing shifting needs, resources, and expectations will be critical to the success of strategy administration. The strategy administrator must be prepared to recognize these changes and incorporate them into the overall plan.

EVALUATING PERFORMANCE

Need to Measure Results

The strategy must unfold in an effective and timely manner. Success will depend to a large extent on the organization's ability to evaluate progress. This means holding accountable those charged with executing certain tasks. Evaluating the effectiveness of the strategy means more than this, however. Are the resulting deliverables useful to the organization? Do certain resulting structures and processes create more problems than they solve? Many times objectives that look good on paper do not translate well into constructive components of the finance function. If tasks and initiatives yield unusable deliverables (processes, systems, etc.), the organization must be careful not to frame this as failure. Failure would be maintaining the unsuitable deliverables in spite of their lack of usability. The finance strategist and administrator (if they are not one and the same) must be prepared to create metrics and evaluation measures to ensure that strategy follow-through occurs in the best interest of the business. Evaluating progress on strategy objectives will mean creating metrics and measures as well as standards for determining the success or failure of the overall strategy effort. The strategy document will be the primary tool for creating such measures.

Translating the Document into Metrics

How will metrics and measures be put in place to gauge progress? Consistent with any project that spans a long time period and/or employs significant resources, the finance strategy must employ reliable measures to evaluate performance and progress. The strategy document will serve as the primary tool for developing relevant metrics and performance measures. Three types of important performance measures can be developed from the document:

1. *Timing.*   Overall strategy time lines and workflow schedules will serve as crucial measures of performance. Although the strategy document may contain high-level time schedules, it also will serve as a basis for developing more specific time lines and workflow schedules. The key to establishing these types of metrics lies in the consistency of timing requirements. All work plans and time schedules must be consistent or conflict will arise. Time schedules in the strategy document should serve as the basis for all time and workflow schedules.

2. *Resources.*   All projects must stay within budget; those that do not must be examined. Aside from poor planning and lack of leadership, poor resource allocation is the greatest barrier to strategy success. Resource allocations and requirements must be unambiguous to all involved in the administration of supporting strategy initiatives. Budgets are not enough

to ensure success. Periodic reporting that evaluates the resources that have been utilized and those that are needed must be a part of project coordination and follow-through. It may be that original budgets and expectations were inadequate. This fact will become evident as projects unfold and resources are evaluated. Budgets and resource allocations defined in the strategy document will serve as the basis for evaluating resources throughout strategy implementation.

3. *Objective achievement.* The strategy's success will hinge on whether tasks are achieved and deliverables are realized. It is easy for the organization to get distracted by initiatives and subinitiatives and the challenges they pose. The final measure of success will be the achievement of objectives that are defined by the finance strategy document. This type of objective measure *must* be a part of overall performance of the strategy implementation. Combining this with timing and resource-oriented metrics will provide a reliable way to measure progress throughout what can be a lengthy and complex effort.

What Is Considered Success/Failure?

The organization's relationship with its finance strategy will be marked, ultimately, by a realization of success or failure. Depending on the size and sophistication of the organization, as well as the expectations of the strategy effort, success and failure can be defined in many ways. Any organization taking on the challenging task of developing and implementing a finance strategy has already realized that the business will not survive without a value-added finance function. The small and emerging business, whether it succeeds in addressing the myriad of tasks and initiatives a finance strategy spawns or not, will benefit by developing the high-level perspective and data-centric approach that strategy development demands. Cultivating a strategic-minded approach to managing financial information and a customer-centric view of the reporting and decision support function will generate a constructive culture within the business in areas beyond finance.

The organization ultimately will seek ROIs and achievements, through the finance strategy, that go beyond moral victories and translate into real improvements to the business. The organization must be comfortable with the fact that certain tasks and initiatives will have to be abandoned as the strategy is administered, which may translate into lost resources. The finance strategist and the organization must keep a high-level perspective when it comes to judging overall success or failure of the strategy in the interim. Doing this will mean looking beyond tasks and initiatives and focusing on data customer satisfaction and organization buy-in as well as initiative administration. Maintaining a constructive outlook will ensure that the ultimate objectives will be achieved and the organization will reap the benefit of both the overt and subtle ROIs the finance strategy offers.

Maintaining Urgency and Follow-through

Success can breed complacency. The finance strategist/administrator must remain focused on the tasks at hand and remain vigilant when it comes to addressing strategy initiatives. Certain achievements marked by strategy follow-through may seem colossal, especially for the small and emerging business owner. The temptation is to focus on certain major achievements and ignore lesser tasks and initiatives. The strategy, however, will not be successful unless all scheduled initiatives are addressed adequately. Often the more subtle components of strategy enable its success. Many times these are the components that are abandoned or discounted when early success is encountered or major initiatives are accomplished early.

Leadership of the organization must recognize that commitment to thorough completion of all finance strategy tasks is imperative. The finance strategist's best tool for maintaining focus and keeping the organization on track is the strategy document. Because a carefully crafted document will illustrate how the significant and less important initiatives make up the whole strategy, it will help make a case for continued commitment to follow-through, even if major achievements have already been realized.

ENABLING FUTURE DEVELOPMENT

Laying a Reliable Foundation

The finance strategist's lasting contribution to the organization will be the future development of the finance function. The true test of a successful finance strategy lies in its capacity to expand/change as the organization changes. Many small and emerging businesses are without a finance function prior to strategizing. Although this may seem to handicap the organization, from a planning perspective it may be an advantage. A clean slate will enable a solid, logical finance foundation to be established on which future development can be based. A well-thought-out finance function will consist of a reliable, scalable core that will endure for the life of the company. This scalable core foundation will manifest itself in many forms, whether it is a reliable system infrastructure or a solid base of knowledgeable professionals.

Developing Discipline and Know-how

One of the enduring factors of the finance strategy will be the body of knowledge and know-how and the process discipline developed as the finance function matures. The finance function will demand and enable the development of knowledge specific to the business's financial condition. Knowledge related to data flow, specifically analysis of data and the analysis paradigms that dictate business decisions, will beget the need for further development of the finance function. The more information provided to the organization, the more it will demand. This may appear to be a never-ending challenge to the finance strategist; however, as the finance strategy unfolds, knowledgeable components of the finance function will prompt thoughtful, relevant enhancements. Development that follows this model will allow for intelligent, customer-centric finance function upgrades that, to a certain extent, will be owned by the user community and/or data customers. These self-directed upgrades will serve not only to decentralize certain aspects of finance function development but to establish ownership for upgrades.

Similar to leveraging off an internally generated knowledge base for finance function enhancements, the strategy will benefit from input from participants who recognize the need for efficient and timely data flow management. The best ideas come from within, however. The organization must beware of exception-oriented or myopic solutions. Suggestions to accommodate exceptions will rarely benefit the finance function as a whole. Professionals who are part of the finance function and recognize the need for uniformity and discipline will understand that enhancements and upgrades must be tethered to good discipline that benefits the entire organization.

Rolling with the Changes

An agile finance strategy may be the organization's most valuable asset. Agility means the ability to be flexible in the face of shifting needs and changing business parameters. How suited is the proposed infrastructure to changes or shifting parameters? Will changes in the business dictate the need to adjust historical data? How difficult a task will this be? Reliable, out-of-the-box data management applications may be easy to implement and simple to learn, but they may be highly inflexible when it comes to moving data around. Extended downtime of critical applications may not be acceptable from a user standpoint. The finance strategist should know what aspects of the finance function must be flexible and incorporate this flexibility into the structure. Whether this agility refers to process, system, or finance organization design, the capacity for change must be contemplated.

Facilitating the ability to change finance strategy initiatives or existing finance function components will hinge on the long-term nature of proposed solutions. While quick, easy solutions may be a priority, especially for the small and emerging business owner, the strategist must weigh the potential cost of rework or the likelihood of irrelevance. Avoiding shortsighted solutions will pay off as time passes. The strategist will have to weigh the cost of surrendering an easy solution for a more complex or expensive one against the long-term payoff of a reliable application that will endure and be maintained easily.

Communication with key users and data customers is necessary to successfully manage shifts in the finance strategy and/or existing finance function. Change is inevitable, whether it is related to needs or general business parameters.

The finance strategist must do everything possible to make this change as predictable as possible. Establishing open communication links with the user community is necessary in order to understand shifting needs before they become critical. The strategy document may be the most effective mode of communication with the user community. Referring to a well-circulated strategy document on a regular basis will provide an ongoing dialog throughout the organization that is relevant and contextual.

Keeping Up with Business Changes

The finance strategist and strategy administrator are faced with the challenge not only of implementing the strategy originally conceptualized but also keeping it relevant. Although this dual challenge applies to the mid- and long-term life of the finance function, for the small and emerging business, it is crucial during the original implementation of the strategy. Maintaining credibility and maximizing resources depends on the strategy team administering usable initiatives and tasks. The initial phases of development are marked by considerable change, as parameters and needs are defined, redefined, and modified as the business evolves. The pressure is on the strategist to provide assurance that the initiatives-in-progress will satisfy a need. During follow-through, should the team pull the plug on an unnecessary initiative or task? When should the task be reassessed and adjusted?

Often users or data customers play a role in an initiative or task rollout. They understand, sometimes well before completion, whether a particular initiative will benefit them. The strategist must maintain adequate communication with such elements of the organization and ensure that processes and systems development suit the purpose for which they are being created. The strategist and administrator must have the courage to adjust, reassess, or even discontinue certain initiatives, if necessary, to ensure the objectives are met and resources are being used wisely.

FINAL THOUGHTS

Crafting a finance strategy document is vital to strategy design, implementation, and future development. For many small and emerging businesses, this process will spur the initial strategy design as philosophies, concepts, and proposed initiatives are translated to written form for the first time. The document will serve as a guide for future initiatives and tasks as well as the single tangible representation of the finance strategy, whether it is still in the inception/development phase, has been put in motion, or is somewhere in between.

The strategy document will serve as the source for all relevant subinitiatives and tasks that define the strategy itself. It also will serve as the basis for the development of all metrics and performance measures that will provide a framework for management/owners to evaluate the suitability of the strategy. The most fundamental benefit to be reaped from a comprehensive, relevant strategy document is the unambiguous statement of strategy objectives and the depiction of the status of the business at inception of the strategy. Ultimately the written finance strategy will protect the organization from relying exclusively on the memory of a small group to dictate the strategic direction of the business enterprise.

_____ Appendix _____

FINANCE STRATEGY: DOWNEY INTERIORS

BUSINESS SUMMARY

Downey Interiors seeks to enhance its market presence as a full-service interior design firm that specializes in commercial and nonresidential space planning and furnishings. Growth has been constant as annual revenues have gone from just under $1 million to nearly $10 million annually in less than five years. Full-time and temporary staff are employed throughout the year depending on the season and workload. The 77 full-time employees include:

- 20 staff designers
- 15 drafters
- 10 expeditors (logistics)
- 20 warehouse workers
- 10 truck drivers
- 2 administrative staff

Most temporary help comes in the form of nonskilled warehouse workers and expeditors. The administrative staff support all back-office matters including the finance function. Net equity of the company is unknown (most recent tax return of Deborah Downey unavailable), although the company has approximately $2 million in receivables, $500,000 in inventory, and $150,000 in cash (per 9/30/01 bank reconciliations) against approximately $1.5 million in lease commitments (office space, warehouse, and trucks).

The company is considering expanding the business model into the retail furniture arena, which will complement the designing and decorating business. Although no formal business model has been developed to analyze the financial dimensions of this strategic move, informal surveys of peer companies indicate that such an expansion could push the business to the $50 to $100 million-dollar range within five years of commencing such a plan. It is estimated that company revenue will grow at approximately 50% annually for an indefinite period beyond this, due to the expected development in the Southeast, particularly Florida. This growth is estimated to occur in equal portions in both the business/commercial and condominium/apartment segments of the business. The challenge in meeting these growth estimates is to create and maintain adequate infrastructure to handle the volume of business. The growth projections are:

- Year 1: $15 million
- Year 2: $22.5 million
- Year 3: $35 million
- Year 4: $50 million
- Year 5: $75 million
- Year 6: $110 million
- Year 7: $165 million
- Year 8: $248 million
- Year 9: $372 million
- Year 10: $558 million

The estimated growth in revenue is marked by the expansion of the business model to include retail furniture sales in Year 3 which will sustain revenue growth in the 40 to 50% range to Year 5. Beginning in Year 5, a nationwide expansion will be undertaken as the company seeks to expand into the Northeast, Midwest, and Rocky Mountain regions. The growth methodology will be organic as the company will seek funding and invest in infrastructure and intellectual capital to expand into the retail furniture market (beginning in Year 3) and into various geographic regions (beginning in Year 5), although acquisitive expansion will not be ruled out.

The primary mode of financing will be debt. Expansion in the short term will consist of the need for the following:

- *Year 1.* $2 million to finance expansion of the physical plant, particularly the warehouse facility
- *Year 3.* $5 million to finance expansion into the retail furniture industry
- *Year 5.* $10 million to finance expansion into geographic regions

Financing requirements are estimates and subject to change given the status of cash flow.

Deborah Downey is and will continue to be the primary strategic force behind operations. All decisions related to product sales and customers will be made by Deborah for the indefinite future. Although she will continue to be intimately involved in all aspects of the business, a board of directors will be formed and a hierarchy of operations personnel will be put in place to steer the company into the five- to 10-year time horizon.

The company is in need of a strong finance function that can buoy the organization into continual, organic growth and position it to expand the current business model in Year 3. The company has pressing needs in the area of cash management. In addition, the organization must develop the capacity to generate accurate, auditable financial statements to submit to financial institutions for financing. The need for financial statements that can be prepared in U.S. GAAP form will be realized within the next 12 months when financing is sought for physical plant expansion. The ability to budget and forecast will be paramount, as the business is vulnerable to downswings in the economy. Overall systems development also must be a priority throughout the organization in the logistics, operational, and finance areas. Key periods for growth, which will demand accurate analysis, will occur in Years 3 and 5.

PROBLEMS/OBJECTIVES

Scope Statement

The current finance function is light, bordering on nonexistent. The overall objective of this finance strategy is to establish scalable infrastructure, particularly processes and systems that can enable the reliable management of cash and translation of the business to financial statements. The organization looks to leverage the infrastructure established to allow for key operational areas to enhance effectiveness through careful analysis and reporting.

Key Challenges

The company lacks a formal controllership function, instead relying on part-time administrative staff to manage the finance aspect of the back office. Remnants of accounting software exist, but there is no capacity or know-how to perform project accounting or manage operating expenses.

There are a limited number of data customers to date. Internal data customers are relatively unsophisticated, consisting of Deborah Downey, the administrative staff, and the team of designers. The data needs of the administrative staff center on the amount and timing of vendor payments as well as the amount and timing of customer payments. The data needs of the designers relate to the budgeting and costing of jobs. The data needs of Deborah Downey focus on the overall financial state of the company. The needs of the internal data customers are not being met. There is no mechanism in place to track vendor payments and terms, nor is there a methodology to track and age receivables. The designers must rely on their own business acumen and manual methodologies to budget and cost jobs, not to mention monitor interim progress. The company does not have the capacity to create

U.S. GAAP financial statements. Although a balance sheet and tax P&L is created by the CPA preparing Deborah Downey's tax return, it is not prepared using GAAP and hence would not hold up to formal review or audit procedures.

The only external data customer the company encounters is the IRS, which receives all company data on Deborah's tax return. The company will file a separate tax return after it incorporates in the coming year. External data customers will expand to financial institutions as debt financing is sought in the next 12 months and beyond. The capacity to generate auditable U.S. GAAP financial statements will be critical as the loan review process is undertaken.

Near-term needs of data customers will center on the ability to track and analyze vendor accounts/payments and customer receivables. Internally, the capacity to budget and cost jobs must be established for the designers. The ability to create GAAP financial statements is critical as the process for acquiring financing will dictate the need for an accurate, auditable balance sheet, P&L, and cash flow statement. Long-term needs will focus on the ability to analyze business activity among the current and prospective business divisions. The finance function must have the capacity to track data from the transactional level up to the summary level by Year 3, when expansion into the retail furniture market will begin.

On a more basic level, the organization lacks many fundamental components of a sound finance function. Organization and division of duties represent the greatest shortcomings of the as-is finance function. The following shortcomings must be addressed in the near future:

- No formal controllership function exists.
- No regular accounting is done on a monthly, quarterly, or annual basis.
- A sustained, auditable approach to cash management does not exist.
- Professionals cannot perform analysis on the profitability of jobs and customers.
- The company cannot compile auditable financial statements.
- Although the firm has few receivables, it cannot age the receivables it holds.
- Roles in the cash disbursements/collections area are poorly defined.
- No clear cash management policies exist.

Proposed Solutions

The organization is in need of systems (hardware and software) and the know-how to use them to create an efficient finance function. The overall solution will require the procurement of reliable, scalable accounting software to facilitate the gathering, processing, and analysis of financial data. Additionally, the organization must develop sound processes and develop disciplines that will facilitate good reporting and cash management. The following must be achieved in the short term:

- Incorporate the business, limiting the liability of owners and establishing distance between the administrative affairs of the business and owner

- Utilize the accounting software (AccPac) that is in place (but rarely used)
- Establish a process of booking daily activity, particularly cash transactions, on a daily basis and key accruals on a monthly basis
- Establish a disciplined closing process that will close the books in one business day
- Purchase a reliable consolidation and reporting software—Hyperion Enterprise
- Create analysis models that break the business into the two main divisions—condominium/apartment and business/commercial
- Establish a central repository of data and auditable transaction trails
- Create clear, accountable division of duties as they relate to the cash function

The benefits received in achieving the above will be a mixture of overt and subtle. The major benefits will relate to cash management through the analysis of receivables and vendor payment schedules. The more subtle benefits will stem from the enhanced discipline and capacity to understand the financial profile of the organization, which will allow for analysis of variations of the business model. The strategy will produce the following benefits:

- Reliable and efficient cash management
- Better analysis of receivables and vendor terms
- Reliable central repository of data
- A reliable reporting scheme
- Availability of operating expense analysis tools
- Capacity for profitability analysis of jobs by individual designer
- Enhanced availability and quality of financial data
- Historical and prospective analysis models
- Fully automated monthly closing process
- Disciplined production of reliable, U.S. GAAP financial statements

AS-IS FINANCE FUNCTION

The current finance function consists of two administrative staff (secretaries) who manage the checkbook as well as cash deposits. They keep track of vendor invoices and prepare all customer billings. The company invested in AccPac bookkeeping software three years ago, but the secretary/bookkeeper who advocated its use left the company shortly after it was installed on her computer, which is the only PC in the administrative area. The remaining administrative staff members have neither the time nor the inclination to learn and use the software. The only bookkeeping that occurs is the annual compilation prepared by the CPA at the end of the year on Schedule C of Deborah's 1040 tax return. This compilation consists of supplying the CPA with all cash receipts and disbursements as well as all sales contracts. No receivables subledger or inventory record is kept. The administrative area has one computer, a Pentium 120 with 64Mb of RAM and 500Mb of hard drive space. The users have no Internet access and use the computer for limited spreadsheet preparation for schedules and meetings.

TO-BE FINANCE FUNCTION

The finance function must employ a controller to develop and manage the monthly closing process as well as cash. This person also must develop analysis tools for the overall business, individual jobs, and prospective business models. The immediate priority will be the administration of cash.

The core of the data flow process will be the utilization of the AccPac software to perform daily cash bookings and monthly accruals. The transactional data gathered in this software will be transferred to Hyperion Enterprise, which will facilitate the monthly closing process and allow for robust reporting and analysis. Hyperion Enterprise is a Windows-based consolidation and reporting tool that is easy to use and maintain. It can be designed to house data in varying ways. Its report creation module is extremely user friendly, enabling a novice finance user to create reports quickly and easily. The combination of AccPac and Hyperion Enterprise will allow the business to create divisional or product-oriented reporting, which will result in a well-thought-out expansion into the retail furniture business. Additionally, it will allow the designers to budget and cost jobs.

Monthly reporting will be facilitated by a small staff of either part-time workers or paraprofessionals. The key success factor is the establishment of a seamless automated process that allows for smooth data flow from AccPac to Hyperion Enterprise. The discipline created with a monthly reporting regimen will parlay into the capacity to develop accurate GAAP financial statements on a regular basis (quarterly). The need for a more powerful data gathering tool at the transaction level will demand that an enterprise resource planning tool be installed by Year 3. The planning for the installation of such a tool must begin at the end of Year 1.

PROPOSED ACTIONS

This finance strategy will focus on conceptualizing, implementing, and maintaining key aspects of the finance function over a 12-month time period. Key components of the finance strategy are the implementation of Hyperion Enterprise and the development of AccPac reporting procedures. The establishment of reliable network and hardware components to support these applications will be critical. A basic server and PC configuration must be established, accompanied by a clear data flow system design (see Exhibit A1 for hardware/software requirements). The de-

Exhibit A1 **Hardware/Software Requirements**

Description	Specifications	Cost
8 PCs	PIII 933 /20GB/ 125 MB/ 48XCDR/ 17″ monitor	$12,000 (1,500 × 8)
3 printers	HP Laserjet 4100N 25ppm 32MB 1200DPI 10/100	$4,500 (1,500 × 3)
Hyperion Enterprise software (plus limited consulting)	Version 6.0; multi-site license	$300,000
ACCPac software	Application as-is	NA
Server	PIII Xeon 500/100MHz 256MB (4GB max), (3 slots free)/ 10-100TX LAN, CD-ROM, Dual Chann. NetRaid 12 Mass Storage shelves (288GB Max)	$15,000

Note: All price quotes above are estimates and subject to change.

velopment of data flow process steps will stem from the implementation and development of these hardware and software tools. The major undertakings in the immediate future include:

- Enhancing AccPac software application.
- Purchasing and installing Hyperion Enterprise software.
- Establishing network and hardware systems configurations.
- Developing data flow process.
- Developing training/knowledge transfer programs.
- Developing a system maintenance program.

It is vital that the necessary people are put in place as quickly as possible to allow for early planning and development. The most critical of these personnel are the controller, AccPac developer, Hyperion Enterprise developer, and systems developer. Although support staff will develop along with the central staffing needs, the vital personnel requirements must be the focus of the organization's efforts (see Exhibit A2).

Systems needs fall into five basic areas. The organization must invest in eight PCs in the near term to accommodate the Hyperion Enterprise and AccPac application development. Additionally, three printers must be purchased to handle user needs. The organization also must prepare to invest in a strong, scalable server to act as the platform for the main financial applications and future financial/nonfinancial applications. The Hyperion Enterprise software also must be purchased. Exhibit A1 outlines software and hardware needs in detail.

Exhibit A2 **Personnel Requirements**

Resources	Roles	Team
Dan Walters, consultant	Chief finance strategist	MCD consulting
Deborah Downey	Organization liaison	Owner/manager
TBD*	Application development	Hyperion/AccPac Implementation Team
TBD*	Application development	Hyperion/AccPac Implementation Team
TBD*	Controller	Finance
Wilma Adams	Admin/support	Finance/general operations
Felicia Williams	Admin/support	Finance/general operations
TBD*	Network support	MIS—Network Support (consultant)
Laura Timmons	Operations liaison	Designer/drafters team
Wendy Sterner	Operations liaison	Logistics/expediter
William "Billy" Pattmore	Operations liaison	Warehouse/supply chain team
TBD*	Network development support	Extended systems/network development team

*Compulsory project resources. Timing of needs dependent on further strategy development.

Budgeting for this undertaking must begin immediately. Initial investments will be necessary for personnel and hardware/software. Exhibits A1 and A3 outline the estimated cost of the initial components of this finance strategy. The initial, up-front investment will be critical in enabling the achievement of the projected revenue growth. Although margin and net income data is not available, it is estimated that the initial investment in software and hardware of approximately $332,000 and $100,000 in first year consulting will be paid off in Year 2. This investment along with the investment in key personnel of $490,000 will be critical to enabling the 50% revenue growth and expansion into the retail furniture market.

The execution of the various initiatives and tasks over the next 12 months will depend on the development of numerous work plans. Exhibit A4 outlines the timing of critical deliverables, which will dictate the timing parameters of succession of work plans. In particular, detailed project plans must be created for the PC/network installations, Hyperion Enterprise implementation, and the reengineering of the AccPac software. Additionally, the development of the processes that will underscore the overall data flow will require detailed timetables and completion targets.

Exhibit A3   **Resource Requirements for Proposed Personnel**

Resource Description	Projected Salary
One year commitment to MCD Consulting (Dan Walters)	$100,000
Controller	$ 80,000
Hyperion Enterprise Implementer	$ 75,000
AccPac software Implementer	$ 50,000
IS administrator	$ 80,000
Network development support senior	$ 60,000
Network development support staff	$ 45,000

Exhibit A5 identifies the 10 key components of the overall finance strategy, who is charged with addressing them, and the deliverables sought. This exhibit will enable the development of work plans and incentives for achieving the overall strategy objectives. This exhibit must be updated as initiatives change or have been completed.

A full suite of analysis tools (reports and metrics) also must be established. Analysis paradigms and performance analysis tools will be developed that will aid in understanding the business. The tools themselves are dependent on the parameters laid out in the data flow process design. The needs will be defined in more detail by the controller function. These tools will come in the form of reports to be developed in the Hyperion Enterprise database. The following analysis tools must be created in the next 12 months:

- Job budgeting/costing
- Cash flow reporting/model
- Accounts receivable aging
- Days sales outstanding
- Operating expense model
- Vendor payment schedules

Education and knowledge transfer tools will be established as well. User manuals and educational curriculums must be developed to train current and prospective employees in using the AccPac and Hyperion Enterprise databases to facilitate the data flow process. These programs cannot be developed, however, until the network, databases, and data flow process are in place.

Future development of the finance function will hinge on the design and implementation of a powerful enterprise resource planning tool. The organization must be prepared to have this tool in place to support the expansion into the retail furniture market. Planning for this must begin in the latter part of 2002 (see Exhibit A4).

Exhibit A4   **Strategy Time Line**

Task/Initiative	Begin	End
Develop first draft of strategy document	1/1/02	2/1/02
Search for and hire controller	1/1/02	2/1/02
Search for and hire IS consultant	1/1/02	2/7/02
Search for and hire Hyperion Enterprise developer	1/1/02	3/1/02
Search for and hire AccPac developer	1/1/02	3/1/02
Develop Strategy Executive Summary	2/4/02	2/11/02
Develop schedule of supporting initiatives/tasks	2/11/02	2/15/02
Develop communication strategy	2/15/02	2/19/02
Develop Chart of Accounts	2/15/02	3/21/02
Create data flow process document	2/15/02	3/15/02
Create hardware development plan	2/21/02	3/7/02
Create network development plan	2/21/02	3/21/02
Create data flow system design	3/15/02	4/1/02
Create a preliminary Hyperion Enterprise application	3/15/02	4/15/02
Develop Hyperion Enterprise Server interface configurations	4/1/02	4/8/02
Develop Hyperion training manual	4/16/02	6/21/02
Create Hyperion application documentation	5/1/02	5/31/02
Create Hyperion installation documentation	4/8/02	5/8/02
Load two years worth of historical data	5/1/02	6/7/02
Build edit checks, validation routines	6/14/02	7/1/02
Create preliminary AccPac application	3/15/02	4/1/02
Create AccPac server interface configurations	3/21/02	4/1/02
Develop AccPac training manual	3/22/02	4/30/02
Create AccPac application documentation	4/1/02	5/1/02
Create upgrade documentation	3/22/02	4/15/02
Develop data transfer routine (from AccPac to Hyperion Enterprise)	5/1/02	5/15/02
Training/rollout prep	7/1/02	7/8/02
Report building, edit checks, application validation	7/1/02	7/15/02
User training session	7/22/02	7/29/02
User rollout	7/31/02	N/A
Go live	8/1/02	N/A
Begin planning ERP design	11/1/02	N/A

Exhibit A5 **Major Components and Deliverables**

Description	Resources	Deliverables
Planning • Strategy planning by initiative and phase	MCD Consulting	• Strategy document • Executive summary • Schedule of supporting initiatives
Coordination and Communication • Coordinate related projects/initiatives • Coordinate with various organization liaisons	• MCD Consulting • Controller	Communication strategy
Data Flow Process Development • Chart of Accounts • Data flow process development	• MCD Consulting • Controller • Finance/general operations	• Chart of Accounts • Data flow process document
PC/Network Specifications • Determine PC requirements company-wide to support AccPac and Hyperion • Document server requirements for AccPac and Hyperion • Define system flow for data collection/delivery • Document general need for network peripherals	• MCD Consulting • Controller • MIS—Network Support • Hyperion/AccPac Implementation Team	• Hardware development plan • Network development plan • Data flow system design
Design Reporting Model • Design data analysis process • Determine management reporting schema • Design information sharing model	• MCD Consulting • Controller • Hyperion/AccPac Implementation Team • Finance/general operations • Designer/drafters team • Warehouse/supply chain team	• Suite of financial reports • Analysis paradigms and performance analysis tools

(continued)

Exhibit A5 **Major Components and Deliverables (Continued)**

Description	Resources	Deliverables
Hyperion Application Development/Implementation • Develop core parameters of Hyperion Enterprise • Develop interfaces • Network/server development	• MIS—Network Support • Hyperion/AccPac Implementation Team	• Preliminary application • Data transfer methodology (from AccPac to Hyperion Enterprise) • Server interface configurations
Hyperion Knowledge Transfer/Documentation • Documentation • Training	• Controller • Hyperion/AccPac Implementation Team	• Training manual • Application documentation • Installation documentation
AccPac Application Development/Upgrade • Re-design core parameters of AccPac • Develop interfaces	• Controller • Hyperion/AccPac Implementation Team	• Preliminary application • Server interface configurations
AccPac Knowledge Transfer/Documentation • Documentation • Training	• Controller • Hyperion/AccPac Implementation Team	• Training manual • Application documentation • Upgrade documentation
Maintenance • Develop procedures to maintain applications, network, and PCs	• MCD consulting • Controller • MIS—Network Support	• System maintenance procedures • Problem escalation plan • AccPac maintenance procedures • Hyperion Enterprise maintenance procedures

ISSUES TO MONITOR

This finance strategy is subject to many dependencies and issues that may derail or alter the direction of the endeavor. The most critical dependency is that the industry is sensitive to the economy. A sluggish economy will dampen both commercial and residential development, especially multidwelling units. The finance function must be prepared to track cash needs and report on the cash position accurately. The major challenge will relate to maintaining knowledge transfer throughout the organization. Because this strategy avoids an outsourcing model, the need to retain the knowledge of systems design and development is critical. In the event growth projections change (for the worse), the strategy may shift to employ an application service provider to serve the company's finance needs. The following points must be taken into account:

- Developing a comprehensive network platform of finance and other non-finance applications
- Developing knowledge transfer and retention program
- Developing documentation of specific system configurations
- Set up a high-level technical support team to manage network setup, PC configuration, and ongoing maintenance.
- Identifying GAAP issues that relate specifically to the business (i.e., long-term contract accounting)
- Developing a logical chart of accounts for AccPac and Hyperion applications
- Being aware of the pressure for quick fixes and time constraints that are not consistent with long-term goals
- Multitasking of general administrative staff between application development and daily duties
- Keeping track of nondedicated resources/turnover throughout the various projects
- Coordinating the development of parameters between the AccPac and Hyperion Enterprise database
- Maintaining control of the scope of the project
- Developing/retaining network expertise

INDEX